# Agility and Discipline Made Easy

# The Addison-Wesley Object Technology Series

Grady Booch, Ivar Jacobson, and James Rumbaugh, Series Editors

For more information, check out the series web site at www.awprofessional.com/otseries.

# The Component Software Series

Clemens Szyperski, Series Editor

For more information, check out the series web site at www.awprofessional.com/csseries.

# Praise for *Agility and Discipline Made Easy*

"The Japanese samurai Musashi wrote: 'One can win with the long sword, and one can win with the short sword. Whatever the weapon, there is a time and situation in which it is appropriate.'

"Similarly, we have the long RUP and the short RUP, and all sizes in between. RUP is not a rigid, static recipe, and it evolves with the field and the practitioners, as demonstrated in this new book full of wisdom to illustrate further the liveliness of a process adopted by so many organizations around the world. Bravo!"

—Philippe Kruchten, Professor, University of British Columbia

"The Unified Process and its practices have had, and continue to have, a great impact on the software industry. This book is a refreshing new look at some of the principles underlying the Unified Process. It is full of practical guidance for people who want to start, or increase, their adoption of proven practices. No matter where you are today in terms of software maturity, you can start improving tomorrow."

—Ivar Jacobson, Ivar Jacobson Consulting

"Kroll and MacIsaac have written a must-have book. It is well organized with new principles for software development. I encounter many books I consider valuable; I consider this one indispensable, especially as it includes over 20 concrete best practices. If you are interested in making your software development shop a better one, read this book!"

—Ricardo R. Garcia, President, Global Rational User Group Council,
www.rational-ug.org/index.php

"Agile software development is real, it works, and it's here to stay. Now is the time to come up to speed on agile best practices for the Unified Process, and this book provides a great starting point."

—Scott W. Ambler, practice leader, Agile Modeling

"IBM and the global economy have become increasingly dependent on software over the last decade, and our industry has evolved some discriminating best practices. Per and Bruce have captured the principles and practices of success in this concise book; a must for executives, project managers, and practitioners. These ideas are progressive, but they strike the right balance between agility and governance and will form the foundation for successful systems and software developers for a long time."

—Walker Royce, Vice President, IBM Software Services–Rational

"Finally, the RUP is presented in digestible, byte-size pieces. Kroll and MacIsaac effectively describe a set of practices that can be adopted in a low-ceremony, ad hoc fashion, suited to the culture of the more agile project team, while allowing them to understand how to scale their process as needed."

—Dean Leffingwell, author and software business advisor and executive

"This text fills an important gap in the knowledge-base of our industry: providing agile practices in the proven, scalable framework of the Unified Process. With each practice able to be throttled to the unique context of a development organization, Kroll and MacIsaac provide software teams with the ability to balance agility and discipline as appropriate for their specific needs."

—Brian G. Lyons, CTO, Number Six Software, Inc.

# Agility and Discipline Made Easy

## PRACTICES FROM OpenUP AND RUP

Per Kroll
Bruce MacIsaac

✦✦ Addison-Wesley

Upper Saddle River, NJ • Boston • Indianapolis • San Francisco
New York • Toronto • Montreal • London • Munich • Paris • Madrid
Capetown • Sydney • Tokyo • Singapore • Mexico City

---

**This Book Is Safari Enabled**

The Safari® Enabled icon on the cover of your favorite technology book means the book is available through Safari Bookshelf. When you buy this book, you get free access to the online edition for 45 days.

Safari Bookshelf is an electronic reference library that lets you easily search thousands of technical books, find code samples, download chapters, and access technical information whenever and wherever you need it.

To gain 45-day Safari Enabled access to this book:

• Go to http://www.awprofessional.com/safarienabled

• Complete the brief registration form

• Enter the coupon code DMHE-JV4G-SSLH-X4HU-FA95

If you have difficulty registering on Safari Bookshelf or accessing the online edition, please e-mail customer-service@safaribooksonline.com.

---

Visit us on the Web: www.awprofessional.com

*Library of Congress Cataloging-in-Publication Data*

Kroll, Per.
    Agility and discipline made easy : practices from OpenUP and RUP / Per Kroll, Bruce MacIsaac.
        p. cm.
    Includes bibliographical references and index.
    ISBN 0-321-32130-8 (pbk. : alk. paper)
    1. Computer software—Development. 2. Software engineering. I. MacIsaac, Bruce. II. Title.
    QA76.76.D47K746 2006
    005.1—dc22

                                                                    2006003472

ISBN 0-321-32130-8
Text printed in the United States on recycled paper at Courier in Stoughton, Massachusetts.
First printing, May 2006.

*To Natasha, Per's wonderful daughter,*
*conceived at the same time as this book—almost*

*and*

*To Mary MacIsaac, Bruce's grandmother,*
*who turns 112 as this book is completed*

# CONTENTS

# FOREWORD

Since that first day when the first software development team collaborated to deliver the first economically viable software-intensive system, there has been and continues to be a philosophical as well as a pragmatic battle over how best to organize a team and how to orchestrate its work. At one extreme are those who advocate high-ceremony processes involving rigidly defined artifacts and a strict ordering of activities; at the other extreme are those who embrace low-ceremony processes involving a fierce focus on coding, with everything else considered irrelevant or inconsequential. The pendulum has swung between these two extremes for years.

The good news is that, with decades of experience in delivering software-intensive systems behind us, it is now possible to identify what has worked for successful organizations and reject what is common among unsuccessful ones. This is the essence of the Unified Process, in both the Rational Unified Process (RUP) and its simpler open-source version, Open Unified Process (OpenUP): RUP and OpenUP are both simply elaborations of a small set of best practices that have proved themselves in practice.

In this book, Per and Bruce explain the six key principles that serve as the foundation of RUP and OpenUP. For each of these principles, the authors discuss the points of pain that each principle addresses, the context for that principle, and pragmatic advice on applying it. Since no single process can work in the same fashion for every conceivable combination of domain and development culture, the authors go on to describe how each of these principles can be adapted across the full spectrum of low- to high-ceremony use.

Per and Bruce are well suited to this task: both have engaged in a multitude of projects over the years, and both have been deeply involved in the formulation of RUP and OpenUP. I can think of no authors better qualified to bring you the essence of these processes.

Grady Booch
IBM Fellow

# PREFACE

The goal of this book is to describe a set of well-defined practices that you and your team can start adopting today. You can choose to adopt only one practice or adopt all of them over a period of time. The practices in this book have been shown to improve the quality, predictability, speed, and/or cost of software development.

## Why We Wrote This Book

During more than a decade of assisting companies in improving their software development practices and leading the development of the Rational Unified Process (RUP), we have had the opportunity to see what works and what doesn't. We have seen the rewards of successful adoption of RUP, and we have seen the challenges that projects and team members may encounter along the way. Over the last few years, we have also learned a lot from the agile movement, with its increased focus on people and low-ceremony approaches to software development. More recently, we have also been key drivers of an open source project, the Eclipse Process Framework (EPF), which includes the Open Unified Process (OpenUP)—an open-source version of the Unified Process. One of the objectives of EPF is to create a repository of industry practices, which are customizable and can be assembled into a set of out-of-the-box processes reflecting different development styles. Through all of this work, we have gained valuable experiences in what works and what doesn't, as well as how to package that knowledge into pragmatic practices that can be easily adopted.

We have found that many companies view improving their software development capabilities as a staggering task. It seems to be like eating an elephant: where do you start, and how do you go about it? The answer? You pick a tender spot and take one bite at a time. The "tender spot" is where you have the most pain; the "one bite at a time" is one or two practices, one or two software disciplines, and/or one or two tools. In other words, take "good bites." You don't want to choke on them. You want to be just a little bit hungry for the next bite.

This book describes a number of "good bites" that will allow you to start improving your software development capabilities today. You can take one bite or a larger number of bites, all based on your appetite.

We want to reduce the initial anxiety and cost associated with taking on a software improvement effort by providing an easy and unintrusive path toward improved results, without overwhelming you and your team. At the same time we want to show early results that keep the momentum going, thus maintaining the interest and commitment of everyone involved.

The practices in this book are written independently of any one specific process. Taken together, however, they do cover many key aspects of RUP and OpenUP. We believe that this book will be an asset for projects and companies interested in adopting some or all of RUP or OpenUP. Each of the practices described in this book distills knowledge from RUP, OpenUP, and other sources to provide pragmatic guidance on how to solve a particular software development problem. They help you in your software improvement effort by attacking one problem at a time. Each practice describes how OpenUP and RUP can help you adopt the practice and also references other methods such as eXtreme Programming (XP)[1] and Scrum,[2] so that you can understand differences and similarities in relation to other methods. This book can also be valuable for projects and companies with no interest in RUP or OpenUP. You can simply take any number of the practices in this book and adopt them on their own.

---

1. See Beck 2004.
2. See Schwaber 2002.

## What Will You Learn from This Book?

This book will familiarize you with the following:

- A number of key principles for software development, which have been validated by thousands of successful software projects of different sizes in a variety of industries.
- A number of concrete practices that you and your team can adopt today that support the key principles. Each of the practices described provides information on the following categories:
  - The problem the practice addresses
  - How you practically go about adopting the practice
  - Related practices
  - Where to read more about the practice
  - How to incrementally adopt practices with minimal risk, and how to leverage RUP and OpenUP

## Who Should Read This Book?

This book is aimed specifically at the following readers:

- All members of a software development team who would like to learn some practices that can be applied today.
- Team members who would like to learn RUP or OpenUP, one practice at a time. This book does not give you an understanding of the complete RUP or OpenUP, but if you have understood the practices described in this book, you have come a long way in learning about RUP and OpenUP.
- Managers, process engineers, and others who want to understand *how key practices can be adopted* in their organization, one practice at a time.

## Structure and Content of This Book

The book is divided into eight chapters. Chapter 1 provides an overview of six key principles for software development that are used as a base for the structure of this book. Chapter 1 also provides an overview of RUP, OpenUP, XP, and Scrum.

Chapters 2 through 7 review each of the six key principles in turn. For each principle, we describe a number of practices that support it. Most practices can be adopted individually, allowing you to understand how to make quick improvements in your development without having to implement too much change. Chapter 8 describes how to adopt and benefit from these practices.

## How to Read This Book

This book can be read using any of three approaches:

1. Read only the parts that make sense for your team. Start by reading Chapter 1. Determine which key principle you think would add the most value to you and your team. Go to the corresponding chapter. Look through the practices listed for that chapter, and read those you find of most interest. Does the problem addressed by each practice coincide with a problem you are facing, and is it worth fixing? If so, share those with your team members and get agreement to adopt the ones that pertain to your situation.

   Once you have adopted the identified practices, use the same approach to identify the next set of practices to read up on. This approach is described in more detail in Chapter 8.

2. Read the parts that are relevant for your role. Note that since software development is a team effort, it is good to be at least somewhat familiar with practices for other roles. The list below identifies the chapters and practices that probably are the most applicable for each of the roles on a software team.
   - Project Manager: read Chapters 1 and 8 and Practices 1–4, 7–10, 12–13, and 19–20.

- Architect: read Chapter 1 and Practices 1, 2, 10–11, 15–18, and 20.
- Analyst: read Chapter 1 and Practices 1–2, 7–10, 12, and 20.
- Developer: read Chapter 1 and Practices 1–2, 5–9, 11–12, 14–18, and 20.
- Tester: read Chapter 1 and Practices 1–2, 4–9, 12, and 20.

3. Read the book from start to finish to learn as much as possible about practices applicable for all members on your team

## For More Information

To learn more about or to download EPF and OpenUP, go to the Eclipse Foundation Web site at www.eclipse.org/epf/.

RUP is delivered through the product IBM Rational Method Composer (RMC). Additional information about RUP or RMC, including a data sheet and a product demo, can be obtained from IBM at http://www.ibm.com/software/awdtools/rmc/.

Information about the Rational Software Global User Group Community can be found at http://www.rational-ug.org/index.php.

Academic institutions can contact IBM for information on a special program for including RUP in a software engineering curriculum at http://www.ibm.com/university/.

## Acknowledgments

The ideas and thoughts synthesized in this book have been derived from many sources. We have learned a lot from the many talented individuals inside and outside IBM who have helped shape RUP and make it work in the trenches. We have also learned from the agile community, Eclipse, and the various process communities. We especially appreciate those who challenged our ideas, helping us to evolve and sharpen what we present in this book.

This book would not have been written if not for the RUP product and its current product team: Amanda Brijpaul, Ricardo Balduino, Trevor Collins, Carlos Goti, Michael Hanford, Peter Haumer, Margaret Hedstrom, Kelli Houston, Russell Pannone, Thierry Paradan, Cecile Peraire, Dan Popescu, Michael Stern, Pawan Rewari, Jim Ruehlin, Jeff Smith, John Smith, and Gordon Schneemann.

Over the years, the Rational field teams and technical experts have accumulated a lot of experience in implementing and using RUP. We are grateful for the many perceptive review comments and ideas from these experts, who have added many insights into what does and does not work out in the trenches. We would especially like to recognize David Alvey, Kurt Bittner, Bill Cottrell, Peter Eeles, Bill Higgins, Kelli Houston, Saif Islam, Walker Royce, and John Smith.

Our external reviewers provided invaluable feedback, forcing us to rethink the structure and content of the book and hopefully helping us to create a book that is easier to read and addresses the most relevant issues for a book about agility and discipline. These insights were provided by Scott Ambler, Joshua Barnes, Lisa Crispin, Jim Dunion, Ivar Jacobson, Philippe Kruchten, Tom Poppendieck, Dan Rawsthorne, Chris Soskin, Christoph Steindl, Garth Richmond, Dave Thomas, David Trent, and Michael Vizdos.

Heath Newburn, Ted Rivera, and Scott Will assisted us through their deep expertise in testing, each contributing a practice to this book, for which we are most grateful.

Catherine Southwood and Deborah Fogel deserve special thanks for making a proper manuscript out of our scribbles, as did Mike Perrow.

Writing a book always takes more time than you think it will, and we want to thank our wives and kids, Susan and Natasha Kroll, along with Kathy, Blaise, and Courtney MacIsaac, for being patient with the many weekends and nights spent writing and rewriting the book.

Finally, many thanks to our editor, William Zobrist, for corralling us through the writing process; to Mary O'Brien, for taking on this book; and to the production and marketing teams at Addison-Wesley, notably Tyrrell Albaugh, Stephane Nakib, and Kim Silvestro, for helping us to get this book out.

# ABOUT THE AUTHORS

 **Per Kroll** is the project leader on the Eclipse Process Framework Project, an open-source project, and development manager for RUP and IBM Rational Method Composer. He is responsible for IBM Rational's strategy in the process area, including integration between methods and tools, and method integration within IBM. Per has twenty years of software development experience in supply chain management, telecom, communications, and software product development. He is the coauthor of the highly acclaimed *The Rational Unified Process Made Easy* (Addison-Wesley).

Per lives in Los Gatos, California, with his wife, Susan, daughter, Natasha, and golden retriever, Copper. He enjoys running, playing floorball (a common Nordic sport centered around beating other middle-aged men over the shins), hiking, and any type of board game. He is known to have an occasional beer, and he loves to dance.

 **Bruce MacIsaac** is the technical lead and manager for RUP and OpenUP content development at IBM Rational. Over the last twenty years, Bruce has served in a variety of management and technical roles, leading both small and large software development teams. More recently, he developed the first version of IRUP, the IBM internal-tailored instance of RUP, co-developed the initial version of OpenUP, and led the migration of RUP to its most recent incarnation in Rational Method Composer. He is now responsible for realizing IBM process

strategy, integrating existing methods in a scaleable framework, and developing new content to cover the needs of different kinds of projects and businesses.

Bruce left the rain of Vancouver, British Columbia, in 2004 with his wife, Kathy, and children, Blaise and Courtney, to dry out in San Jose, California. He enjoys roller-blading, skiing, tennis, and all styles of dance. Although Bruce and Per enjoy many of the same things, they are easy to tell apart—Bruce has more hair and is a better dancer.

# CHAPTER 1

# Leveraging Key Development Principles

This book provides a set of software engineering best practices that your project can start using right away to improve the way you develop software. The practices can be adopted individually, but they also support each other. This means that you can pick a set of practices to adopt and be able to make sense of them without having to adopt all of the practices. As you adopt more and more of the practices, you will start to notice the synergy among them. Each practice becomes a piece of a puzzle, and taken together, though not complete, they constitute the backbone of a process that is iterative, agile, and scales to your project needs. See the Preface for how to use this book.

*Practices can be adopted individually.*

## Where Do the Practices Come From?

We have chosen the best practices in this book based on principles gleaned from a huge number of successful projects and distilled into a few simple guidelines that we call key development principles (see the section Key Development Principles later in this chapter). Grouping the practices under these key development principles allows you to identify proven principles that address the issues your project is facing and review the practices supporting each principle to see how you can make progress toward adopting the principle. We will discuss the topic of adoption in more detail in Chapter 8, "Making Practical Use of the Best Practices."

These practices borrow from a large number of iterative and agile processes, all sharing a focus on iterative development; continuous integration; early and continuous testing; addressing customer needs; people and team collaboration; and minimizing process overhead.

*OpenUp is an open-source version of the Unified Process.*

*EPF is an open source process framework.*

The practices capture much of the thought that was formative in the creation of the **Open Unified Process (OpenUP)**, especially its most agile and lightweight form, OpenUP/Basic, targeting smaller and collocated teams interested in agile and iterative development. OpenUP is a part of the **Eclipse Process Framework**[1] **(EPF)**, an open source process framework developed within the Eclipse open source organization.[2] It provides best practices from a variety of software development thought leaders and the broader software development community that cover a diverse set of perspectives and development needs. Some of the practices in the EPF may differ from the ones you find in this book, because they were produced by people with a different view of how to develop software or targeted a different type of project. This is one of EPF's strengths: allowing diversity of ideas, while encouraging learning from each other, thereby driving unification and evolution of best practices. We believe that reading this book will help you gain insights into key aspects of OpenUP/Basic as well as EPF; see the section OpenUP/Basic later in this chapter and Appendix A for more detail.

*RUP is a continually evolving process framework that extends EPF.*

The key development practices also have a strong connection to RUP. RUP is a continually evolving process framework. It started in 1987 as the Objectory Process[3], a use-case-driven and object-oriented process, and in 1996 was integrated with the Rational Process[4], an iterative and architecture-centric process. Since 1996, it has integrated best practices

---

1. www.eclipse.org/epf/.
2. www.eclipse.org.
3. See Jacobson 1992.
4. See Devlin 1995.

from a broad set of sources, including processes for testing, configuration management, agile development, service-oriented architecture, and business engineering[5]. RUP extends EPF with in-depth process content for specific technologies and tools, such as J2EE and IBM tools; for specific domains, such as packaged application development, systems engineering, and program management; and for process maturity standards and frameworks, such as SEI CMMI.

Some of the practices in this book are more appropriate for projects that need to follow a higher-ceremony process, making them better reflect RUP than the lighter-weight guidance in EPF. We believe that RUP users will find the practices in this book valuable, because they articulate a clear set of principles for developing software. Unfortunately, too many RUP users do not adhere to these principles (see Key Development Principles later in this chapter) and so misinterpret the underlying spirit of RUP.

Other iterative and agile processes, including eXtreme Programming (XP),[6] Scrum,[7] Agile Modeling,[8] Crystal,[9] Agile Data Method,[10] and Dynamic Systems Development Method (DSDM)[11] have influenced the practices in this book, just as they have influenced RUP and OpenUP.

*XP, Scrum, Agile Modeling, Crystal, Agile Data Method, and DSDM have influenced this book.*

## Using Practice Descriptions

Each key development principle is discussed in its own chapter and contains the practices that support that principle. For example, the principle Demonstrate Value Iteratively is supported by the practice Manage Risk, which gives concrete guidance on one of several practices

---

5. See Appendix B and Kroll 2001 for the history of RUP.
6. See Beck 2004.
7. See Schwaber 2002.
8. See Ambler 2002.
9. See Cockburn 2002
10. See Ambler 2003.
11. See Stapleton 2003.

that will help you to adhere to the principle effectively. Each practice description discusses the following:

- **Problem:** the problem that the practice addresses
- **Background:** background information
- **Application:** how to apply the practice
- **Comparison with other practices:** how the practice compares with practices found in major iterative and agile development processes, including XP and Scrum
- **Adoption:** how to implement the practice at different levels of adoption
- **Related best practices:** additional supporting practices
- **Additional information:** additional reference information available in OpenUP and RUP, and in books relevant to the practice

There may be practices that do not fit your project or organization at this time for technical, cultural, business, or other reasons. You may find that you are already following other practices. Most practices can be adopted at different levels, allowing you to adopt more practices over time as well as implement them at a higher level. We believe that gradually adopting a distinct set of practices at a level appropriate for your organization will enable you to start improving today, and to continue improving over subsequent projects, without requiring that you change everything at once. See the following section for more information on the different levels of adopting a practice.

Before we dive into the practices, let's discuss the process of adopting the practices: iterative development, levels of ceremony and agility, followed by the key development principles. We will then provide an overview of the Unified Process lifecycle, followed by an overview of OpenUP/Basic, RUP, XP, and Scrum in turn.

## Adopting the Practices: Iterative Development, Levels of Ceremony, and Agility

A key aspect of this book is to allow you to move incrementally from where you are today to where you would like to be a couple of years from now, adopting the practices at your own pace.

## Levels of Adopting the Practices

Each practice can be adopted at three different levels: basic, interme-diate, and advanced. The basic level represents a level of adoption we think most projects can adhere to with limited investments, that is, with a limited skill set and with no or small amounts of tool invest-ments. This level thus represents a reasonable starting point on your journey toward improved ability to develop software effectively, but it is not necessarily an acceptable end goal. As you move to the interme-diate and advanced levels of adoption, you will have to make addi-tional investments in building skills and/or tools. For some teams and practices, the basic or intermediate adoption level is preferable. Other teams should aim at adopting advanced-level practices for maximum productivity.

*Each practice can be adopted at three levels: basic, intermediate, and advanced.*

## Process Map

To understand the level that is appropriate for your team, we will use a process map (see Figure 1.1) characterized by two dimensions dis-cussed below:[12]

- **Low ceremony/High ceremony**[13] dimension on the horizontal axis. **Low ceremony** produces minimum supporting documenta-tion and has little formality in the working procedure; **High cere-mony** has comprehensive supporting documentation, traceability maintained between artifacts, Change Control Boards, and so on.

- **Waterfall/Iterative** dimension on the vertical axis. **Waterfall** is a linear approach with late integration and testing; **Iterative** is a risk-driven development approach with early and continuous implementation, integration, testing, and validation of software that delivers concrete value to the stakeholders.

---

12. See Chapter 3 in Kroll 2003 for an in-depth discussion on the process map.

13. Cockburn refers to "Ceremony" as "Methodology Weight." See page 123 in Cockburn 2002 for an interesting discussion on this topic.

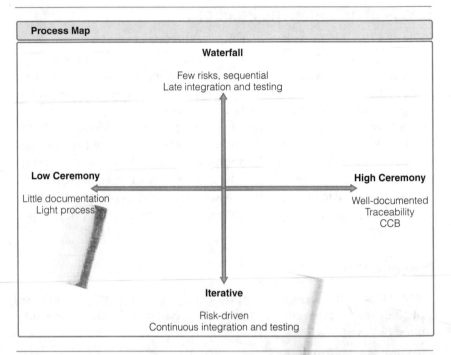

**FIGURE 1.1 Process Map for Process and Practice Comparison.** *By organizing processes and practices along two dimensions—Low ceremony/High ceremony and Waterfall/Iterative—you can compare them and analyze which are more suitable for your project or organization. Agility translates to being in the lower-left quadrant on the map. (Adapted from Kroll 2003.)*

## Agility and Ceremony

*Agility is the ability to respond rapidly to risks and change.*

We define agility as *the ability to respond to risks rapidly; changing requirements or stakeholders needs, or other changes impacting the application we are building.*[14] Agility translates to being in the lower-left quadrant in our process map. Iterative development provides us with the rapid and timely feedback we need to understand when and what to

---

14. Compare Larman 2004, page 25, "agility—rapid and flexible response to change."

change, and the low ceremony provides us with the ability to execute changes rapidly.

So, do we always want to be in the lower-left "agility" corner? If you are two developers building an application with a short life span, you may choose to save time by not documenting many of the requirements or the design. This may allow you to be more productive and to make rapid changes to the application. However, if you are doing distributed development with twenty people in different time zones, you will probably be more productive if you document the requirements and key design decisions. But the added ceremony will add time and cost when you have to implement a change. You therefore choose to move to the right on the process map to gain productivity, while losing agility. By deploying the right tools, however, you can counter this loss and reduce the cost of change, allowing you also to move down on the scale.

Most projects[15] benefit from being as low as possible on the waterfall/ iterative axis to ensure rapid feedback, but not so low that the cost associated with the overhead of each iteration becomes prohibitive. One of the aims of iterative development is to reduce the overhead cost of each iteration so that you can do more iterations, and many of the practices in this book help you achieve that goal. As Professor Barry Boehm points out in *Get Ready for Agile Methods, with Care,*[16] each project should choose the appropriate level of ceremony to fit its specific needs (Boehm used the term "agile" to mean roughly the same as what we refer to as "ceremony.") This means that each project should be as agile as possible based on its specific characteristics, but not more agile.

Most, but not all, advanced practices lead to higher levels of ceremony. *If your project is better off following a low-ceremony process, you should probably not adopt an advanced practice if it leads to higher level of*

---

15. A few projects with very well understood requirements and architecture, facing very limited risk, are exceptions to this rule and may benefit from waterfall development.

16. See Boehm 2002.

*ceremony.* On the other hand, there are many reasons why projects may benefit from more ceremony, including large project size, regulatory requirements, distributed development, complex projects, long application life span, or complex stakeholder relations. In some cases an advanced adoption level leads to less ceremony and shorter and more frequent iterations, which is probably beneficial for most projects that are willing to take on the investment.

## Where Does a Level of Adoption Take You on the Process Map?

We describe the levels of adoption for each practice, as well as giving an indication of the direction in which the adoption level will take you on the process map. Let's look at examples of some of the symbols we use:

 If the arrow goes down and to the left, it means that adopting the practice at this level will lead to, or enable you to have, shorter iterations with a decreased level of ceremony. This is typical for many of the practices at the basic level but could also be true for the intermediate and advanced levels.

 If the arrow goes down and to the right, it means that adopting the practice at this level will lead to, or enable you to have, shorter iterations, while increasing the level of ceremony or learning curve for new team members. This outcome may be desirable if your project needs more ceremony, or if team members need to build more skills, but if that is not the case, your project should consider not adopting the practice at this level.

 If the arrow goes up and to the right, it means that adopting the practice at this level will increase the level of ceremony you are working with, as well as the overhead associated with doing shorter iterations, potentially forcing you to increase the iteration length. These are typically not good changes for a project, but the benefits of implementing the practice may be valuable enough to counteract the drawbacks.

## Key Development Principles

The practices in this book are organized according to six fundamental principles observed by IBM to characterize the most successful projects in the software development industry.[17] Many of the following principles (see Figure 1.2) are found to some degree in most iterative and agile processes:

*Six fundamental principles characterize the most successful projects in the software industry.*

1.  **A**dapt the process.
2.  **B**alance stakeholder priorities.
3.  **C**ollaborate across teams.
4.  **D**emonstrate value iteratively.
5.  **E**levate the level of abstraction.
6.  **F**ocus continuously on quality.

Adapt the process.

Balance stakeholder priorities.

Collaborate across teams.

Demonstrate value iteratively.

Elevate the level of abstraction.

Focus continuously on quality.

**FIGURE 1.2 Principles for Business-Driven Development.** *These six principles characterize the software development industry's best practices in the creation, deployment, and evolution of software-intensive systems. They have been derived by IBM through workshops with thousands of development managers and executives and by synthesizing input from a large number of technical leaders within IBM who are working with software development organizations across all industries.*

---

17. These six principles are an evolution of what IBM Rational previously called the 6 Best Practices.

*Each principle and supporting practices is described in a separate chapter.*

Each of these principles is described in a separate chapter giving an overview of the principle, outlining the patterns of behavior that best embody each principle, and listing the most recognizable anti-patterns that can harm software development projects. The primary focus of each chapter is a set of supporting practices that will help your team to adhere to the principle. To provide a more logical sequence for the book, we have chosen to present the chapters in a different order from the alphabetical order in which the principles are listed above. There is no particular significance to the ordering of practices within a chapter. The principles and their supporting best practices are listed below in the order in which they appear in the book.

- **Demonstrate value iteratively.**
  Each iteration should deliver incremental capabilities that are assessed by stakeholders. This enables you to get feedback from stakeholders as well as on progress made so that you can adapt your plans as required. Iterative development also allows you to focus each iteration on addressing the key risks that the project is currently facing, allowing you to increase predictability.

  Practice 1    Manage risk.

  Practice 2    Execute your project in iterations.

  Practice 3    Embrace and manage change.

  Practice 4    Measure progress objectively.

- **Focus continuously on quality.**
  Continuously improving quality requires more than just testing to validate fitness for use. Rather, it involves all team members throughout the lifecycle—having them build quality into the process and the product. An iterative approach focuses on early testing and test-and-build automation throughout the lifecycle as a means to reduce the number of defects, provide fact-based quality metrics early on, and allow you to plan and adapt your product more effectively based on reality.

  Practice 5    Test your own code.

  Practice 6    Leverage test automation appropriately.

  Practice 7    Everyone owns the product.

- **Balance stakeholder priorities.**
  There will always be many competing stakeholder priorities, such as producing a solution rapidly and inexpensively versus address-

ing all the business requirements. We need to work closely with the stakeholders to make sure that we understand their priorities and to prioritize the right projects and the project requirements. We also need to strike the right balance between leveraging existing assets and building custom software, acknowledging that in some cases the former may require compromising on what requirements to address.

Practice 8    Understand the domain.

Practice 9    Describe requirements from the user perspective.

Practice 10   Prioritize requirements for implementation.

Practice 11   Leverage legacy systems.

- **Collaborate across teams.**
  We need to enable people to work at their best. This means that we need to equip talented people with the right skills, break down walls that prevent a project team from collaborating effectively, and put in place the right environments to facilitate meaningful collaboration. As software becomes increasingly critical to how we run our business, we also need to make sure that we work well together across business, software, and operational teams.

Practice 12   Build high-performance teams.

Practice 13   Organize around the architecture.

Practice 14   Manage versions.

- **Elevate the level of abstraction.**
  Complexity is a major enemy to project success, and minimizing the amount of code, data structures, components, model elements, or other constructs humans produce during a project is crucial to reducing complexity. You can achieve this goal by reusing existing assets—such as business models, components, patterns, and services—instead of custom-building new ones. You can also leverage higher-level languages, frameworks, and tools that can generate code from higher-level models; automate unit testing; and manage the complexity of configuration management. Another approach to reducing complexity is to promote implicity. You can do this by refactoring, keeping code and models clean, and implementing key aspects of the architecture first in what we call architecture-driven development.

Practice 15   Leverage patterns.

Practice 16   Architect with components and services.

Practice 17   Actively promote reuse.

Practice 18   Model key perspectives.

- **Adapt the process.**
  More process is not necessarily better. Rather, you need to adapt the process to the specific needs of your project, based on size, complexity, needs for compliance, and so on. In addition, you need to adapt the process to different lifecycle phases, so you may, for example, use less ceremony at the start of a project and more ceremony toward the end. You must also continuously improve the process, for example by assessing how well it works at the end of each iteration.

Practice 19   Rightsize your process.

Practice 20   Continuously reevaluate what you do.

## Unified Process Lifecycle

*The Unified Process lifecycle divides a project into four phases: Inception, Elaboration, Construction, and Transition.*

Throughout this book you will see references to the **Unified Process lifecycle.** This is the lifecycle used in RUP and OpenUP, and all other processes part of the **Unified Process** family. It is one of several lifecycles supported in the EPF. Even though the practices in this book typically apply to any iterative lifecycle, they work particularly well with the Unified Process lifecycle.

The lifecycle describes the time dimension of project, that is, how a project is divided into phases and iterations. It divides a project into four **phases: Inception, Elaboration, Construction,** and **Transition,** each ending with a well-defined milestone.[18] Each phase has specific objectives:

1. **Inception.** Establish the scope of the system, including a good understanding of what system to build, by reaching a high-level understanding of the requirements. Mitigate many of the business

---

18. See Kroll 2003 for an in-depth overview of what is done in each phase.

risks and produce the business case for building the system and a vision document to get buy-in from all stakeholders on whether or not to proceed with the project. This is similar to what many agile processes refer to as *Iteration 0*.

2. **Elaboration.** Reduce major risks to enable cost and schedule estimates to be updated and to get buy-in from key stakeholders. Mitigate major technical risks by taking care of many of the most technically difficult tasks. Design, implement, test, and baseline an executable **architecture,** including subsystems, their interfaces, key components, and architectural mechanisms such as how to deal with interprocess communication or persistency. Address major business risks by defining, designing, implementing, and testing key capabilities, which are validated with the customer. Do not define and analyze all requirements at this time, as doing so would lead to waterfall development. Detail and analyze only the requirements required to address the above risks.

3. **Construction.** Undertake a majority of the implementation as you move from an executable architecture to the first operational version of your system. Deploy several internal and alpha releases to ensure that the system is usable and addresses user needs. End the phase by deploying a fully functional beta version of the system, including installation and supporting documentation and training material (although the system will likely still require fine-tuning of functionality, performance, and overall quality).

4. **Transition.** Ensure that software addresses the needs of its users by testing the product in preparation for release and making minor adjustments based on user feedback. At this point in the lifecycle, user feedback focuses mainly on fine-tuning, configuration, installation, and usability issues; all the major structural issues should have been worked out much earlier in the project lifecycle.

Each phase contains one or more **iterations** (see Figure 1.3), which focus on producing a product increment, that is, the working code and other deliverables necessary to achieve the business objectives of that phase. There are as many iterations as it takes to adequately address the objectives of that phase, but *no more*. If objectives cannot

*Each phase contains one or more iterations, each producing a product increment.*

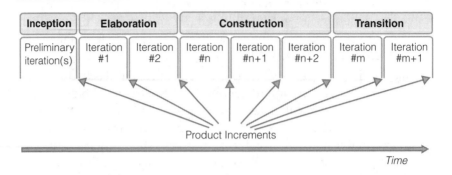

**FIGURE 1.3 The Unified Process Lifecycle.** *Each of the four phases in the Unified Process lifecycle consists of one or several iterations. Each iteration builds on the result of previous iterations, delivering a product increment one step closer to the final release. Product increments should include working software, with a possible exception being the product increments produced in the Inception phase for new applications.*

be adequately addressed within the planned phase, another iteration should be added to the phase, but this will delay the project. To avoid such a delay, make sure that each iteration is sharply focused on *just* what is needed to achieve the business objectives of that phase, but no less. For example, focusing too heavily on requirements in Inception is counterproductive; so is not involving stakeholders.

The Unified Process lifecycle provides a great deal of flexibility. Product increments may be internal only and may be demonstrated or deployed only to select project stakeholders. Other product increments may also be released for use by customers. For example, some projects benefit from the deployment of several product increments to the production environment, which allows end users to adopt the most critical capabilities more rapidly. You can do this by rapidly moving into the Transition phase and having several Transition iterations, each deploying a release into the production environment (see Figure 1.4).

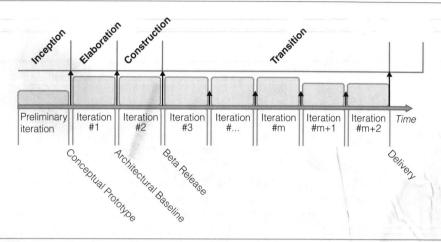

**FIGURE 1.4 Incremental Delivery Using the Unified Process Lifecycle.** *Projects that deliver product increments into the production environment often rapidly move into the Transition phase. Once in Transition, they deliver a new product increment to production at the end of each iteration. The milestone at the end of the Construction phase aims at ensuring that all pieces are together so that the system can be deployed. You should pass this management milestone before undertaking deployments into the production environment.*

## OpenUP/Basic

OpenUP is an open-source process framework that over time is expected to cover a broad set of development needs.[19] OpenUP/Basic is a subset of OpenUP, and provides a simplified set of artifacts relative to RUP and a much smaller set of roles, tasks, and guidelines. Let's look briefly at the key artifacts, the essentials of the process, and how these relate to the practices in this book.

*OpenUP/Basic is an agile and iterative process focusing on the needs of small collocated teams.*

*See Practice 19.*

The project team maintains a **work item list**[20] of all work that needs to be done, including requirements and change requests to be addressed and random tasks, such as delivering training. At the beginning of

*See Practices 1 and 10.*

---

19. At the time of this book's printing, OpenUP is almost equivalent to OpenUP/Basic, and we have chosen to primarily refer to OpenUP/Basic for the remainder of this book. OpenUP is expected to grow over time, while OpenUP/Basic will continue to be a small process.

20. Work item list corresponds to product backlog in Scrum; see Schwaber 2002.

**FIGURE 1.5 Managing an OpenUP/Basic Project.** *The project manager is responsible for producing a high-level project plan, maintaining a work item list of all things to be done, prioritizing work items into an iteration plan, and assessing the result of the iterations. The entire team is typically involved in producing each of these artifacts.*

each iteration, the team prioritizes which work items should be addressed within that iteration, and that subset of the work item list is called the *Iteration Plan* (see Figure 1.5). The team prioritizes work items to drive down risks and to deliver high-priority end-user capabilities in each iteration.

*See Practices 2, 3, 4, and 20.*

An iteration is typically a few weeks long, and each iteration will deliver an executable that is one step closer to the final product, with the potential exception of the first iteration. During an iteration, the team will work on defining, designing, implementing, and testing the requirements listed in the iteration plan, as well as any other planned work items. At the end of each iteration, the team will assess what was accomplished and demonstrate the executable to stakeholders. The resulting feedback will enable the team to improve upon the solution and understand what are the most important work items for the next iteration. Lessons learned during the retrospective improve the process for the next iteration.

*See Practices 5–6, 8–10, 14, and 18.*

A *vision* outlines stakeholder needs and high-level features, establishing a common understanding of the domain. Functional requirements are documented as use cases and scenarios, and other requirements are documented as supplementary requirements. The requirements are incrementally implemented by growing the design and implementation in stages, while continuously testing and integrating the code into builds. A strong emphasis is placed on test-and-build automation to enable frequent and high-quality builds.

OpenUP/Basic is steeped in the belief that the team needs to take responsibility for the end product, to which everybody chips in as needed. To improve productivity and quality, the team should reuse existing assets, such as patterns and common components, as appropriate. OpenUP/Basic also puts a strong emphasis on the architecture; a stable architecture is established early in the project and evolves continuously along with the application. Components and services are leveraged as appropriate, and the architecture also impacts how responsibilities are divided within the team.

*See Practices 7, 11–13, and 15–17.*

OpenUP/Basic is a subset of OpenUP, and is delivered through the EPF (see Appendix A). It is also the basis for RUP.

## Rational Unified Process (RUP)

RUP is a widely adopted process framework used by tens of thousands of projects ranging from teams of two to teams with hundreds of members, in a broad variety of industries worldwide. It extends EPF with a large volume of additional process content, allowing development teams to scale their process to do the following:

*RUP extends EPF with additional process content.*

- Carry out distributed or large-scale development requiring more ceremony, such as requirements traceability, analysis models, model-driven architecture (MDA), or comprehensive testing of load and performance.
- Develop systems using IBM tools, providing specific guidance on relevant technologies such as J2EE and .NET, and using IBM and partner tools.
- Develop systems adhering to industry standards such as ISO 9001, SEI CMMI, or SOX.
- Scale from project-oriented processes to enterprise processes, such as program and portfolio management; systems engineering;

enterprise reuse; business modeling and simulation; or enterprise-scale SOA.

*RUP provides a collection of processes that can either be used "out of the box" or further customized.*

RUP follows the Unified Process lifecycle and adheres to the key principles described above. RUP emphasizes the importance of adapting the process to the needs of your project. Rather than providing one process, such as OpenUP/Basic, RUP provides a collection of processes that can either be used out-of-the-box or further customized. These processes are variations built on OpenUP/Basic and include processes for Large-Scale Custom Application Development, Commercial-Off-The-Shelf (COTS) Packaged Delivery (see Figure 1.6), Service-Oriented Architecture Development, Systems Engineering, Small Projects, Maintenance Projects, Portfolio Management, and so on. More processes are continually being added. RUP allows you to customize these processes or build your own process through the product IBM Rational Method Composer, which is the delivery vehicle for RUP. The product is described in more detail in Appendix B.

One of the key ideas behind RUP is that a process is much more valuable when automated by tools. Therefore, a fundamental aspect of RUP is the tight integration with developer tools through context-sensitive process guidance available within the tools and tool-specific guidance available in the process, which makes RUP an integral part of the development environment. RUP is also tightly integrated with tools that allow teams to instantiate their process, enabling adaptive planning of projects and collaborative software development (see Appendix B for more information). Even though RUP is integrated with IBM and other tools, it does not require the use of any one set of tools.

RUP is described in a variety of white papers and books.[21] The most comprehensive information can be found in the Rational Method Composer (RMC) product, which contains detailed guidelines, examples, and templates covering the full project lifecycle. However, RUP underwent extensive modernization in 2005, and material or product versions predating 2006 may use different terminology.

---

21. See Kruchten 2003 and Kroll 2003.

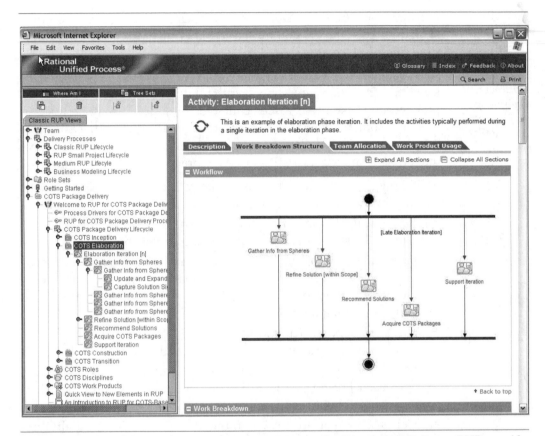

**FIGURE 1.6  RUP for Commercial-Off-The-Shelf (COTS) Packaged Application Delivery.** *RUP provides many out-of-the-box processes for different types of projects, including COTS packaged application delivery. For COTS development, RUP provides specific guidance on how to evaluate commercial components or packages, how to deal with a Request for Information (RFI) and a Request for Proposals (RFP), and how to make trade-offs to balance the many conflicts between stakeholder needs, architecture, program risk, and market concerns.*

# eXtreme Programming (XP)

**eXtreme Programming (XP)** is one of the best-known agile processes. Created by Kent Beck,[22] it is considered by many to be "glorified hacking,"

---

22. Beck 2004.

but that is far from the case. XP is a disciplined approach, requiring skilled people who are committed to adhering closely to a core set of principles.

*XP is a disciplined approach, requiring skilled people adhering to a core set of principles.*

XP articulates five values to guide you in your project: *communication, simplicity, feedback, courage,* and *respect.* Further, it prescribes a set of practices to make these values concrete. Although it may be unclear whether somebody really adheres to a value, you can easily tell whether somebody adheres to the practice. XP practices are divided into *primary* and *secondary.* The primary practices are listed below.

- *Sit together* helps you to communicate more effectively by being physically collocated in the same room or office space.
- *Whole team* talks about the importance of building a cohesive team with a diverse set of skills required to complete the project.
- *Informative workspace* tells you that if an outsider spends 15 seconds in your workspace, he or she should be able to get a general idea of how the project is going. What are the issues you are facing and items you are working on?
- *Energized work* guides you in adjusting your work hours so that you function effectively when working and avoid burnout.
- *Pair programming* tells you to write all production code in pairs, with each person taking turns watching and assisting the other programmer write code.
- *Stories* allow you to specify, in one or two sentences, capabilities that typically take one or two days to implement. The customer prioritizes which stories to implement and in what order.
- *Weekly cycle* means that at the beginning of each week you plan what should be accomplished for that week by assessing status, prioritizing user stories, and dividing user stories into tasks that programmers sign up for.
- *Quarterly cycle* allows you to step back and determine how to improve process, remove bottlenecks, focus on the big picture of where to take the projects, and do coarse-grained planning for the next quarter.
- *Slack* is built in to the schedule as tasks that can be dropped or by assigning certain time slots as slack time.

- *Ten-minute build* forces you to trim your automated build and automated tests so that they take no more than 10 minutes.
- *Continuous integration* aims at reducing the overall cost of integration by forcing it to happen at least once every couple of hours.
- *Test-first programming* tells you to write automated tests before writing the code to be tested.
- *Incremental design* guides you in doing a little bit of design every day, but designing only for what you need today rather than for future possibilities.

XP also articulates a set of fourteen principles that function as the bridge between values and practices, guiding you in how to apply the practices effectively in order to adhere to the values. The principles are humanity, economics, mutual benefit, self-similarity, improvement, diversity, reflection, flow, opportunity, redundancy, failure, quality, baby steps, and accepted responsibility.

## Scrum

**Scrum**[23] was introduced in 1996 by Ken Schwaber and Jeff Sutherland.[24] The term *scrum* is derived from rugby, in which it refers to restarting play after the game is stuck in a so-called maul. Scrum focuses on the management of a project without describing the specifics of how to undertake design, implementation, or testing. Consequently, it can be combined with a number of different processes, such as XP or RUP.

*Scrum focuses on the management of a project.*

Each iteration is 30 days long and is referred to as a sprint. The sprint starts with a half-day planning meeting to determine what should be done within the sprint. During the planning meeting, the Product Owner provides a prioritized **Product Backlog,** which is an evolving list containing all requirements, defects, tasks, and change requests. The development team will then determine how many of the high-priority items they can take on within that sprint, which constitutes

---

23. Schwaber 2002.
24. Scrum was formalized and presented at OOPSLA'96.

the **Sprint Backlog,** and a sprint goal is crafted. The sprint goal provides the team with a clear focus by establishing an objective that will be met by implementing the backlog.

After the planning meeting, the team spends 29 days developing an executable that delivers incremental functionality. The sprint ends with a half-day Sprint Review Meeting, at which the team and management inspect the product increment together and capture lessons learned. The team will then start the next sprint, delivering an executable every 30 days that is one step closer to the final product.

During a sprint the team will get together for a daily 15-minute meeting, also called scrum. During the scrum, each team member will briefly answer three (and *only* three) questions:

1. What have you done since last meeting?
2. What will you do between now and next meeting?
3. What obstacles stood in the way of doing work?

The "scrum master" makes sure that the meeting is kept on track, makes decisions as appropriate, and is also responsible for ensuring that identified obstacles are addressed as soon as possible. As issues arise that need further discussion, the scrum master sets up additional meetings with involved parties to continue the discussion, to ensure that the daily scrum is kept to 15 minutes. The scrum master also makes sure that no outside changes are imposed on the plan during a sprint, so that the team can focus on executing the plan without any distracting interruptions.

The team in scrum should have seven (give or take two) members. If your team has more, split the team into several teams and divide their work so that they can operate semi-independently. Scrum teams should be cross-functional so that each team can do the necessary analysis, design, implementation, testing, and documentation.

Scrum teams are self-organized, meaning that the team is left loose during the sprint to use whatever approach is considered appropriate to convert the Sprint Backlog to a product increment. Management should not intervene. At the end of the sprint, management can assess what was done and make changes as necessary.

Scrum focuses on collaboration. Open workspaces are preferred, and each team member should attend the daily scrum meeting in person. No titles or job descriptions are used, and people are asked to leave their egos at home.

*Scrum focuses on collaboration. Each team member attends the daily scrum meeting.*

## Summary

This chapter introduces key principles and practices that support them. It also presents the framework for this book, as outlined below:

- **Comparison with other methods.** For each practice, we describe how the practice is similar to, or different from, other methods.
- **Levels of adoption.** Each practice can be adopted at three levels: basic, intermediate, and advanced. The advanced level typically requires a combination of more advanced skills, more advanced tooling, or a higher-ceremony process.
- **Process map.** For each level of adoption of a practice, we indicate whether the practice enables agility or discipline and whether it enables shorter iterations.
- **Information in the Unified Process.** For each practice, we describe how OpenUP/Basic and RUP support these practices.

To enable you to make better use of this framework, this chapter provides a summary of the Unified Process lifecycle, OpenUP/Basic, and RUP and explains how they fit together in the family of Unified Process methods built on EPF and RMC. This chapter also summarizes Scrum and XP, because we have chosen to focus on these methods as part of the "comparison with other methods" section in each practice.

With this background, we hope you can now pick and choose a practice chapter of interest and gain valuable insight into how to improve your process. We recommend that you start with the basic level of adoption and incrementally adopt some intermediate and advanced practices based on whether you need to be more iterative, agile, or disciplined.

## CHAPTER 2

# Demonstrate Value Iteratively

| | |
|---|---|
| *Benefits* | • Early risk reduction.<br>• Higher predictability throughout the project.<br>• Trust among stakeholders. |
| *Patterns* | 1. Enable feedback by delivering incremental user value in each iteration.<br>2. Adapt your plans using an iterative process.<br>3. Embrace and manage change.<br>4. Attack major technical, business, and programmatic risks early. |
| *Anti-Patterns* | • Plan the whole lifecycle in detail, track variances against plan (can actually contribute to project failure).<br>• Assess status in the first two thirds of the project by relying on reviews of specifications and intermediate work products, rather than assessing status of test results and demonstrations of working software. |

The principle of demonstrating value iteratively explains why software development greatly benefits from being iterative.[1] An iterative process makes it possible to accommodate change easily, to obtain feedback and factor it into the project, to reduce risk early, and to adjust the process dynamically.

Several imperatives underlie this principle. The first is that we must *demonstrate incremental value to enable early and continuous feedback*. We achieve this goal by dividing our project into a set of iterations. In each iteration we perform some requirements, design, implementation, and testing of our application, thus producing a deliverable that is one step closer to the final solution. This process allows us to demonstrate the application to end users and other stakeholders, or have them use the application directly, enabling them to provide early feedback on how we are doing. Are we moving in the right direction? Are stakeholders satisfied with what we have done to date? Do we need to change the features implemented so far? And finally, what additional features need to be implemented to add business value? If we can answer these questions satisfactorily, we are more likely to build trust among stakeholders that the system we are developing will address their needs. We are also less likely to overengineer our approach or to add capabilities that are not useful to the end user.[2]

The second imperative is to leverage demonstrations and feedback to *adapt our plans*. Rather than relying on assessing specifications, such as requirements specifications, design models, or plans, we need instead to assess how well the code developed thus far actually works. We must therefore use test results and demonstrations of working code to stakeholders to determine how well we are doing. Following this procedure provides a good understanding of where we are, how fast the team is progressing, and whether we need to make course corrections to complete the project successfully. We can then use this information to update the overall plan for the project and develop detailed plans for just the next iteration, rather than for the entire project.

---

1. Material appearing in the introductions of Chapters 2–7 adapted from Kroll 2005. Used with permission.

2. According to the Standish Group's *Chaos Report* (2003), 45 percent of features implemented on the average project are never used.

The third underlying imperative is to *embrace and manage change.* Today's applications are too complex for the requirements, design, implementation, and testing to align perfectly the first time through. Instead, the most effective application development methods embrace the inevitability of change. Through early and continuous feedback, we learn how to improve the application, and the iterative approach provides us with the opportunity to implement those changes incrementally. By having the processes and tools in place, we can effectively manage all this change without confining desired creativity.

The fourth imperative underlying this principle is the need to *drive out key risks early* in the lifecycle, as illustrated in the diagram in Figure 2.1. We must address the major technical, business, and programmatic risks as early as possible, rather than postponing risk resolution toward the end of the project. This stage is accomplished by continuously assessing what risks we are facing and addressing the top remaining risks in the next iteration. In successful projects, key business risks are mitigated in early iterations by involving stakeholders to ensure buy-in to a vision and high-level requirements, and key technical risks are mitigated through design, implementation, and testing of key aspects of the architecture. It is also important to retain

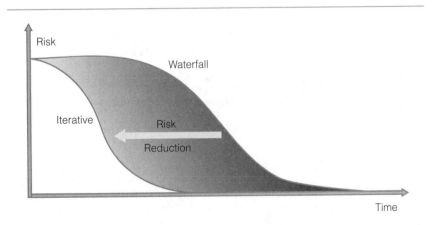

**FIGURE 2.1 Risk Reduction Profiles for Waterfall and Iterative Developments.**
*A major goal with iterative development is to reduce risk early on by analyzing, prioritizing, and attacking top risks in each iteration. (Adapted from Royce 1998.)*

information required to force decisions about what major reusable assets or commercial-off-the-shelf (COTS) software to use.

The anti-pattern to following this principle would be to plan the whole lifecycle in detail up front and then track variances against plan. Another anti-pattern would be to assess status in the first two thirds of the project by primarily relying on reviews of specifications, rather than assessing status of test results and demonstrations of working software.

This chapter will walk you through a number of best practices that will assist you in demonstrating value iteratively.

- *Practice 1: Manage Risk* explains how to identify and prioritize key risks. These risks are used to determine the focus of the next iteration.
- *Practice 2: Execute Your Project in Iterations* describes how to plan iterative development and how to divide your project into a series of iterations in which early iterations address high risks.
- *Practice 3: Embrace and Manage Change* suggests what changes to encourage and discourage at each stage of a project, as well as techniques to maximize change freedom.
- *Practice 4: Measure Progress Objectively* discusses how to leverage the right measures to avoid getting a false perception of status.

# Manage Risk

by Per Kroll

*Identifying and addressing top risks in each iteration increases predictability and lowers overall cost.*

## Problem

A risk is a variable with an unknown or uncertain value that could endanger or jeopardize a project's success.[3] The key idea in risk management is not to wait passively until a risk materializes and becomes a problem or kills the project, but rather to seek out and deal with risks.

Ignoring or procrastinating in this area may lead you to invest in the wrong technologies, a bad design, and/or a set of requirements that may not meet stakeholder needs. Unaddressed risks may mean that you run your project with staff that do not have the skills required to do the job, or that you build an application different from the one that stakeholders expect. This is bad software economics. Failure to address risk early in the project means spending more on rework down the road, as many risks become major issues.

## Background

I grew up in a very small town, and once a year a fair came to town for the weekend. My favorite game had a bunch of green frogs that kept popping up, the object of which was to knock down the frogs with the hammer provided as rapidly as possible. Managing risk effectively is very much like that game. New risks always keep popping up. As a team, you need to drive them down as fast as you can, focusing on the major risks first.

*As a team, you need to drive down risk as fast as you can.*

---

3. See Concept: Risk in the Rational Unified Process product.

Just as those green frogs kept coming, you will never be finished dealing with risk. Because risks are volatile, you need to monitor and reassess your situation constantly. Are there any new risks that you need to address? Which risks are more serious than others? Just as you get more points for knocking down some frogs than others, in real life some risks are more serious than others. We want to rig the game of software development to enable us to knock down the biggest frogs early, so that we maximize our points even if we run out of time.

Many risks become a problem due to lack of communication: people do not speak up or, worse, remain silent because they fear retaliation or being ignored by managers or peers. I remember my first major iterative development project. We were building a huge scheduling system that controlled broadcasting distributed across a series of satellites. Our project was divided into two subprojects; mine was responsible for building a system that scheduled all the broadcasting, while the other was building a real-time system for feeding the scheduling information from our system to a series of satellites. The problem was that a Sunday football broadcast, for example, might require last-minute changes to the schedule if the game was running late. We had to decide whether to do late changes in the upstream scheduling system and have the information transferred to the downstream real-time system through a very fast interface, or provide the functionality for making scheduling changes directly in the real-time system. Unfortunately, we didn't resolve these issues until late in the project, because even though several of us were aware of the risk early on, we never escalated the risk to ensure that it received the right level of attention. Once we eventually decided how to proceed, we had to rework parts of the architecture, which took us several months.

Some risks, such as staff turnover and schedule slip, are a reality in most projects and should be taken into account in advance, for example by putting in buffers in the schedule. Other issues are outside the control of the project. If you have no way of influencing something or its consequences, it is not a risk, but rather a constraint that you have to live with.

Now that we have discussed the nature of risks, the need to attack them early on, and the importance of continuously reassessing what risks you are facing, let's look at some concrete guidelines for managing risk.

## Applying the Practice

Managing risk requires a multifaceted approach involving the entire team.

- Identify the risks you are facing.
- Document serious risks.
- Openly discuss them inside and outside your team.
- Develop plans for how to address the most serious risks, that is, those that are deemed the most harmful to the project.
- Focus your extended team on addressing risks.

Let's explore each of these activities and discuss some of the benefits of effective risk management.

## Identify Risks

At the beginning of each iteration, all team members should jointly consider what risks they are facing and make a list of top risks (or revise an existing list). But how do you find risks? It is good to look for risks by type. You may, for example, look for risks related to resources, business, technical issues, and scheduling. You can then walk through a standard set of risks that often occur in each of these categories.

*Make a list of top risks at the beginning of each iteration.*

Finding risks should be everybody's responsibility, and each team member should make contributions to the risk list to ensure that all serious risks have been found. It is, however, important to involve people with the right experience from the domain where the risk originates. Otherwise, you will have problems both finding and addressing the risk. Following is a partial list of risks found in RUP.

*Organization*

- Is there sufficient commitment to this project (including management, testers, QA, and other external but involved parties)?
- Is this project the largest this organization has ever attempted?
- Is there a well-defined process for software engineering, including requirements capture and management?

*Funding*

- Is the funding in place to complete the project?
- Has funding been allocated for training and mentoring?
- Are there budget limitations that require the system to be delivered at a fixed cost or be subject to cancellation?
- Are cost estimates accurate?

*People*

- Are enough people available?
- Do they have appropriate skills and experience?

## Document Serious Risks

Risks can be documented in many ways: on whiteboards, on a Wiki,[4] in a spreadsheet, or in a risk management tool. For each risk specify:

- A *name* or label for the risk.
- A *brief description* of the risk.

---

4. A Wiki is a Web site that can be edited by the viewers through their Web browser; see www.wiki.org.

- The *impact* of the risk, that is how seriously its occurrence will affect your project outcome.
- The *probability* of the risk occurring.
- The *magnitude* of the risk, that is, its impact times probability. This field is typically used to sort the risk list, ensuring that risks of the greatest magnitude are addressed first.
- The *owner* of the risk, that is, the person responsible for ensuring that the risk is mitigated (mitigating a risk is typically a team effort, but somebody needs to manage that effort).
- The *management strategy* or *plan* for addressing the risk. This could include steps to *mitigate*, *avoid*, or *transfer* the risk. We will discuss those three risk strategies more below.

Based on your needs, you may choose a subset of the above attributes, or a number of additional attributes, such as whether it is a technical, nontechnical, architecturally significant, or legal risk.

You should prioritize the risk list according to magnitude and then determine what you need to do to address, typically, the top three to five risks. Table 2.1 provides an example of how to compile a risk list. As you prioritize the list based on magnitude, it is important to understand that your end goal is to identify which risks the team needs to focus on first. Resist the urge to argue about whether the probability is 65 percent or 70 percent, or whether the impact should be a 2 or a 3. Just choose a value that is in the right ballpark (for most projects, this is not a very exact science); if the risk is among the top 15, assess whether you consider it prioritized appropriately, and if not, adjust the probability and/or impact to make sure that your top 5 or 10 risks represent the ones you should focus on.

*Prioritize the risk list and address the top three to five risks.*

Table 2.1 shows suggested column headings, but you can use whichever headings are useful for your project, or add more columns as appropriate. Additional columns that could be useful include risk category and status. It is generally worth starting with less information to minimize overhead, and adding more as necessary. Later in this practice we'll add a management plan for each of these risks.

**TABLE 2.1 Sample Risk List.** *Key risks are listed with name, description, impact, probability, magnitude, and owner. Impact represents the seriousness of the risk occurrence on the project outcome; probability represents the likelihood of the risk occurrence; magnitude is the impact times probability. More columns, such as category and status, may be added if useful. (Adapted from Kroll 2003.)*

| Name | Description | Impact | Probability | Magnitude | Owner |
|---|---|---|---|---|---|
| **Lack of stakeholder buy-in** | Based on past experience, key stakeholders in Department X may not understand or agree to the requirements their own representatives have specified, and as a result will request major changes *after* beta software is delivered. | 3 (High) | 90% | 2.7 | Per, the analyst |
| **Integration with system Y** | We do not understand how we can integrate with legacy system Y. | 3 (High) | 80% | 2.4 | Bruce, the architect |
| **Training material** | We do not have the competency to develop high-quality training material, which may lead to poor training. | 2 (Medium) | 100% | 2.0 | Ellen, the manager |
| **Lack of .NET experience** | We risk developing a technically inferior solution due to lack of experience with the Microsoft .NET platform. | 2 (Medium) | 60% | 1.2 | Heath, the developer |

## Openly Discuss Risks

*Addressing risks should be a priority for everyone.*

Addressing risks should be a priority for everyone throughout the project, but for that to happen, everyone first needs to be aware of the risks to be faced. Many project managers avoid exposing the extended project team to the risk list or are in denial about the existence of the risk. They are afraid that revealing it will look bad to stakeholders and team members and will indicate that they are managing the project poorly. And unfortunately, many company executives do more readily criticize than praise project managers who are open about risks.

This is where the XP value "courage" becomes crucial.[5] It should be each team member's responsibility to be both brave enough to speak up and responsible enough not to criticize others who do so, even though the risk may point to a flaw in their area of responsibility. To be successful with iterative development (or any project), you need to foster a culture in which you can openly discuss risks and how to address them. Every project faces risks, and living in denial by avoiding the topic of risk makes your project more likely to fail.

An example of a very effective mechanism for increasing risk visibility to ensure that risks are properly discussed is to put up a huge sign in a common place such as the lunchroom or team room, a so-called information radiator,[6] listing the top ten risks on the project and who is responsible for addressing each one. As a result, everybody knows what risks the project is facing and feels encouraged to discuss the best way to deal with them.

## Develop a Plan for Addressing the Most Serious Risks

Typically, risks need to be addressed from multiple perspectives—for example, business perspectives such as scope, funding, and resources as well as technical perspectives such as requirements, design, and testing. For each of these perspectives, start with a coarse solution and successively refine it to diminish the risk. Table 2.2 shows examples of actions in the risk management plan that you can take to deal with the risks identified in Table 2.1.

As with all software development activities, it is important to focus more on execution than planning. Plan enough about how to address the most serious risks so that you can effectively mitigate the top risks. If you are able to focus on only three to five risks at a time, there is no point in doing detailed planning of the top 15 risks.

---

5. See Beck 2004.
6. See Cockburn 2002.

**TABLE 2.2 Example of Risk Management Plans.** *Each risk should have an associated action in the risk management plan that articulates how to manage the risk. There are three basic management strategies to choose from: risk mitigation, risk avoidance, and risk transfer. (Adapted from Kroll 2003.)*

| Name | Description | Management Plan |
|------|-------------|-----------------|
| **Lack of stakeholder buy-in** | Based on past experience, key stakeholders in Department X may not understand or agree to the requirements their own representatives have specified, and as a result will request major changes *after* beta software is delivered. | **Strategy: Risk Mitigation** (Reduce magnitude of risk.)<br><br>As use cases requested by Department X are described, complement them with a UI prototype and partial implementations. Set up a meeting with key stakeholders in Department X and walk them through use cases as they are completed, using the UI prototype and partial implementations as a storyboard. Make sure that you get meaningful feedback from key stakeholders. Throughout the project, keep Department X in the loop on progress and provide them with early prototypes and/or alpha releases. |
| **Integration with system Y** | We do not understand how we can integrate with legacy system Y. | **Alternative A—Strategy: Risk Mitigation**<br>Have a "tiger team" of one or two skilled developers build an actual prototype that validates how to integrate with legacy system Y. The integration may be a throwaway, but the prototype should prove that you actually can integrate with the legacy system. Design, implement, and test appropriate use-case scenarios throughout the project to validate the integration with legacy system Y.<br><br>**Alternative B—Strategy: Risk Avoidance**<br>(Modify project to prevent risk occurrence.)<br>Cut the scope of the project so that you do not have to integrate with legacy system Y. |
| **Training material** | We do not have the competency to develop high-quality training material, which may lead to poor training. | **Strategy: Risk Transfer** (Reorganize project so that some other organization owns the risk.)<br>Outsource development of training material to external organization. (Note that this action may introduce another set of risks.) |

**TABLE 2.2 Continued**

| Name | Description | Management Plan |
|---|---|---|
| **Lack of .NET experience** | We risk developing a technically inferior solution due to lack of experience with the Microsoft .NET platform. | **Strategy: Risk Mitigation**<br>Send a couple of people for training on Microsoft .NET, and find the budget to bring in a .NET mentor two days per week for the first three weeks of the project. Recruit a team member with an understanding of the .NET platform. |

## Focus the Extended Team on Risk Management

Now that you are aware of the risks you face and have a plan for addressing each risk, how can you focus your extended team, including project sponsors and external experts, on using this information to bring about changes in behavior? Here are some considerations:

- Always keep in mind what Tom Gilb[7] said: "If you don't actively attack the risks, they will actively attack you."
- As you plan an iteration, look at what you would "normally" do for the iteration at hand and then slightly modify the plan to make sure that you deal with your risks. Schedule activities that will mitigate risk. This provides the right focus on risk mitigation, as well as allowing you to understand how much time is spent on it.
- In your daily status meetings (scrums) or weekly staff meetings, use the risk list to help determine what actions to take and what code to develop and test next. Because the risk list represents issues that may make or break the project, it deserves a lot of attention in your staff meetings. Make sure to include updates on key risks as you report risk status.
- Make sure that each team member has access to a current version of the risk list. As necessary, use large, visible charts to ensure that all team members are aware of and react to the most serious risks. Involve extended team members who may be able to help the

---

7. Gilb 1988.

team mitigate risks—business sponsors, higher-level management, external experts, and members from other teams you are collaborating with, such as development teams for systems that you are integrating with.

*Attacking risk is a constant battle.*

One thing to keep in mind is that the risk list continually changes. Attacking risk is a constant battle; in each iteration you will be able to reduce or remove some risks, as others grow and new ones appear.

## Make Your Ability to Manage Risk a Key Differentiator

*If you can effectively manage and mitigate risk, you can take on higher-risk projects.*

One of the key points DeMarco (2003) makes is that if you can effectively manage and mitigate risk, you can take on higher-risk projects, that is, you can assume the risk of being more innovative, leverage newer technologies, undertake more complex projects, take on more challenging business environments, and so on. Effective risk management thus not only allows you to execute your projects more effectively but also enables you to go down roads that others are unable or unwilling to take.

## Other Methods

Waterfall processes differ from iterative processes in that they defer integration and testing activities to the latter half of the project, which results in fewer risks being identified early on, as well as making it more difficult for the team to verify that an identified risk has been sufficiently addressed.

*All agile and iterative processes focus on the need to manage risk.*

All agile and iterative processes focus on the need to manage risk, but with some variations. As an example, in *Planning Extreme Programming* Kent Beck and Martin Fowler find that "Programmers want to do high-risk stories first, and customers want to tackle high-value stories first. . . . It is the programmers' task to make the risk visible, not to make the decision." XP provides limited guidance on the topic of managing risk, but several practices are designed to drive down risk:

- Make risks widely visible to the team, for example by dedicating whiteboard space for a risk list.

- Use short one- to two-week iterations with continuous integration and testing to provide quick feedback loops.
- Make customers a part of the project team to ensure that both business and technical people evolve and validate the application together.

One difference between the Unified Process and XP is that the Unified Process lifecycle puts greater emphasis on prioritization based on risk, especially technical risk, whereas XP emphasizes less early investment in mitigating technical risk in favor of customer prioritization of what problems to address. Each of the four phases in the Unified Process—Inception, Elaboration, Construction, and Transition—carries a distinct focus on mitigating a different type of risk. For example, risks associated with understanding the overall project scope, business case, and gaining stakeholder buy-in are the primary focus of the Inception phase.

Scrum does not emphasize risk management as a discipline; it does, however, place a strong emphasis on removing impediments through the daily scrum meetings, at which each team member identifies issues standing in the way of progress on the project. It is the scrum master's job to eliminate these issues rapidly. Scrum also emphasizes mitigation of the specific risk of churn within an iteration by strongly discouraging new change requests to be addressed within an iteration. Instead, change requests are considered for implementation in the next or other future iteration.

## Levels of Adoption

This practice can be adopted at different levels:

- **Basic.** Work on risky areas earlier rather than later. Don't ignore risks as they show up. Determine which risks to focus on in each iteration.

  Prioritizing your work according to risk makes it easier to have shorter iterations by providing a structure for dividing your work into smaller chunks that can fit within an iteration. As an example, identify the minimum steps you need to take to address your top three risks, and use that as a starting point for what to do within the next iteration.

- **Intermediate.** Update the risk list for every iteration, and make sure that you list at least a handful of risks. Make the risk list clearly visible to all team members. Walk through and update the list in team meetings, and make it a primary tool for discussing status and what actions to take.

At this level, start to introduce more formality or discipline. The emphasis on risks enables you to determine effectively just what you need to focus on in the next iteration, and thus also what you do *not* need to focus on. This emphasis typically leads to the ability to have shorter iterations.

- **Advanced.** Use a risk management tool and a risk management plan to allow a more comprehensive and consistent treatment of risk within your organization. Maintain traceability links between risks and related artifacts and activities that will either help mitigate the risk or are affected by it. As an example of traceability, if you have scheduled five different tasks all related to mitigating a risk, you should be able to find those tasks and their status by calling up the risk on the risk management tool.

As you introduce yet more formality and tooling, you will increase the learning curve for new team members, hence moving you to the right on the process map. The overhead with the practice is limited, however, and does not significantly affect the length of iterations. This level is appropriate for larger projects and projects that need more ceremony.

## Related Practices

- *Practice 2: Execute Your Project in Iterations* describes how to plan iterative development and divide a project into a series of iterations. Risk drives the actions taken in each iteration.
- *Practice 3: Embrace and Manage Change* describes what changes to encourage and discourage at what time within a project. Discouraging certain types of changes late in the project is essential to manage risk effectively.

- *Practice 10: Prioritize Requirements for Implementation* shows how to determine which requirements to address in early iterations to drive the architecture and to mitigate key risks.

## Additional Information

## Information in the Unified Process

The project management discipline in OpenUP/Basic describes how to identify and manage risks and how to use risk to drive iteration planning. It also provides basic templates for risk management. The project management discipline in RUP expands on this content by adding more elaborate templates and guidelines, as well as examples of risk lists. Formal projects may also leverage the risk management plan in RUP to ensure that risk is properly identified, analyzed, documented, mitigated, monitored, and controlled.

## Additional Reading

The following book provides a good understanding of how risk can be used as a competitive differentiator:

Tom DeMarco and Timothy Lister. *Waltzing with Bears: Managing Risk on Software Projects.* Dorset House, 2003.

The following books provide a good overview of the discipline of risk management:

Barry W. Boehm. "Software Risk Management: Principles and Practices." *IEEE Software,* January 1991, pp. 32–41.

Marvin Carr et al. *Taxonomy Based Risk Identification.* Software Engineering Institute, 1993.

Robert Charette. *Software Engineering Risk Analysis and Management.* McGraw-Hill, 1989.

Capers Jones. *Assessment and Control of Software Risks.* Yourdon Press, 1994.

Dale Karolak. *Software Engineering Risk Management.* IEEE Computer Society Press, 1996.

# Execute Your Project in Iterations

by Per Kroll

*Iterative development cycles give rapid and timely
feedback so that the software can be continually improved
along the development lifecycle.*

## Problem

Today's software applications are too complex to allow you to sequentially define the requirements, come up with an architecture and design, do an implementation, carry out testing, and get it all right. Whether you use waterfall or iterative development approaches, your initial requirements, architecture, design, and code will be suboptimal. With waterfall development, you typically do not get meaningful feedback on what improvements can be made until it is so late in the project that it is too costly to make them. By contrast, dividing the project into a series of time-boxed iterations allows you to deliver incrementally capabilities that can be assessed by stakeholders at the end of each iteration. This approach provides rapid and timely feedback loops enabling issues to be addressed and improvements made at a lower cost while budget and time still allow, and before the project has gone so far ahead that major rework is required.

## Background

Assume that you want to write a book. How would you go about it? You could start by writing page 1 and then continue page by page until you have completed the entire book. You could then give it to people to read and review.

But what might happen if you followed such a process? Your publisher might say that there is no market for your book, at least not without a major rewrite; your reviewers might point out that the book needs major restructuring to be readable; and your editor might ask you to write in a different style altogether. In the end you might need to scrap half of the manuscript or more and do it all over again.

This sounds like a crazy approach, right? But many teams develop software this way. Let's look at an alternative approach to writing a book—the one we used when writing this one. The main idea was to get rapid feedback on key elements of the book so that we could rethink and improve it. We wanted to get this feedback *before* we invested the time required to write the complete text. We therefore divided the writing into a number of succinct iterations, each of which resulted in a well-defined deliverable that could readily be assessed, to ensure that we all understood the status of our book project and to get meaningful feedback on how to improve the book. The iterations included the following:

- **Iteration 1.** Get buy-in on the idea that this book is worth writing. Write the preface, a brief outline of each chapter with an enumeration of potential practices, and a sample practice. Get OK from publisher.

- **Iteration 2.** Get initial buy-in on what practices to include and how to structure a practice. Write a couple of paragraphs for each potential practice. Have each author lay out one or two practices in detail to ensure agreement on overall style. Make a preliminary selection of which practices to include in the book.

- **Iteration 3.** Validate that we have a stable book outline and structure. Draft half of the most fundamental practices, ensuring that reviewers obtain a good understanding of what the end result may look like. Send for internal technical review.

- **Iteration 4.** Validate key messages and understand what additional fine tuning and rework are needed. Complete a draft of 75 percent of the book. Address comments from first review. Send for external technical review.

- **Iteration 5.** Produce a complete version of the entire book. Incorporate external reviewers' suggestions for improvements, among other things aligning the book more closely with other writing in the agile community. Produce a stable version of the entire book. Do initial edit of the book. Send for second external review.

- **Iteration 6.** Polish the book. Address review comments. Edit the book. Finalize artwork, index, bibliography, and any other remaining work. Send to production team for completion.
- **Iteration 7.** Review final editing of the book and address feedback from production team. Send out for production and publication.

As you can see, each iteration has a well-defined deliverable that can be readily assessed. Based on that assessment, we may scrap some of the work done and then determine what changes we should make to the overall project, including modifying the timeline or scope of the book. You can also see that we first flesh out a broad solution and then keep detailing and refining it. Finally, we keep spearheading the effort by picking critical, but narrow, areas where we provide detailed solutions to drive out risk and to understand what the overall solution will look like.

The above iterations map well to the Unified Process lifecycle, where Inception is iteration 1; Elaboration is iterations 2 and 3; Construction is iterations 4 and 5; and Transition is iterations 6 and 7.

Many software teams, however, are in effect still writing the book straight through from the first page to the end by using a *waterfall* process for development projects. They complete each phase in strict sequence: requirements analysis, then design, then implementation/integration, and then testing. Or, more commonly, they use a modified waterfall approach, with feedback loops added to the basic overall flow described above. Such approaches defer integration and testing until the end of the project lifecycle, when problems tend to be tough and expensive to resolve, as well as posing serious threats to release deadlines and project budgets.

*Each iteration has a well-defined set of objectives and produces a partial working implementation of the final system.*

By contrast, an iterative approach divides a project into a sequence of iterations, each of which evolves through the requirements, analysis, design, implementation, and testing assets, as you can see in Figure 2.2. Early iterations place a greater emphasis on requirements, analysis, and design; later iterations focus more on implementation and testing. Each iteration has a well-defined set of objectives and produces a partial working implementation of the final system. Further, each successive iteration builds on the work of previous iterations to develop and refine the system until the final product is complete.

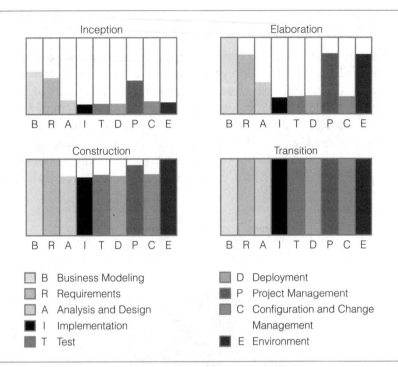

**FIGURE 2.2 Iterative Development.** *Each iteration involves some requirements, analysis, design, implementation, and testing. Each iteration builds on the work of the previous one to produce an executable that is one step closer to the final product.*

## Advantages of the Iterative Approach[8]

Some project managers resist the iterative approach, seeing it as a kind of endless and uncontrolled hacking. The risk-driven iterative approach is, however, very disciplined: the iteration length is fixed; the objectives of iterations are carefully planned; and the tasks and responsibilities of participants are well defined. Additionally, objective measures of progress are captured. Some reworking takes place from one iteration to the next, but this too is done in a structured fashion.

---

8. This section adapted from Kroll 2003.

The iterative approach has proved itself superior to the waterfall approach for a number of reasons[9]:

- **You are more likely to build an application that addresses user needs**. Early specification of requirements often leads to unused features. The Standish Group has researched thousands of application development projects and has found that more than 45 percent of features are never used, while another 19 percent are used rarely[10] (see Figure 2.3). In other words, typically more than half of the development effort is wasted on developing nonessential capabilities. To avoid this problem, you need to involve the cus-

**Features and Function Usage**

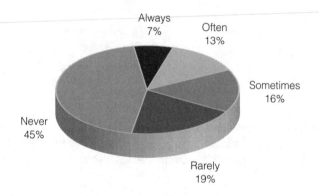

**FIGURE 2.3 Most Features Implemented Are Never or Rarely Used.** *An amazing 45 percent of features implemented are never used, while another 19 percent are used only rarely. If features never used were not implemented in the first place, development time would be cut in about half. Further, since productivity is typically measured in the form of lines of code or functionality delivered, this improvement would not register as a productivity increase using standard productivity measures.*

---

9. For comprehensive coverage of the motivation and evidence that iterative development is more effective than waterfall development, see Larman 2004, Chapters 5 and 6.

10. Chaos 2003.

tomer in the development project and use an iterative approach that allows you to implement and validate the capabilities deemed most essential in each iteration. This approach allows not only early validation of key capabilities but also addition of new capabilities late in the project.

- **Integration is not one "big bang" at the end of a project.** Leaving integration to the end results in time- and budget-consuming rework. To avoid this, an iterative approach breaks a project down into smaller iterations, each evolving executable code that is continuously integrated to enable rapid feedback and minimize later rework.

- **Risks are usually discovered or addressed during early iterations**. With the iterative approach, risks are more likely to be identified and addressed in early iterations. As an example, if there is a risk that a stakeholder will not be happy with the functionality you are developing, iterative development will encourage you to implement the most essential capabilities partially and demonstrate them to key stakeholders to make sure that you are on the right track.

- **Your ability to work effectively is fine-tuned.** During early iterations, team members are walking through all lifecycle activities, from requirements capture and test definition to development, implementation, and testing. Consequently, they can make sure they have the tools, skills, organizational structure, and so on to work effectively.

- **Management has a way of making tactical changes to the product.** Management can make changes to the product along the way—to compete with other new products, for example. Iterative development allows you to evolve partial implementations of the end product quickly and use these for quick release of a reduced-scope product to counter a competitor's move.

- **Reuse is facilitated.** It is easier to identify common parts as they are being partially designed or implemented in iterations than to recognize them at the beginning. Discussions and reviews of the design in early iterations allow team members to spot potential

*During early iterations, team members are walking through all lifecycle activities, making sure they have the tools, skills, and organizational structure to work effectively.*

opportunities for reuse and then develop a mature common code for these opportunities in subsequent iterations.[11]

- **Defects can be found and corrected over several iterations.** This capability results in a robust architecture and a high-quality application. Flaws are detected in early iterations, rather than during a massive testing phase at the end. Performance bottlenecks are discovered while they can still be addressed instead of creating panic on the eve of delivery.

- **Project personnel are better used.** Many organizations match their use of a waterfall approach with a pipeline organization: the analysts send the completed requirements to designers, who send a completed design to programmers, who send components to integrators, who send a system to testers. These many handoffs are sources of errors and misunderstandings and make people feel less responsible for the final product; see *Practice 7: Everyone Owns the Product!* for more information. An iterative process encourages widening the scope of expertise of the team members, allowing them to play many roles and thus enabling a project manager to make better use of the available staff and simultaneously remove problematic handoffs.[12]

- **Team members learn along the way.** The project members have several opportunities within a development cycle to learn from their mistakes and improve their skills from one iteration to another. More training opportunities can be discovered as a result of assessing the earlier iterations.

- **The development process itself is improved and refined along the way.** The end of iteration assessment not only looks at the project status from a product or scheduling perspective but also analyzes what can be improved in the next iteration in both the organization and the process—the agile community often refers to this as "retrospective."[13] See *Practice 20: Continuously Reevaluate What You Do* for more information.

---

11. A lot of reuse also happens cross-project.
12. Ambler 2002.
13. Kerth 2001.

## Applying the Practice

To build your project effectively in iterations, you need to (1) decide how many iterations you need and the appropriate length of the iterations; (2) determine what risks you are facing and how they could impact your iterations; (3) figure out what executables and deliverables should be produced in each iteration; and (4) assess the iterations and leverage the experiences gained during the execution to fine-tune your plan for the next iteration. Let's explore each of these activities.

## Decide the Number of Iterations and Their Length

To decide on the number of iterations and the iteration length suitable for your project, you need to have an idea of the staffing level and duration of the project. First, size the project using the estimation approach of your choice, such as function points, COCOMO,[14] or expert opinion, where past experiences from similar projects are used to estimate future projects. Then determine a rough staffing profile, and use this information to assess the approximate project duration.

Next, you need to determine what is an appropriate iteration length for your project. We recommend using four weeks (this is the default recommendation by RUP and Scrum, while XP recommends one or two weeks) as a starting point for your discussion around iteration length. Then analyze factors that will impact the iteration length. Table 2.3 provides an overview of many of these factors.

You also want to keep the total number of iterations to a reasonable number. Project teams new to iterative development may have problems handling a project with more than three to four iterations, whereas project teams experienced in iterative development may have projects with ten or more iterations.

Based on the above factors, you could find that the appropriate iteration length is two weeks for a four-month long project with four collocated,

---

14. COCOMO is a Software Cost Estimation Model; see Boehm 2000.

**TABLE 2.3 Factors Impacting Iteration Length.** *The appropriate iteration length is influenced by a large number of factors, including team size and organization, the sophistication of the supporting tool environment, the experience of team members, and the complexity of the domain and architecture.*

| Factors Leading to Reduced Iteration Length | Factors Leading to Increased Iteration Length |
|---|---|
| Small teams | Large teams |
| Collocated teams | Distributed teams |
| Strong configuration management system | Poor configuration management system |
| Dedicated, full-time resources | Matrixed or part-time resources |
| Automated testing | Lack of automated testing |
| Integrated tool environment | Absence of good automation and tool integration |
| Team experienced with iterative development | Team inexperienced with iterative development |
| Fast decision making | Policies and bureaucracy preventing fast decision making |
| Unclear requirements | Well-understood requirements |
| Unclear or brittle architecture | Well-defined and stable architecture |
| New and poorly understood technology | Well-understood technology |

experienced team members with a good tool environment. Meanwhile, a two-year, technically complex, distributed project with sixty team members, inexperienced in iterative development and with a poor tool environment, may require an iteration length of six weeks. Large projects should, however, consider breaking up the project into several smaller projects, each delivering a part of the end solution. See also the section Iteration Profiles for Very Long Projects on page 53.

## Determine What Risks Need to Be Addressed and in What Order

Each iteration should produce the working software and, potentially, other deliverables required to address a set of risks, but what risks should be addressed at what time? You want to address the most serious risks first—those that will most severely impact the project outcome. But how do you handle risk that is not known early in the project? This is where the four phases in the Unified Process lifecycle come in handy.

*Address the most serious risks first.*

The Unified Process lifecycle provides a consistent approach to managing projects when the phases are coupled to risk mitigation. These phases are also powerful tools in iteration planning. They are, in order:

*The Unified Process lifecycle phases are coupled to risk mitigation.*

1. **Inception phase.** Mitigate business risks, understand the scope of the project, build the business case, and get stakeholder buy-in to move ahead. This phase corresponds to Iteration 0 in many agile approaches. Note that the Unified Process lifecycle allows you to have more than one iteration in the Inception phase if needed.

2. **Elaboration phase.** Mitigate major project risks. Major technical risks are mitigated by creating a baseline executable architecture, allowing you to understand what it takes to build the system. Major business risks are, among others, mitigated by delivering the most important end-user capabilities.

3. **Construction phase.** Mitigate risks related to the ability to produce a complete product. Build the first operational version of the product.

4. **Transition phase.** Mitigate risks related to whether the product is acceptable to the customer. Build the final version of the product and deliver to the customer.

Using the iteration length and number of iterations, you can now determine how many iterations you need in each phase to address the type of risks and produce the type of results expected from each phase. If your project is facing a lot of risk associated with the business case, scope, and stakeholder buy-in, plan for more iterations in

**TABLE 2.4 Examples of Iteration Profiles for Different Projects.** *This table shows an example of different iteration profiles. We see that higher architectural risk drives up the number of iterations in the Elaboration phase. The number and length of iterations depend on many different factors.*

| Project Length (months) | Iteration Length (weeks) | Architectural Risk | Number of Iterations Per Phase | | | |
|---|---|---|---|---|---|---|
| | | | Inception | Elaboration | Construction | Transition |
| 4 | 2 | Low | 1 | 1 | 4 | 2 |
| 24 | 6 | High | 2 | 4 | 8 | 2 |

the Inception phase. If your project is facing a lot of architectural risk, plan for more iterations in the Elaboration phase, and so on.

It could be that the four-month project with two-week iterations will have an iteration profile of 1, 1, 4, 2, that is, one iteration in Inception, one in Elaboration, four in Construction, and two in Transition (see Table 2.4). This profile would indicate that the project planners expect to produce stable requirements, a business case, and a baselined architecture very quickly. On the other hand, the two-year project with six-week iterations may have an iteration profile of 2, 4, 8, 2, meaning that the planners expect to need a lot of time to get the architecture right and expect to make steady progress once that is done.

## Determine a Series of Executables and Deliverables That Will Take You to the End Point

*Outline at a high level the expected end result of each iteration.*

Once you have established the initial iteration profile (which you will have opportunities to rethink later in the project based on progress made), outline at a high level the expected end result of each iteration, primarily expressed as what capabilities should be implemented and tested with favorable feedback from customer representatives. These are similar to Sprint Goals in Scrum (Schwaber 2002). It is often enough just to document a few bullets. The Background section at the beginning of this chapter provided a good example of such a brief list in relation to our book project, showing what should be accomplished in each iteration. This is a part of what the Unified Process calls the Phase Plan,[15] and there is *one* such plan for the entire project. The

Phase Plan is purposely kept at a high level, typically only one or two pages long, for small projects.

## Assess Iteration and Plan the Next Iteration

Project managers who produce detailed iteration plans for entire projects at the start of a project are usually wasting everybody's time conveying false precision where there can be none. Instead, detailed planning should be carried out incrementally, when sufficient information is available.[16] Toward the end of each iteration, the team produces a detailed plan of the next iteration and outlines what capabilities should be implemented and tested, including how to assess the iteration through, among other means, test cases, and demonstrations to key stakeholders.

At the end of each iteration, assess the iteration by analyzing test results, reviewing what was produced, and collecting feedback from customer representatives. The iteration assessment gives you an objective and precise reading of where you are. You can now compare where you are with where you expected to be and where you need to go; and you can then use this information to update the Phase Plan as needed. The Phase Plan is hence used as a high-level and evolving roadmap, showing where you expect to be at the end of each iteration and where you need to end up at the completion of the whole project. Using a Phase Plan in combination with iteration assessments is a very powerful tool that allows you to understand overall project performance and helps you decide whether you need to make changes to the project, or even to kill it altogether.

*Using a Phase Plan in combination with iteration assessments allows you to understand overall project performance.*

## Iteration Profiles for Very Long Projects

Some large or long projects may be difficult to break up into smaller projects. For these projects, we use the notion of super-iterations and mini-iterations. A super-iteration is typically several months long and

---

15. Phase Plan was previously referred to as a Coarse Project Plan in RUP.

16. See Chapter 12 in Kroll 2003 for more information on how to plan using two levels of detail, coarse project planning, and iteration planning.

provides a well-defined integration point for the entire project that is formally assessed, resembling what XP calls quarterly cycles. In contrast, mini-iterations are typically a few weeks long and provide subteams with the benefits of short iterations with quick feedback loops.

Let's look at an example: A 100-person project lasting two years may have super-iterations that are three months long: every three months there is a very well-defined and well-tested deliverable integrating everything that has been done and delivering something of tangible value to the end users. These super-iterations are tracked in the Phase Plan and used as a major decision point for the project.

The project may be divided into ten or so subteams. Each subteam will divide its work into, for example, three-week mini-iterations, with four mini-iterations in each super-iteration. Each mini-iteration is tested and validated with the stakeholders specifically interested in that set of capabilities. The subteam thus receives quick and timely feedback on what it is doing, as well as gaining increased maneuverability by becoming less dependent on the work of other teams.

Projects should aim to integrate and test all code frequently, ideally creating a build and automatically testing it after each check-in, as recommended by XP. In our experience, this method is not feasible for many larger or legacy projects, due to lack of skills, lack of test automation, poor build processes,[17] or the complexity of larger projects in which meaningful automated test suites may take too long to run. Other examples include distributed development, or development done across organizational borders, leveraging different infrastructures, or cases where some subprojects develop components, such as hardware components, that cannot be evolved continuously as software can. The mini- and super-iterations provide a framework for managing these situations by having subteams do frequent integration and testing of their set of components, while doing integration and testing of the larger systems less frequently. Comprehensive testing, such as

---

17. The cost of changing the basic environment and retraining people is often too prohibitive to be carried by one project and makes it necessary to implement the change over a series of projects. The time, however, is well worth the investment, at least if the system will be maintained for some time.

load and performance testing, may be carried out primarily toward the end of super-iterations, with the last few weeks focusing solely on stabilizing the build and making quality improvements.

## Other Methods

A strict waterfall project runs a project as one iteration, with a strict sequence of requirements, design, implementation, and testing. Often, such a project is forced to add one or several bug-fixing iterations at the end to deal with unexpected integration and quality issues.

In practice, few projects do strict waterfall development. Instead, many apply mini-iterations as part of a larger waterfall project. As issues are identified, teams are assembled to do a mini-iteration to drive out a specific risk. At any given time zero to several teams may be doing mini-iterations, often without synchronization in terms of common iteration ends.

In 1988 Professor Barry Boehm[18] introduced the spiral model, which is an incremental and risk-driven development approach. In this model a project is divided into a number of iterations, each of which goes through planning, requirements, design, implementation, integration and testing, and so on sequentially. Each iteration is hence a mini-waterfall project, delivering a product increment.

*In the spiral model, each iteration is a mini-waterfall project.*

Iterative and agile methods such as RUP, Scrum, XP, and OpenUP/Basic apply an iterative approach in which each iteration continuously develops the requirements, design, implementation, and testing without a sequential order. Sometimes you do a little coding to understand how to improve the design, only to do more coding the next day, followed by some testing, and then some requirements work. RUP, Scrum, XP, and OpenUP/Basic vary, however, in their recommendations for iteration lengths and how individual iterations are executed.

*RUP, Scrum, XP, and OpenUP/Basic apply an iterative approach in which requirements, design, implementation, and testing evolve without a sequential order.*

XP recommends short one- to two-week iterations with continuous integration and testing to provide quick feedback loops. The work of

---

18. Boehm 1988.

each iteration is prioritized by the customer or customer representative, and should deliver what is deemed most important to the customer. Approaches using the Unified Process lifecycle, on the other hand, prioritize based on a combination of risk and customer importance. Each iteration delivers an executable that may be put into production.

Scrum recommends four-week iterations. Scrum projects focus on continuous communication, with a short daily stand-up meeting with the entire project team at which each person briefly reviews status and discusses any roadblocks that need to be resolved. Each iteration has a well-defined objective, and no changes to the objectives are allowed during the iteration. Scrum manages large projects through a "scrum of scrums," in which representatives of each subteam get together daily to resolve cross-team issues.

The Unified Process has many similarities to Scrum. It recommends four-week iterations but advises you when to consider longer or shorter ones. Iterations in both Scrum and Unified Process should be executed without changes to the objectives, except in extraordinary circumstances. There are also some notable differences between the two methods, though. The Unified Process lifecycle defines four distinct phases, each having a well-defined business objective and containing one or several iterations. Another key difference is that the Unified Process integrates the management lifecycle with a process for how to carry out the technical work, to facilitate practical implementation of the management process, and ensure that the management process works well with the technical process. Scrum, on the other hand, addresses only the management aspect, allowing integration with a variety of processes.

## Levels of Adoption

The iterative development practice can be adopted at three levels:

- **Basic.** At the basic level, move toward incremental delivery of capabilities, and replan your project to reflect lessons learned along the way.

In many projects the easiest way to move toward incremental delivery is first to do one or two iterations primarily focusing on requirements and high-level architecture, and then to divide the projects into chunks of functionality, where each functionality set is detailed, designed, implemented, integrated, tested, and validated in each iteration.

Using the Unified Process lifecycle, this approach could be translated as primarily doing waterfall development through Elaboration (still trying to build some prototypes during Inception and Elaboration) while adopting the iterative approach in Construction and Transition. In our experience, it is normally easier for new teams to do iterative development in the Construction phase, since they have a stable architecture and a good understanding of the requirements, allowing for an easier discussion about what to do in which iteration.[19] This level should be seen as only an interim step toward the intermediate level, and never as an end goal. Projects able to go directly to the intermediate level should do so.

- **Intermediate.** Use risk as a primary driver for your iteration planning. Produce an executable architecture early in the project to mitigate technical risks. This means that early on you should design, implement, and test some of the most essential components, the interfaces of your subsystems, and relevant architectural patterns. Deliver high-priority capabilities in early iterations to ensure that you deliver continuous value to end users. All projects should try to reach this level.

- **Advanced.** At the advanced level, very large or long projects may introduce the concept of super-iterations and mini-iterations. This approach will allow you to have shorter iterations, since the mini-iterations have a minimum of overhead. It does, however, also introduce some additional management complexity, increasing the required skill level of your managers and thus moving you to the right on the process map.

---

19. Note that many of the earlier iterative processes followed this pattern, such as HP's Fusion, early versions of DSDM, and many homegrown iterative processes we have run into.

Projects of all sizes fine-tune their ability to do shorter iterations by, for example, improving build and test automation, accelerating decision making, increasing high-bandwidth communication or other means of reducing ceremony, and hence reducing the cost of doing iterations.

## Related Practices

- *Practice 1: Manage Risk* talks about identifying and prioritizing key risks. Key risks are used to determine what to focus on in the next iteration.

- *Practice 3: Embrace and Manage Change* describes what changes to encourage and discourage at what time within a project. Discouraging certain types of changes late in the project is essential to manage risk effectively.

- *Practice 4: Measure Progress Objectively* shows how to assess progress better through iterative development.

- *Practice 6: Leverage Test Automation Appropriately* describes how automating appropriate amounts of the test effort can realize improved product quality and shorter product development schedules, including what tests to automate in early iterations and the benefits of automated regression testing.

- *Practice 7: Everyone Owns the Product!* addresses how all team members need to orient their mindset to enable effective iterative development.

- *Practice 10: Prioritize Requirements for Implementation* shows how to determine which requirements to address in early iterations to deliver high-priority capabilities early, drive the architecture, and to mitigate key risks.

- *Practice 14: Manage Versions* describes how to keep track of changes and various versions of assets. This is crucial in iterative development, since your assets will go through a large amount of churn, and you need to be able to create builds easily.

## Additional Information

### Information in the Unified Process

OpenUP/Basic guides you in how to divide your project into iterations, and how to plan iterations by balancing the continuous need to deliver end-user capabilities with the need to mitigate risk. RUP provides more in-depth guidance on iteration planning, issue, and exception management and how to deal with problem resolution. RUP also provides guidance on formal reviews, Project Review Authorities, and monitoring and control processes appropriate for larger or more complex projects or projects concerned with compliance. Future versions of RUP will provide explicit guidance on mini- and super-iterations.

### Additional Reading

The following books provide guidance on iterative development leveraging the Unified Process lifecycle:

Per Kroll and Philippe Kruchten. *The Rational Unified Process Made Easy: A Practitioner's Guide to the RUP.* Addison-Wesley, 2003.

Scott Ambler, John Nalbone, and Michael Vizdos. *The Enterprise Unified Process: Extending the Rational Unified Process.* Prentice Hall, 2005.

Walker Royce. *Software Project Management: A Unified Framework.* Addison-Wesley, 1998.

The following books provide guidance on other iterative approaches:

Craig Larman. *Agile and Iterative Development: A Manager's Guide.* Addison-Wesley, 2004.

Alistair Cockburn. *Agile Software Development.* Addison-Wesley, 2002.

Ken Schwaber and M. Beedle. *Agile Software Development with SCRUM.* Prentice Hall, 2002.

Kent Beck with Cynthia Andres. *Extreme Programming Explained: Embrace Change, Second Edition.* Addison-Wesley, 2004.

# Embrace and Manage Change

by Per Kroll

*Embracing change helps you to build a system that addresses stakeholder needs, and managing change allows you to reduce costs and improve predictability.*

## Problem

Physical systems, like bridges and skyscrapers, are very difficult to change. Adding a lane to a bridge or expanding a building is extremely costly once construction has begun. For this reason, detailed planning is critical to the success of physical engineering projects.

*Use the working product as a communication medium to help determine what is really needed.*

Software, however, can be changed far more easily. Software can be designed to be configured. Early prototypes can demonstrate behavior, which can then be modified for the final system. Rather than try to design software in detail up front, it is often far better to build some software and use the working product as a communication medium to help determine what is really needed.

Nevertheless, although the ability of software to support changes provides a great opportunity to evolve it to meet changing stakeholder requirements, continuous change presents a challenge to software development teams. Changes can introduce costs that need to be managed. They can also cause developers to thrash around, unable to progress with the software because the requirements are changing faster than they can keep up.

This practice describes how to manage change and keep chaos at bay while embracing necessary and important changes.

## Background

My wife and I are currently in the middle of a garden and house renovation project. We started by writing down a rough sketch of what we wanted to have done—a new deck, a large balcony—and some rough ideas for landscaping our garden. We discussed the project with a few different contractors, asking each to come up with a design. We picked one design (with an associated price tag), and worked with that contractor to refine it to our exact requirements. The contractor was very open to making whatever changes we wanted to ensure that we would be happy with the end result, and we threw around a lot of ideas, while sticking to the overall agreed-upon price.

As the project progressed, we ran into unexpected problems. We did not get a permit for building as large a balcony as we wanted, so we needed to change the plans and design a smaller one. Then, once we changed the structure of the balcony, we decided to alter slightly the dimensions and placement of our deck. At a later stage, our neighbors insisted we plant a few trees as a condition for their approval of the construction of our balcony. All these changes were reasonable, as they did not alter the fundamental parameters of what we were trying to achieve, but some resulted in changes that needed to be approved by all stakeholders, that is the contractor, my wife, and me. For these the contractor produced a "change order," describing in one or two sentences what revisions were being made to the original plan, which we all signed. Sometimes the change order meant a revision to the overall cost of the project, sometimes it did not; but it ensured that we all agreed on what needed to be changed.

As the construction and landscaping project progressed, other, more minor issues needed to be resolved, such as what flowers to plant, exactly where to put plants, what type of stain to use on the deck, and so on. Most of these decisions could be handled without a change order, but for all major revisions we used a change order, not only to make sure that we all agreed on the changes but also to allow us to go back later and understand the end result.

Sometimes my wife and I wanted changes that would have been very expensive. When we first saw the size of the deck, after it was almost completed, we felt that we had gone overboard with the size. Maybe we should have more grass, and less deck. A quick discussion with the contractor made us realize the cost of introducing such a change so late in the project. We decided that we should move ahead with the plans as they were. Project members need to have the guts to inform a customer honestly of the impact of a change (see Figure 2-4).

**FIGURE 2.4 Some Changes Can Be Very Costly.** *The Swedish navy launched a new grand royal flagship, Vasa, in 1628. The Swedish king asked the builder to add a second gun deck after the project was initiated. Nobody dared to tell the king about the associated risk, even though those involved knew that this change would make the ship too top-heavy to be seaworthy. The Vasa sank on its maiden voyage. Always remember to provide your customer with reliable information about the potential impact of a change.*

Running a project like the one above is similar in many ways to running a software project. So what can we learn from the above?

*Major changes can be made early in a project at a very limited cost.*

• Major changes can be made early in a project at a very limited cost. Major alterations carried out later in the project become increasingly expensive to implement. Note that some people in the agile community claim that changes can be made at any time with no cost increase. We will give several examples in this practice showing why this assertion is untrue. Agile techniques, including the ones introduced in this book, aim at reducing the cost of making changes, but they will not completely eliminate the cost of most changes, nor will they allow you to make any type of change at any given stage in a project without potentially serious negative effects.

- To satisfy customer needs, you typically need to introduce a fair amount of change to the original plans. You also need to inform the customer fully of the cost and schedule implications of carrying out changes (especially late in the project) and allow the customer to use this information to determine whether the change is really necessary or not.

- For certain projects, such as those with a contract, as in the construction and landscaping example above, you may need to formalize the changes; in other cases, informal discussion with key stakeholders may be enough. In general, less formality is needed regarding changes at the beginning of a project, but as the project progresses, you should document requested changes with appropriate formality to ensure that their impact is properly understood and agreed on by all stakeholders.

## Applying the Practice

In this practice we will walk through concrete guidelines allowing you to embrace and manage change more effectively. We will first look at different types of change and their associated cost profile and then examine how the Unified Process lifecycle can help you to manage change. We will describe how to adapt the process of managing change to the characteristics of your project and the phase you are in. We will then review some techniques to maximize change freedom, provide guidelines for reducing thrashing by minimizing change within an iteration, and explain how to increase productivity by fixing defects as they are found, rather than maintaining a backlog of defects to be fixed sometime in the future. Let's take a closer look at these topics!

## Understand the Cost Profile of Different Types of Changes

Different types of changes have a different cost based on when in the project they occur, and it is important to understand the cost profiles when prioritizing project work to avoid costly changes at a late stage. Let's look at some examples.

*Understand cost profiles to avoid costly changes at a late stage.*

- **Major changes to the business solution.** Major change to the business solution involves extensive rework of requirements to address a different set of users or user needs. As an example, let's assume that you plan to replace three existing applications with one new application. The cost of replacing each application is $25,000. If on day 1 of the project you decide not to replace one of the applications, the cost is close to $0. If instead you make that decision on the last day of the project, the cost is $25,000 (assuming you cannot reuse the code later on). There is thus a fair amount of flexibility in making this type of modification early in the project, before you have started to invest in requirements, design, implementation, and testing of a specific business solution.

- **Major changes to the architecture.** Major architectural rework is frequently very expensive when done late in the project. Examples of such changes include switching from a rich-client to a thin-client, making a buy-versus-build decision for a major component, or changing strategy for recovery of a safety-critical system. If you decide to make such a change late in the project, you may have to rework vast amounts of code, potentially delaying the project. It is therefore important to validate architectural decisions by partially implementing the application early on. By realizing early what architectural decisions may be suboptimal, you can modify them early on and avoid later rework. Other modifications to the architecture can be made inexpensively. For example, by isolating persistency to be handled by a persistency layer in your architecture, you can change how to deal with persistency with minimal impact to your application at a reasonably late stage. One goal of architectures is to minimize the cost of future changes. Refactoring can also reduce the cost of change, but it only goes so far, as discussed in the section Techniques Maximizing Change Freedom on page 68.

- **Change to the design and implementation.** If you do component-based development, leverage service-oriented architectures, or use other well-structured design approaches that localize the impact of change, you can make limited changes to your design and implementation at fairly low cost up until the end game of the project, when you need to stabilize and fine-tune your application.

- **Reduction of scope.** The cost of cutting scope—and hence post-poning features to the next release—can be relatively inexpensive throughout the project. This method assumes that you use an iter-ative approach whereby you develop the most essential capabili-ties first, and that you cut scope by de-scoping the least essential capabilities first. Project teams should use de-scoping as a key tool to ensure on-time project delivery of the most essential capabilities.

Focusing early iterations on building the prototypes, developing and testing key capabilities, and achieving close collaboration with stake-holders will reduce the likelihood of costly shifts in direction late in the project.

*Focusing early iterations on prototypes and collaboration with stakehold-ers will reduce the likelihood of costly shifts late in the project.*

## The Unified Process Lifecycle and Change

The phases in the Unified Process lifecycle are designed to force the costly changes discussed in the previous section to occur early (see Figure 2.5), while allowing you to make critical decisions as late as safely possible, as discussed in the section Techniques Maximizing Change Freedom.

- The *Inception* phase aims to drive out risks associated with major changes to the business solution. Its purpose is *not* to force detailed specification or prevent later changes to requirements.

- The *Elaboration* phase aims to drive out risks associated with major changes to the architecture by validating a viable architec-ture through implementation of a minimum amount of code. The purpose is not to prevent later changes to the architecture, but to minimize costly changes late in the project.

- The *Construction* phase aims to drive convergence around what constitutes an acceptable operational version of our application, with continuous feedback from early versions of the system lead-ing to the release of a beta version of your application by the end of this phase.

- The *Transition* phase aims to drive out the last issues with the release, with the primary goal of stabilizing the release and addressing last-minute concerns from stakeholders. There may be incremental releases in Transition.

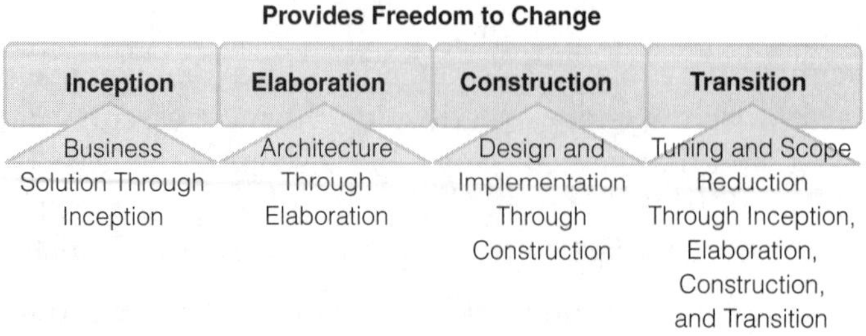

**Provides Freedom to Change**

| Inception | Elaboration | Construction | Transition |
|---|---|---|---|

| Business Solution Through Inception | Architecture Through Elaboration | Design and Implementation Through Construction | Tuning and Scope Reduction Through Inception, Elaboration, Construction, and Transition |

**FIGURE 2.5 Phases Are Optimized to Minimize Overall Cost of Change.** *The cost of introducing a change varies according to the lifecycle phase, and each type of change has its own cost profile. The Unified Process lifecycle is optimized to minimize overall cost of change, while maximizing the freedom to make changes. In general, as the project progresses, you should be more careful about introducing change, especially to the overall business solution and the architecture.*

The above guidance should *not* be interpreted as preventing you from carrying out the necessary changes in a later phase than desired. For example, if you notice during Construction that you need to rethink the business solution and make extensive changes to the requirements to be able to deliver a satisfactory application, naturally you should consider implementing that change. But during Inception, you would not really think twice about it. If you need to change the business solution during Construction, it is reasonable to consider the following actions:

- Understand the cost of change.
- Understand the consequence of not making the change. If the impact is severe, it warrants taking on a big cost for the change.
- Formalize the decision around making the change to ensure that it is not done on a whim, or without appropriate management control. The following section elaborates on this step.
- Analyze whether you can improve your process to avoid these late and costly changes in future projects.

## Adapt the Change Management Process Suited to the Phase and Project Type

For some applications, the cost of making any type of late change can be quite prohibitive. Consider the following:

*For some applications, the cost of making any type of late change can be quite prohibitive.*

- A safety- or business-critical system where you cannot accept defects. A late change could compromise the quality, and the resulting cost or impact may not be acceptable.

- A broadly deployed shrink-wrapped product. A shrink-wrapped product that is broadly deployed typically has a lot of supporting collateral, a large number of people who need to be trained in services and support organizations, extensive beta testing, and localization to many languages. All of these things make it expensive to introduce late changes.

- A technically highly complex application, or an application developed by a very large team. Due to its complexity and size, testing may be quite comprehensive, requiring a considerable amount of time to stabilize the application.

- An application with a large number of stakeholders that need to be consulted before major changes are made. When changes are carried out late in the project, there may not be sufficient time to allow every stakeholder to be heard.

In the section Understand the Cost Profile of Different Types of Changes we also saw that major changes late in the project, especially to the business solution and the architecture, can be particularly costly. The above are examples of project types for which you need to formalize changes late in the project. So how should you go about formalizing the decision to make a change? Change approvals are carried out through a combination of manual procedures (for example, through Change Control Boards), and through tools such as Configuration and Change Management software.

Early in the project, you should ensure that the right stakeholders are aware of the change. This may require nothing more formal than an e-mail going out to appropriate stakeholders, or frequent demonstrations of working software to the stakeholder that allow you to show the changes already made and mention future planned changes, providing stakeholders with the ability to interject if they so desire. For larger and more formal projects, you may need to set up separate meetings to ensure proper handling of issues requiring contract renegotiations, or to guarantee that the right procedure is being followed from an auditing perspective due to FDA[20] or other regulations.

*As projects near the end, you want to assess the potentially negative impact of any changes.*

As projects near the end, you often want to make sure that you properly assess the potentially negative impact of any changes. For small projects, for example, a quick daily meeting may suffice to discuss major changes briefly and enable each team member to express any concerns. Larger projects, or projects requiring more formality, may instead leverage a Change Control Board with representatives from all key constituencies. This board discusses potential changes to make sure that the board members understand the pros and cons of any change. The board will then agree on whether or not to carry out the change.

Through configuration and change management tools, you can set up rules governing what changes can be made and by whom, and what process these changes need to follow. As an example, you may specify in your change and configuration management tooling that all defect fixes in the Transition phase require approval by a certain board or person before they can be included in a build.

## Techniques Maximizing Change Freedom

The underlying assumption with iterative development is that the only way to build the right application is by getting feedback and then making changes to the solution to accommodate this feedback. Even though changes late in the project can be costly, you want to maximize your ability to accommodate change. Here are some techniques proven to maximize change freedom:

- **Partial implementation.** You should always strive to implement capabilities only partially before you get feedback, so that you can improve upon the solution before investing too much time on a

---

20. Food and Drug Administration in the United States of America.

capability. Consequently, you should implement perhaps only 10 percent of the code for a use case before you show it to end users for feedback. You will then have a good vehicle for discussing what the requirements really are for the use case and will be able to make changes to the use case with a minimum of rework.

- **Refactoring.** The cost of architecture or design changes can be reduced by continually improving your architecture, design,[21] and data[22] through refactoring. The principle behind refactoring is that the first design should address only the requirements you know you need today. As requirements evolve, you will also evolve the design in small increments to address additional capabilities. You may therefore first develop a design to accommodate a single-user scenario of an application and then gradually improve the design to provide multi-user support. Refactoring will not, however, free you from the need to make the right difficult design decisions early on. For example, if you make the wrong build-versus-buy decision and then invest 200 hours building a component that you later notice could have been completed in 20 hours by leveraging an open source component, refactoring will not allow you to regain your 200 hours. It will, however, allow you to refactor your design incrementally from leveraging your home-grown component to leveraging the open source component.

- **Keep documentation, design, and code simple.**[23] The more documentation you have, the more costly it is to maintain. You should therefore strive to keep your documentation to a minimum. However, having too little documentation can also be costly by leading to miscommunication or endless discussions revisiting issues already solved, so aim to strike the right balance based on your project needs. As a rule, if you cannot clearly articulate how not having a piece of information will hurt you, remove it. The same reasoning applies to your design. Choose the simplest design that addresses your needs. Continually strive to keep your design and

*If you cannot clearly articulate how not having a piece of information will hurt you, remove it.*

---

21. Fowler 1999.
22. Ambler 2006.
23. Kent Beck describes this technique in Beck 2004.

code simple by refactoring it and cleaning it up, making it easier to make future changes.

- **Predict future likely changes.** By spending initial time on assessing likely changes, you can architect your application to minimize the costs of those changes, should they occur. For example, if you are unsure of what persistent storage mechanism you will need, first implement the simplest possible solution, such as file-based storage, and architect your application so that you can easily upgrade to a high-end database solution. You can document such potential changes in your software architecture document, or by using change cases.[24]

- **Effectively manage change requests.** During a project, a lot of people inside and outside the immediate project team will have suggestions for how to improve your application. To leverage this feedback effectively, you need to make it easy for people to suggest an improvement. One solution is to make it easy for people to enter change requests into your change request database. If you are afraid that many suggestions may not make sense, you may choose to apply some type of filter, such as having a customer representative continually interact with key stakeholders, and they enter change requests based on feedback.

- **Automate change management and change propagation.** The cost of change can also be reduced by having procedures and tools in place for managing change. Automatic synchronization between design and code is an example of reducing the cost of change through automation, since it allows you to make some code changes working on a higher level of abstraction—the design. Another example is to have tools that allow you to couple a change request to all the right versions of files impacted by it. Once the designer has implemented a change, a tester can more easily verify that it has been properly implemented by gaining direct access to affected files.

- **Organize your work to understand the impact of change.** A change to, for example, a requirement, may also impact the

---

24. See Bennett 1997.

design, code, user manuals, online documentation, training material, test assets, and so on. You should organize your work to make it easy to understand what impact a change to one artifact may have on other artifacts. You can to some extent achieve this goal through traceability in tools, as well as by following a use-case-driven process. If you have a change to a specific use case, you will be able to see directly its impact on your design (through corresponding use-case realization), on test cases (by organizing test cases by use case), on manuals (by having one user manual chapter for each use case), and so on.

## Minimize Changes to the Current Iteration

As you work in an iteration, you will get a lot of good feedback on capabilities that you should change, and you will realize how you can do things better. You need to be very careful about introducing changes within an iteration, which may lead to churn and thrashing, thus preventing successful completion of the iteration. Here are some guidelines to consider:

*Introducing changes within an iteration may lead to churn and thrashing.*

- Remember that the next iteration is only a few weeks away. Any major changes should be listed and prioritized with all other items considered for the next iteration. If it is an important change, it will go into the next iteration, so it will soon be taken care of. If it is not an important change, you should be really glad you decided not to work on it within the current iteration. Examples of changes that fit within this category are adding a new feature or rethinking the main flow of a use case. These changes would typically impact the iteration plan you established at the beginning of the iteration, listing what you want to accomplish in this iteration.

- If it will take less time to implement a minor change directly than to document and discuss when to implement it later, just do it. Examples of such changes include minor changes to use cases or screen layouts. These changes typically do not impact the iteration plan.

- When in doubt about whether something is a minor or major change, make a note of the change request and delay it to the next iteration.

## Avoid Carrying Many Defects Forward

As you develop your application, you will find a lot of defects. There will always be pressure from various stakeholders to focus on developing new capabilities rather than fixing existing defects. This is true within a project, since spending time on fixing defects from previous iterations will prevent you from developing new demonstrable features in the next iteration. It is also true that if your next project focuses on fixing defects, you will deliver fewer new features.

*Carrying many defects forward will seriously impact your productivity.*

Each defect needs to be documented and managed. The more defects you have, the more time you spend triaging them, explaining to people how to work around them, and discussing whether they should be addressed or not. Carrying many defects forward will thus seriously impact your productivity (see Figure 2.6). To avoid wasting tons of time managing them unproductively, fix defects as you find them, rather than carrying them forward. Many teams—or rather, team leaders, customer representatives, or stakeholders—make the common mistake of not doing this when prioritizing what is to be done. It is the responsibility of the development team to articulate the cost of carrying defects forward, but in the end whether to focus on defects or new features is a business decision.

**FIGURE 2.6 The Cost of Defects.** *The more defects you have, the more costly it is to triage them and bear the cost of describing to people how to work around them through support and other means. You should therefore strive to minimize your defect backlog. Fixing defects may temporarily reduce your ability to develop new features but will improve productivity over time.*

## Comparison with Other Methods

Traditional waterfall development aims to minimize the need for changes through detailed initial specification of requirements and design and thorough subsequent review of those specifications. However, many changes are in fact triggered when stakeholders see partial implementations, rather than through careful review of specifications, and meaningful feedback therefore often comes very late in waterfall projects. Consequently, waterfall development solves problems as they were understood at the beginning of the project. Because change is discouraged, you often have to wait until the next version of the application to incorporate very important changes. Especially when combined with heavy documentation and design approaches, waterfall development often leads either to systems that poorly address user needs, or to expensive cost and schedule overruns.

*Many changes are in fact triggered when stakeholders see partial implementations.*

Scrum focuses on several techniques consistent with this practice. Scrum proposes iterative development in which the most essential capabilities are implemented and tested in early iterations; at the same time it strongly discourages changes during an iteration (called Sprint in Scrum). Changes are captured in a product backlog and high-priority changes for each iteration are included in the Sprint backlog (compare iteration plan in Unified Process). Scrum, however, lacks distinct phases guiding the team in how to think about what type of changes to make at what time, nor does it include concepts such as Change and Control Boards. Further, Scrum does not provide techniques for how to manage and automate change, understand the impact of change, or deal with refactoring.

XP provides guidance and has helped drive evolution around many of the specific techniques mentioned in this practice, including refactoring, keeping things simple, and avoiding carrying defects forward. Beck describes how these techniques help change the cost equation around change.[25] Many people have translated this to mean that with XP, the cost of change is constant, allowing changes at any time in a

---

25. See Beck 2004, pp. 52–53.

project. Several reviewers have heavily criticized some aspects of this practice. We strongly believe that agile practices can improve the cost equation and enable more types of change to be carried out later in most projects, but it is also important to understand that some types of changes will be increasingly costly for some projects, as outlined in this practice, especially those related to business solutions or architecture.

## Levels of Adoption

This practice can be adopted at three levels:

- **Basic.** Ensure that appropriate stakeholders are aware of major change decisions. Use the techniques *Partial implementation* and *Keep documentation, design, and code simple.*

  At this level you are reducing overhead through simplicity and facilitating short iterations through partial implementations, taking you down and left on the process map. This is appropriate for all types of projects.

- **Intermediate.** Use the techniques *Effectively manage change requests, Refactoring,* and *Organize your work to understand change impact.* Follow the Unified Process lifecycle to guide you in which changes to encourage and which to assess more carefully.

  At this level you continue introducing agile practices that reduce overhead and facilitate short iterations, taking you down and left on the process map. This is appropriate for all types of projects.

- **Advanced.** Use the technique *Automate change management and change propagation.* Minimize changes to the current iteration. Introduce a Change and Control Board to manage more effectively what changes to allow late in the project.

  At the advanced level, you introduce technology and practices that require more discipline and learning. The improved automation enables shorter iterations, while the Change and Control Board has the opposite effect by increasing overhead. The net effect is that this level brings you to the right on the process map.

## Related Practices

- *Practice 2: Execute Your Project in Iterations* describes how you plan iterative development and divide your project into a series of iterations so that you can get feedback on what needs to be changed.
- *Practice 10: Prioritize Requirements for Implementation* discusses what type of requirements to focus on in the first few iterations of your project. These requirements will force early decisions in key areas to minimize costly changes late in the project.
- *Practice 14: Manage Versions* describes how to keep track of changes and various versions of assets.

## Additional Information

## Information in the Unified Process

OpenUP/Basic provides guidance for the basic and intermediate levels of this practice. RUP also adds guidelines for the advanced practices, with guidelines and tool-specific information on configuration- and change-management practices such as parallel and distributed development, as well as information about change control boards and other more formal ways of managing change.

## Additional Reading

To understand how the phases in the Unified Process lifecycle help you minimize overall cost of change, see the following:

Per Kroll and Philippe Kruchten. *The Rational Unified Process Made Easy: A Practitioner's Guide to the RUP.* Addison-Wesley, 2003.

Walker Royce. *Software Project Management: A Unified Framework.* Addison-Wesley, 1998.

For other practices that help drive down the cost of change, see the following:

Scott W. Ambler and Pramodkumar J. Sadalage. *Refactoring Databases: Evolutionary Database Design.* Addison-Wesley, 2006.

Kent Beck with Cynthia Andres. *Extreme Programming Explained: Embrace Change, Second Edition.* Addison-Wesley, 2004.

Douglas W. Bennett. *Designing Hard Software: The Essential Tasks.* Independent Publishers Group, 1997.

Martin Fowler et al. *Refactoring: Improving the Design of Existing Code.* Addison-Wesley, 1999.

# Measure Progress Objectively

by Bruce MacIsaac

*Objective measurement of progress helps you to manage cost, schedule, people, and priorities.*

## Problem

A software project's progress is difficult to measure objectively due to a number of challenges:

- Tasks vary widely. How much progress results from requirements work versus coding work?
- Unplanned events often delay projects. How can these be factored into estimating progress?
- There is always pressure to report good progress and to be optimistic about future progress.
- There are competing factors. You can, for example, reduce time to delivery by sacrificing quality or increasing costs.
- Different techniques for measuring progress have their unique strengths and limitations.

This practice describes some approaches to ensure that progress is measured objectively and is therefore providing useful data for project management.

## Background

We explain why progress measures are important, their limitations, and their connection to estimation.

## Why Measuring Progress Is Important

*Progress measures are vital to project management.*

If you don't objectively know how your project is progressing, you don't really know if it's failing or succeeding. A senior vice president at a company I once worked for remarked that the biggest problem the company faced was not that projects failed, but that they failed after the money had been spent. He wanted to identify failing projects while there were still options, such as renegotiating scope, bringing in outside help, or canceling before it was too late. This is where effective progress measures are vital, because they enable management to address key questions, such as the following:

- Can we afford to continue to invest in this project?
- Will the project be available when it is needed?
- Can we beat our competitors to the market?
- Should we drop some lower-priority features in order to meet the schedule?

Progress measures can also serve as an indicator of project health. Poor progress often indicates overall problems that need to be addressed, such as people issues (for example, lack of skills or low morale), and process issues (for example, too much bureaucracy or lack of clear direction). As you address these problems, you can use progress measures to evaluate your success.

## Estimation and Progress Measurement Are Connected

Estimates are directly tied to progress measurement: saying you are 10 percent done means that you estimate that 90 percent of the work remains to be done. Software estimating is difficult, and even the best estimation techniques can yield poor results. Estimates are typically done early in the project, before the problems are well understood, and yet they are then carved in stone. Team members often try to live up to those estimates, even after it becomes clear that they are unachievable.[26] Progress measurement alleviates these problems by allowing original estimates, however poor, to be refined as the project proceeds.

---

26. Glass 2003 cites several studies that identify estimation as a major cause of failed projects.

## Understand the Limitations of the Measures That You Are Applying

There is an Indian legend about six blind men who each went to see an elephant. The one who felt the trunk concluded that elephants are snakelike, the one who felt the tusk concluded that the elephant was spearlike, and so on. Unfortunately, most measures are prone to similar misinterpretations, because they similarly focus on a small part of the overall picture. The following are some experiences I've had with measures misuse.

*Most measures are prone to misinterpretation.*

Once I refactored some badly written code and reduced it to one-fifth its original size. Our team measured productivity by the source lines of code delivered weekly, so by this measure it appeared that I had made "negative" progress. Understandably, I was worried how my "negative" productivity would appear. Similar issues come up when code is reused, rather than created from scratch.

On another project with multiple teams, one team logged only serious defects that would take several days to fix; smaller defects were fixed immediately or were grouped into a few Change Requests. Another team logged every tiny problem. The conclusion? Obviously the first team had higher-quality code, since they had fewer defects! An equally wrong conclusion is that the second team was more productive because it had a higher defect-fixing rate!

The lesson is to understand the limits of the measures that you are applying and to account for these limitations when drawing conclusions.

## Applying the Practice

Several methods can be used to measure progress objectively; we'll describe some basic principles and their limitations. We discuss the following:

- Measure progress by end-user capabilities and materials.
- Extrapolate "like" activities.
- Visualize progress.
- Test progress trend.

- Measure defect-fixing progress.
- Don't measure overall progress in the Inception phase.

## Measure Progress by End-User Capabilities and Materials

The goal of a software project is to deliver a usable software product. So the most objective progress measure is working code that delivers functionality, plus documentation and training materials for using that functionality.

Unfortunately, typical waterfall development projects will happily claim progress based on completion of parts of the development, rather than on working functionality, for example:

- Detailed requirements or design specifications, which later prove unworkable
- Coded and unit tested components, which later do not integrate

*Iterative development allows for more reliable estimation of future work.*

In an iterative approach, the software grows in stages—iterations— with an executing build producing functional software at the end of each iteration. This approach requires some work in each of the disciplines: requirements, analysis and design, implementation, testing, project management, and so on. The key differentiating factor from waterfall development is that because iterative development includes all the work required to deliver working functionality, it allows for more reliable estimation of future work.

The key to measuring progress is breaking down the requirements into increments that can be delivered in each iteration. Requirements are assigned to iterations based on priority, as described in *Practice 10: Prioritize Requirements for Implementation.* The estimated effort includes design, implementation, and test effort and is used to determine how much can be accomplished in the iteration.

So what is the actual measure of progress? The simplest measure is the percentage of work accomplished—add up estimates for completed scenarios and divide these by the estimates for scenarios planned to complete in the iteration.

Measuring progress based on the percentage of estimated work completed, and not counting partial progress on tasks, is called "earned value."[27] However, traditional earned-value approaches allow credit to be taken for completion of any task. A more conservative approach is to give credit only for usable capabilities and materials, that is, integrated and tested scenarios plus end-user documentation and training materials.

## Extrapolate "Like" Activities

One of the main reasons we measure progress is to adjust our estimates of future tasks. When reestimating work, it is important to make the adjustments based on experience with similar tasks.

The simplest way to do this is to adjust estimates at the start of each iteration by the percentage of estimated work completed for the previous iteration. For example, if you completed only 90 percent of planned work in the previous iteration, you should increase your estimates for the next iteration accordingly (dividing your remaining estimates by 90 percent). This usually works well, because the experience of the prior iteration is usually the best predictor of the next.[28]

*Adjust estimates at the start of each iteration, based on progress of similar work in the previous iteration.*

Consider other factors: Will future tasks be performed by similarly skilled staff under similar conditions? Have the data been contaminated by "outliers," tasks that were severely overestimated or underestimated? Is effort being reported consistently (for example, is unpaid overtime included)? Was there a "learning curve" that has since been overcome?

## Visualize Progress

It is often useful to visualize progress. One of the best ways to do this is with a "burn-down" chart,[29] which shows the total remaining work on the $y$ axis and time on the $x$ axis. The goal is to get to zero remaining effort. Burn-down charts can be used within an iteration to visualize progress of work assigned to the iteration (see Figure 2.7).

*Charts can be used to visualize progress for an iteration and for the overall project.*

---

27. For details of "earned value" and related measures, see IEEE 1998 (PMBOK Guide).

28. There may be other factors to consider, as discussed earlier in this practice.

29. Burn-down charts come from the Scrum project management methodology. See Schwaber 2004.

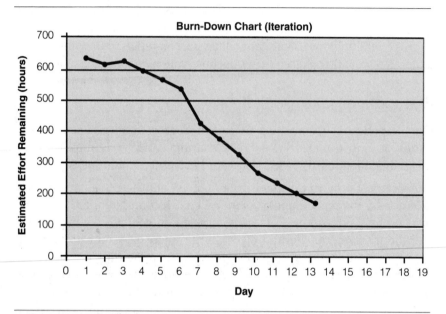

**FIGURE 2.7 Example of a Burn-Down Chart (Iteration).** *Burn-down charts can be used to visualize progress during an iteration.*

Burn-down charts can also be used to visualize progress of the project as a whole[30] (see Figure 2.8).

It can be helpful to show the following points on a project or release burn-down chart:

- Estimated work at the start of the iteration.
- Completed work based on those estimates at the end of the iteration.

The difference gives the "earned value" (see Figure 2.8), and the line can be extrapolated to estimate project completion. The spikes at the end of each iteration show the result of scope changes and reestimation on the remaining work. You can also add a third point to separate reestimated work from scope changes.

---

30. Cockburn 2005.

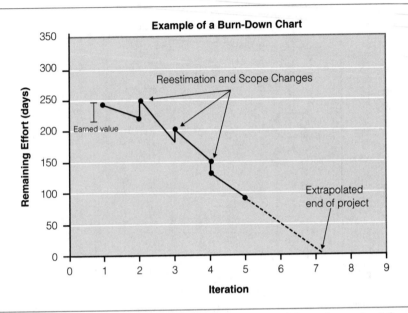

**FIGURE 2.8 Example of a Burn-Down Chart (Project).** *A burn-down chart for a project can be used to visualize progress on the project as a whole and thus help predict when project work will be completed.*

A variation is to use "points" on the *y* axis that reflect the relative effort of scenarios. At the end of each iteration, you add up the "points" for completed scenarios and reestimate the remaining work. Using points is more complicated, but it lets you see changes in productivity: a steeper chart indicates points being delivered at a faster rate.[31] Using points also lets you flip the chart around and show increasing progress as points are delivered. This kind of "earned value" chart is sometimes referred to as a "burn-up" chart.[32]

31. This is "project velocity," as described in Beck 2000.
32. See Cockburn 2005.

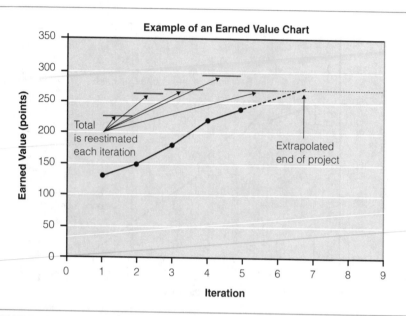

**FIGURE 2.9 Example of an Earned-Value Chart.** *Charts of increasing earned value are an alternative way to visualize progress.*

## Test Progress Trend

*Measure test progress in terms of executing and passed tests.*

If the test function is integrated within the team, and there is thorough testing in each iteration, then "burn-down" or "burn-up" charts can incorporate test progress. However, many organizations have an independent test organization to supplement the testing done by the development team. Test managers can use burn-down or burn-up charts to measure test progress, but in this case, the "delivered" value to be measured is executing tests and passed tests. Less accurate, but simpler, is a count of passing acceptance tests (see Figure 2.10).

Test progress trends are a simple measure of test progress, but they only represent part of the picture. They don't show how much time is spent on different kinds of testing, such as exploratory and performance testing, nor what kinds of testing are most effective. They don't indicate the quality of the build, nor the extent to which tests are blocked because of factors outside the tester's control.

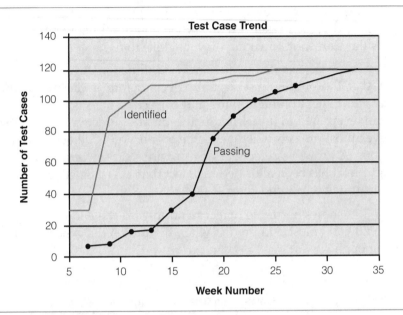

**FIGURE 2.10 Example of a Test Progress Trend Chart.** *From this chart you can see that no new test cases are being added, and progress suggests that in six weeks all test cases will pass, assuming progress remains linear.*

There are a number of techniques for measuring test effectiveness, such as using code coverage, tracking how much effort goes into discovering defects, and noting when discovery of new defects starts to trail off.[33] However, while additional metrics can help, qualitative assessments by the team are key to providing a balanced picture of test progress and test effectiveness. Assessing test effectiveness at the end of each iteration helps to improve test effectiveness in subsequent iterations.

*Assess test effectiveness at the end of each iteration.*

## Measure Defect-Fixing Progress

Defect-fixing progress will occur in all iterations but becomes a key progress measure toward the end game, as the focus changes from

---

33. These techniques, and others, are described in more detail in RUP.

completing code to ensuring good enough quality. But how can you apply earned value to defect fixing when you don't know how many defects there are, nor how long they will take to fix?

*Fix defects as functionality is delivered.*

Start by fixing defects iteratively. That is, as functionality is delivered, also test it thoroughly and fix the defects before declaring victory. Actual effort spent on identifying and correcting defects in one iteration can be applied to future iteration estimates. Practically speaking, however, most projects will defer some proportion of defects to future iterations. A growing defect backlog provides early warning that not enough effort has been allocated to defect fixing. The defect backlog is best illustrated by a trend chart.

Figure 2.11 shows a sample defect trend toward the end of a project. The trend can be used to predict when the product is expected to be good enough.

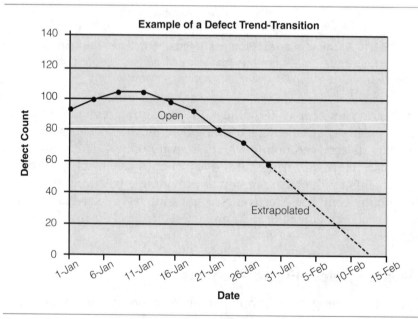

**FIGURE 2.11 Example of a Defect Trend in Transition Phase.** *From this chart we can project that on February 10 about 10 percent of defects will remain.*

One issue with this approach is that change requests will have different weights: one defect may affect a single line of code, whereas another will require major redesign. This problem can be addressed by weighing defects with an "estimated effort to fix," which allows defects to be incorporated into a standard burn-down or earned-value chart, either separate from or together with the overall project progress chart.

> **NOTE:** Defects should be triaged based on how severely they will affect the customer. The sum of estimated effort for all outstanding "must fix" defects is a good measure of remaining work.
>
> A lack of recorded defects may imply a lack of testing. Be aware of the actual level of test effort when examining defect trends.

## Don't Measure Overall Progress in the Inception Phase

The main goal of the Inception phase is to establish the business case for the project by, among other things, establishing an overall vision and rough estimates of cost and duration. Only when the project moves into the Elaboration phase does the focus shift to producing code and detailing requirements.

A common question is how to measure progress during Inception, when there is no delivered functionality. The simple answer is, don't measure *overall* project progress during Inception. Instead, track your progress toward reaching the goals of Inception. These will generally be qualitative measures that assess whether you have identified the stakeholders; outlined needs, features, and risks; and estimated cost and schedule. This process helps you estimate when you can expect to complete the Inception phase, but it does not help you to extrapolate the progress of the project as a whole.

*There is little correlation between Inception work and the remaining work to complete the project.*

The value of the Inception phase from a project management perspective is that it establishes the overall scope of the project, enabling sponsors to decide whether or not the project should proceed. Project estimates at this point are usually based on comparison with similar projects. As much as we might like to extrapolate from the effort and duration of Inception tasks to firm overall project estimates, there is little correlation between Inception work and the remaining phases of the project.

## Other Methods

Traditional project management methods use earned value, along with related measures like "budgeted cost of work performed" to measure project progress. Traditional earned-value approaches allow credit to be taken for completion of any task. In a waterfall development approach this helps to show if the project is tracking according to estimates. However, until working software starts to be delivered, the project hasn't really provided any value, and this "progress" is therefore questionable.

Unified Process, XP, and other agile methods value working code as the primary measure of progress, and developers are encouraged to use their experience in each iteration to estimate what can be achieved in the next. Variants of earned value are common. For example, XP has moved from recommending a relative "points-based" approach[34] to using absolute effort estimates.[35] Completed user stories provide a basic earned-value measure of progress, whether the estimates are points or absolute effort estimates. Unified Process, which uses completed use-case scenarios as the fundamental measure of progress, is similar in this respect.

Scrum[36] recommends burn-down charts for each iteration or "sprint" to track progress during the iteration, as well as a Product Backlog burn-down report at the end of each sprint to report on overall project progress. This is compatible with Unified Process. Both Unified Process and Scrum recommend that progress be measured at the end of each iteration and used to revise project estimates. Scrum burn-down charts are good tools for this. Note that since Unified Process is a method framework, it also allows for additional measures.

34. Beck 2000.

35. Beck 2004.

36. Schwaber 2004.

## Levels of Adoption

This practice can be adopted at three different levels:

- **Basic.** Measure progress iteratively, and update estimates by extrapolating from actual progress in the previous iteration.

  Basic adoption of progress measurement is useful on all projects and most effective when applied iteratively.

- **Intermediate.** Use burn-down charts to communicate progress.

  Optionally use earned-value charts, test progress trends, and defect trends to provide additional insight.

  Intermediate adoption can be useful for many projects but adds some overhead.

- **Advanced.** Automate measurement collection and reporting.

  Select additional measures[37] (such as measures of where time is spent, how and where defects are found, quality measures of individual components, and so on), based on organizational needs and ease of collection.

  Record measurements in a database so that historical data can be used to estimate and gauge progress in future projects.

  Advanced adoption of progress measurement is best applied in larger projects, or to manage programs or portfolios of smaller projects when more formal reporting is required.

## Related Practices

- *Practice 2: Execute Your Project in Iterations* describes the benefits of iterative development. Measuring progress at the end of the iteration helps you to adjust estimates and identify problems while they can still be fixed.
- *Practice 10: Prioritize Requirements for Implementation* allocates work to iterations based on priority.

---

37. See RUP for a list of measures to consider.

- *Practice 20: Continually Reevaluate What You Do* uses progress measurements to help you to evaluate what you are doing.

## Additional Information

### Information in the Unified Process

OpenUP/Basic proposes the basic measures suited to most small projects. The key measures outlined here are proposed for inclusion in OpenUP/Basic. RUP adds descriptions of a large number of candidate measures for measuring the process and the product, along with guidance on when and how to apply those measures. In more formal projects, the RUP project manager selects from candidate measures and documents these selections in a measurement plan.

### Additional Reading

Burn-down charts, burn-up charts, and project velocity:

> Ken Schwaber. *Agile Project Management with Scrum.* Microsoft Press, 2004.
>
> Alistair Cockburn. *Crystal Clear.* Addison-Wesley, 2005.
>
> Kent Beck. *Extreme Programming Explained: Embrace Change.* Addison-Wesley, 2000.

Traditional earned value approaches:

> IEEE Std 1490-1998: *IEEE Guide Adoption of PMI Standard, A Guide to the Project Management Body of Knowledge.* IEEE, 1998.

For additional measures to consider:

> Doug Ishigaki and Cheryl Jones. "Practical Measurement in the Rational Unified Process." *The Rational Edge*, January 2003.
>
> Walker Royce. *Software Project Management: A Unified Framework.* Addison-Wesley, 1998.

## CHAPTER 3

# Focus Continuously on Quality

| | |
|---|---|
| ***Benefits*** | • Higher quality.<br>• Earlier insight into progress and quality. |
| ***Patterns*** | 1. Ensure team ownership of quality for the product.<br>2. Test early and continuously in step with integration of demonstrable capabilities.<br>3. Incrementally build test automation. |
| ***Anti-Patterns*** | • Conduct in-depth peer review of all intermediate artifacts, which is counterproductive since it delays application testing and hence identification of major issues.<br>• Complete unit testing of the entire application before doing integration testing, again delaying identification of major issues. |

The principle of focusing continuously on quality emphasizes that quality, to be achieved, must be addressed throughout the project lifecycle. An iterative process is particularly adapted to achieving quality, since it offers many measurement and correction opportunities.

Improving quality is more than simply "meeting requirements" or producing a product that meets user needs and expectations. Rather, quality also means identifying the measures and criteria that demonstrate how it was achieved and show clearly that the process can be repeated and managed.

Ensuring high quality demands more than the participation of the testing team; it involves all team members and all parts of the lifecycle, and it requires that the entire team *own* quality.

- **Analysts** are responsible for making sure that requirements are testable.
- **Developers** need to design applications with testing in mind, and they must be responsible for testing their code.
- **Managers** need to ensure that the right test plans are in place and that the right resources are in place for building the testware and performing required tests.
- **Testers** are the gatekeepers of quality. They guide the rest of the team in understanding software quality issues by providing objective quality metrics of working software throughout the project. They are responsible for product-level testing—functional, system, and performance.

Every team member should be willing to chip in to address a quality issue.

One of the major benefits of iterative development is that it enables teams to *test early and continuously* (see Figure 3.1). By the end of a project, since the most important capabilities are implemented early on, the most essential software will have been up and running for months and will therefore likely have been tested for months. This early feedback regarding quality also allows you to understand and improve the quality of requirements, design, architecture, and the overall process you follow. It is no surprise that most projects adopting iterative development claim that higher quality is a primary tangible result of the improved process.

As you incrementally build your application, you should also *incrementally build test automation* to detect defects early, while minimizing up-front investments. As you design your system, consider how it should be tested. Making the right design decisions can greatly improve your ability to automate testing. You may also be able to generate test harnesses and drivers directly from the design models. This saves time, provides incentives for early testing, and increases the quality of testing by minimizing the number of bugs in the test software. Automated testing has been a key area of focus for, among others, the agile community; the aim here is to automate all unit testing of code and, to a lesser degree, acceptance testing, and to write tests before the code is written (test-first design).

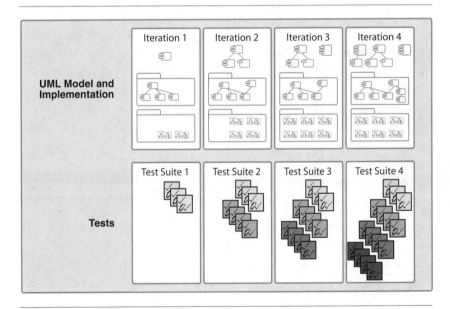

**FIGURE 3.1 Testing Is Initiated Early and Expanded Upon in Each Iteration.** *Iterative development enables early testing. Software is built in every iteration and tested as it is built. Regression testing detects whether new defects are introduced as new iterations add incremental functionality. (Adapted from Kroll 2003.)*

The anti-pattern to following this principle would be to do in-depth peer review of all intermediate artifacts and complete all unit testing before doing integration testing. In-depth peer review of all intermediate artifacts can delay your application testing and can thus be counterproductive. Integration testing is crucial for finding major issues, such as architectural problems, and needs to happen early and often, rather than only after all code has been unit tested.

This chapter describes a series of practices that will help you improve the quality of your application.

- *Practice 5: Test Your Own Code* details how developers can approach testing their own code holistically and includes techniques that will potentially be part of a broader test automation strategy.

- *Practice 6: Leverage Test Automation Appropriately* describes how automating appropriate amounts of the test effort can also realize improved product quality and shorter product development schedules.

- *Practice 7: Everyone Owns the Product!* takes a deeper look at how analysts, developers, architects, testers, managers, and customers need to change their mindset to be successful in building a quality product.

Let's have a look at these practices.

# Test Your Own Code

by Scott Will and Ted Rivera

*Defensive coding techniques and good development
test practices will help you produce higher-quality code
in shorter periods of time and with fewer defects.*

## Problem

A primary motivation for writing this book is set forth in the Preface:

> We want to reduce the initial anxiety and cost associated with taking
> on a software improvement effort by providing an easy and unin-
> trusive path toward improved results, without overwhelming you
> and your team. At the same time we want to show early results that
> keep the momentum going, thus maintaining the interest and com-
> mitment of everyone involved.

Any software improvement or development effort needs to focus also
on the outlook and habits of the individual developer, but the problem is that many improvement efforts tend to overlook this key item,
partly because too many developers think that their job is merely to
write the code and that it's then the tester's job to find defects. However, this mindset is the antithesis of agility, and it results in the need
for additional effort later in the development cycle.

By adopting simple defect prevention and early defect detection techniques, developers can produce immediate improvements in code
quality and productivity, which in turn create momentum for wider
adoption of these techniques as well as other improvement initiatives.

This practice focuses on simple techniques that all developers can use
to prevent defects from occurring and to help find defects before the
code is given to a test team.

## Background

It's a good thing that defensive driving techniques are hammered home in driver's education classes. You may have witnessed drivers running a red light while talking on a cell phone, swerving all over the road while drinking a cup of coffee, or being distracted by kids misbehaving in the back of the car. As part of defensive driving, we quickly learn to anticipate dangerous situations, as well as do our best to avoid them. As part of safe driving preventive measures, we make sure that we wear seatbelts and drive cars equipped with airbags and other safety devices.

*The testing team is a fallback measure if defects escape development teams.*

Defensive driving is a useful analogy for "defensive development." While most of us have been taught defensive driving techniques (and for good reason!), not all developers have been taught defensive development techniques. Sure, cars are equipped with seatbelts and airbags, but these are fallback measures in case the avoidance techniques don't work. Similarly, in software development we use testing teams, but they shouldn't be our first resort for preventing defects from reaching the end user. Rather, the testing team should be seen as the fallback measure if defects make it out of the development teams.

The remainder of this practice addresses both defensive coding techniques and good development test practices that will help you produce higher-quality code in less time and with fewer defects.

## Applying the Practice

First, a "no brainer" question: Which takes less time?

1. Having a test team find a defect and write a defect report, then having a developer fix the defect, and then having the test team confirm that the defect is fixed through subsequent testing.

2. Having a developer find defects on his or her own and fix them before the test team finds them.

3. Preventing the defect from occurring in the first place.

While the theoretical answer to the question is obviously number 3, in actual practice we too often choose answer 1 because of intense schedule pressures placed on us during the initial phases of product development. Such pressures must be resisted: defect prevention should be a top priority for developers and must be consciously and actively pursued along with a strong emphasis on early defect detection.

Following is a discussion of several helpful defect prevention techniques to consider, broken down into three stages.

1. *Prior to writing code:* design considerations, installation and usage considerations, operating system and database considerations, testability considerations.
2. *While writing code:* defensive coding techniques, customer awareness, pair programming, code inspections.
3. *When testing code:* defensive testing techniques, scaffolding code, test-driven development, source-level debuggers.

## Prior to Writing Code

Before you even start writing the code, you should consider the following items in detail: design, installation and usage, operating systems and databases, and testability.

### Think First: Design Considerations

Steve McConnell uses the example of moving enormous blocks for building the pyramids as an analogy for building complex software—there are many ways to move such blocks, and although it may take time to plan such movement up front, you will make far greater progress if you use adequate forethought.[1] Don't be content just to push hard! Ensure that the design is appropriate for the complexity of the method, function, or application to be developed. In some instances this will be no more difficult than forming a clear design in your head or on the whiteboard by identifying a set of test cases to be proved, or, when appropriate, through more formal means.

*Ensure that the design is appropriate for the complexity of the application.*

---

1. McConnell 2004, pp. 7–21.

When looking at the use cases for the product, do any areas appear ambiguous? Is requirements wording vague, or even contradictory? Is anything unclear or confusing? Make sure to resolve these issues, especially if it appears that one developer could interpret an issue one way and a peer could interpret the same item in a different way, thus leading to confusion, incompatibilities, and ultimately delays and dissatisfied users. A great way to obtain an independent assessment of the requirements is to review them with an end user or an end user's representative. Without such input, you might not fully understand the requirements.[2]

*Writing code is a great way to validate requirements and designs.*

One additional point is worth emphasizing: the beginning of a project always has the highest degree of uncertainty. A common mistake is to spend a disproportionate amount of time up front getting the requirements "just right" instead of two days describing them, two days designing, four days implementing, and then a few more days updating the requirements, design, and implementation to make sure all elements are in synch. Writing code is a great way to validate requirements and designs, as long as you are consciously doing so with a plan in mind, but it should not be the only means by which the designs are created. Conversely, a tight schedule is no justification for just "getting started"; on the contrary, appropriate planning and design increases overall project speed.

### Installation and Usage Considerations

*First impressions matter.*

First impressions matter. When users have to install, upgrade, or fine-tune software that is important to their organization, they are often "under the gun." If these activities are awkward or difficult, their perception of the software itself is often permanently skewed. Many defects can be avoided, and many users pleased, by considering installation, migration, and usage up front; however, these are too often tasks that are left to the end of a software project.

Has functionality been changed from an earlier release? If so, how will upgrading from an earlier release to this newer level be affected?

---

2. Note that in some agile projects only high-level requirements are written down.

Have parameters or other options been changed that may cause these upgrades to fail? Has an application programming interface (API) changed? Do other products integrate with this code? Will the latest changes impact that integration?

Your software is often part of a mixed environment, and the ease with which it is deployed contributes significantly to the value users will derive from it and (for those customers who purchase your product) to the positive return on their investment. Understanding what changes have been made, and writing or updating code accordingly, can prevent these high-impact defects from occurring.

As a side note, test teams should be thinking about installation issues early on as part of their test strategy. Scott Ambler has been hammering home for years the necessity of having testers perform comprehensive installation testing. See his discussion of this issue in *The Object Primer: Agile Model Driven Development with UML 2.0*.[3]

### Operating System and Database Considerations

Teams sometimes assume that the code they are developing on the operating system or database in their office or cube will easily port to other similar operating systems or databases. The testing of other such important platforms is often either left to others or never adequately completed, thus frequently creating inconsistent levels of reliability across such platforms. Are there new releases of operating systems or databases that your code is expected to run on? Do you know what changes have been incorporated into these newer versions and whether they will affect your code?

One simple approach to consider wherever possible is having individual developers or independent testers routinely use different combinations of software as their primary development platform or test environment. This approach minimizes the cost and risk of platform testing but, surprisingly, is rarely considered. Regardless, if you are selling software that purports to run on key operating systems or databases, you must give adequate consideration to the necessity of

*Have developers routinely use different combinations of software as their primary development platform.*

---

3. Ambler 2004.

ensuring success in these environments; you cannot treat this as an afterthought if the software is to achieve true success.

### Testability Considerations

*Debugging errors up front is a necessity, not a luxury.*

The increasing complexity of software, the rise of componentization and **service-oriented architectures,** and the need for software to be integrated into sophisticated environments makes figuring out how to debug errors up front a necessity, not a luxury. The harsh alternative is a lifetime maintaining code with weak testability. Do you plan to incorporate testability into your code? If so, do you understand what this entails?

What types of measures should you be considering in terms of *testability?* Here are a few to point you in the right direction:

- **Run-time access to variables.** Allow access to "status" variables (for example, *current state*) by external tools, specifically to those variables needed by testers to verify that the code is working correctly or to help debug a problem.

- **Tracing and logging.** Is there significant emphasis on tracing and logging? The easier you can make it for others to help with defect analysis, the easier it will be for you to fix any defects they find.

- **Automation hooks.** Depending on the automation test tools you have chosen to use, specific "hooks" may be required for the tools to work properly.

No doubt you can come up with other items to add to this list, especially those that may be specific to your product or your organization.[4]

## While Writing Code

There are several techniques to consider using while actually writing code: defensive coding techniques, customer awareness, pair programming, and code inspections.

---

4. See Feathers 2005 for a good discussion of testability techniques.

### Defensive Coding Techniques

Let's face it: defects will make their way into your software. Substantial problems arise from errors in design, architecture, requirements, documentation, complex or erroneous environment setup, and a myriad of other sources. This section focuses primarily on coding defects. A little forethought while writing code can go a long way to minimizing the number of defects injected—and that is what this particular practice is all about. While some defects are inevitable, many can be avoided by the application of defensive coding techniques that require little investment.

*Forethought while writing code minimizes the number of defects injected.*

- **Make the compiler your ally.** One of the best ways to prevent bugs from living very long is to *use* the compiler. Using the lowest level of warning output for compilations is frightening. Instead, crank up the compiler warnings full blast—consider it a challenge to write code that, when compiled, produces absolutely no warnings even when the compiler is configured to complain about *e-v-e-r-y l-i-t-t-l-e t-h-i-n-g.*

- **Defensive coding techniques.** Define a set of appropriate coding techniques that you and your team adhere to. Here are several sample coding techniques for your consideration:

  1. *Initialize all variables before use.* Also, consider listing all the local variables you'll be using at the very outset of your routines and then specifically initializing them at that point as well. You will then leave no doubt as to what you intended when you wrote the code—and most optimizing compilers won't generate any extra runtime code for doing this.

  2. *Ensure return-code consistency.* One area that creates difficulties when debugging problems is when a return code signifying an error is masked (overwritten) by the calling routine. Ensure that all return codes returned to your code are handled appropriately.

  3. *Use a "single point of exit" for each routine.* Simply put, do not use multiple "returns" within a routine—*ever.* This is quite possibly one of the most overlooked and yet most beneficial practices you can include in your day-to-day coding activities. If a routine returns from only *one* place, you have a very easy

way of making sure that all necessary "cleanup" is accomplished prior to returning; debugging problems also then becomes much easier.

4. *Use meaningful "assertions" in your code.*[5] An assertion is nothing more than a programmatic sanity check: is what I expect to be true in fact true?

5. *Write readable code.* Can you recall what you were thinking when coding that method six months ago? What do you think someone who has to modify your code a year from now is going to think? Use names that clearly explain what the named element is for. Factor the code into a series of self-explanatory steps. Follow consistent coding conventions. Use comments sparingly to explain only what is not obvious from the code. If you can change the code so that a comment is no longer needed, do so.[6]

### Customer Awareness

*Customers will use your application in ways you've never envisioned.*

Remember, your customers think about your application differently than you do. They will install it in an environment that your team has likely never considered, or at least has not been able to test against. They will use it in ways you've never envisioned. They will configure it in ways you would never dream of. So your job is to try to make sure they don't get burned. Here are a few items to consider:

- Check and verify the integrity of all incoming parameters. Consider what happens if you're expecting an array, and you get passed a NULL somehow, and you don't check for that possibility prior to indexing the array. Diligence here is especially important if your application permits APIs allowing the customer to write code that provides input into your product. It is so often true that customers do things we do not expect them to do; consequently, APIs represent an often undertested aspect of our software.

---

5. See the following two references in IBM's *developerWorks* that discuss assertions in Java: Zurkowski 2002 and Allen 2002.

6. For the reader interested in exploring further the idea of writing readable code, see the following works on *literate programming*: Knuth 1992 and Knuth 1993.

- Consider all possible error cases. Add code to handle each one you can think of (you want your code to handle error conditions gracefully instead of just choking and then dying). Although the likelihood of errors is small, if one does occur, you can at least attempt to handle it, as opposed to just accepting the inevitable system crash that your customers will see. And for those error conditions you can't think of, include a generic "catchall" error handler (while still ensuring return-code consistency as mentioned above). How many times have you seen an error message that says, "This should never happen. . ."? If your experience is anything like ours, you've seen it many, many times.

  In addition to trying to test for each error condition you can think of, an even better approach would be to write an automated test case for each of these conditions—allowing others to reap the benefits in addition to increasing the pool of automated regression tests that can be run.[7]

- Globalization considerations. If your product is to be translated for use in other countries, make sure your code is "enabled." Even if there is just a small possibility that your product will be translated, consider that attempting to retrofit code to make it enabled is a real *defect generator*. Here are just a couple of enablement considerations to whet your appetite for further research:

  - Do you have any hard-coded strings?
  - Do you handle different date/time formats correctly?
  - What about the different currency representations?[8]
  - What about the icons you will use? Often, an icon you are comfortable with will mean something entirely different in another country.

- Active stakeholder participation. Active stakeholder participation is an expansion of the XP practice of on-site customer participation. This is perhaps the most robust way of obtaining customer awareness, since customers are available to the development team.

---

7. This is a logical area to apply test automation. See also *Practice 6: Leverage Test Automation Appropriately* later in this chapter for additional information.

8. For more details, see Esselink 2000.

- Delivery of working code on a regular basis. Whether your team is able to have customer representatives on site, or you have an established practice of beta releases, one of the best ways to gain customer insight and feedback is to provide prerelease versions of working software to your intended customer set on a regular basis. Customers are not shy about letting you know what works, what doesn't, and what they expect to be done about the feedback they provide.

### Pair Programming

Two heads are better than one—and one implementation of this age-old axiom is pair programming. Pair programming is nothing more than having two programmers sit at the same computer and jointly write code: while one programmer is typing, the other is looking over his shoulder and providing both input and immediate feedback. Although pair programming has been around for years, it has only recently been "mainstreamed" by XP practitioners.

*Pair program-ming "lost" productivity is countered by increases in code quality.*

You might think that having two programmers working on the same code would cut productivity in half. However, as many advocates of pair programming have discovered, the "lost" productivity is countered by increases in code quality. Think of pair programming as simultaneous code writing and code reviewing.

### Code Inspections

Wait a minute: this section of the book was supposed to address easy-to-implement techniques, wasn't it? And isn't the practice of code inspections an enormously time-consuming activity?

*Code inspections range from a buddy looking at your code to for-mal inspections.*

Here's the truth: there's nothing glamorous about doing code inspections, and they *do* take time—especially the highly structured, formal code inspections originally articulated by Michael Fagan of IBM nearly thirty years ago.[9] However, they are also one of the best ways to discover defects. Aside from encouraging you, in the strongest terms possible, to perform code inspections, we'll leave the details concerning various aspects of inspections to those who have written extensively on them. For example, see Karl Wiegers's *Peer Reviews in*

---

9. Fagan 1976.

*Software*[10] for details on the types of existing code inspections (ranging from simply asking a buddy to look at your code to semiformal walk-throughs and desk checks, up to and including formal inspections); ways to implement inspections in your organization; and, especially, the tremendous benefits they provide.

To date, we are not aware of any head-to-head comparisons between teams using a highly structured, formal code inspection process ver-sus teams using a less structured approach like pair programming. Studies have shown that the returns realized from pair programming are worth the investment,[11] and there is an extensive history showing the benefits of formal inspections,[12] so a word of warning is appropri-ate here: in the same way that an organization can become buried in documentation while detailing requirements or designs before ever writing code, so also reviews and inspections can degenerate into an end in themselves. So don't fall in love with the process, but with the goal: driving out defects. Let common sense prevail and choose the technique that best suits you, your teammates, your project, and your organizational culture.

## When Testing Code

When the code is written and you are testing it, consider the following techniques: defensive testing techniques, scaffolding code, test-driven development, and source-level debuggers.

### Defensive Testing Techniques

In this book defensive testing is considered to be any testing and anal-ysis that a developer performs on his or her code, after the code com-piles correctly and before it is handed off to a test team. It is important for developers to pursue such testing actively *and to have a tester's*

*Defensive test-ing is done by a developer before it is handed off to a test team.*

---

10. Wiegers 2002.

11. See Cockburn 2000 and Williams 1998. Williams's work refers to an even ear-lier work by Larry Constantine: "In 1995, Larry Constantine reported observing pairs of programmers producing code faster and freer of bugs than ever before" (p. 20). Additionally, see Padburg 2003.

12. See Wiegers 2002.

*mindset when doing so.*[13] Here is what "developer testing" should include:

- **Static code analysis tools.** The first and easiest way to analyze your code is to have someone else do it for you—or in this case, have some*thing* else do it for you. There are numerous static code analysis tools available, from comprehensive tools that some development organizations actually incorporate into their "build" environments to others that can run on a developer's own machine.[14]

  Static code analysis tools can help you find errors such as *boundary exceptions*, *null pointer dereferences*, *memory leaks*, and *resource leaks* (for example, file handles), and they are actually fairly easy to use. What they can't find are things like missing functionality—which is why code inspections, as well as specific testing against the specified requirements, are needed. However, your code should be run through static analysis tools prior to performing an inspection; let the tools find what they can and highlight potential areas of concern, allowing subsequent code inspections then to focus on the "bigger" items.

- **Runtime and structural analysis.** Static analysis tools are quite good at finding certain types of defects, but they certainly don't find all of them. The only way to find absolutely all memory leaks is to run the code and monitor the memory usage. Many tools exist to help automate what would otherwise be a very intensive manual task. Depending on how your organization is structured, how large your project is, the complexity of the code, and the number of developers working on the project, it may be appropriate to perform runtime analysis. As the overall complexity of a software development project increases, the greater the return on investment from runtime and structural analysis.[15]

---

13. For an excellent perspective of a tester's mindset, see Whittaker 2003.

14. For an example of a very capable, open source static code analysis tool for Java, see the "FindBugs" tool available at http://findbugs.sourceforge.net.

15. For example, IBM's Rational *Purify Plus* has extensive memory leak detection capabilities (http://www-128.ibm.com/developerworks/rational/library/811.html and http://www-128.ibm.com/developerworks/rational/library/957.html).

- **Performance testing.** The mere fact that a section of code compiles and seems free of significant errors doesn't mean that your work as a developer is done. Performance bottlenecks need to be identified, as these problems can be magnified when the code is used with the rest of the application, or used in conjunction with other software, or load-tested with a large group of simultaneous users. While comprehensive performance testing needs to be done at a system level, individual developers can execute limited performance testing along the way. In doing so, design defects leading to performance bottlenecks can often be discovered much earlier.

- **Ways to find bugs.** Remember, these are either bugs *you* created or bugs arising from code you omitted. Here are some helpful ways to "think maliciously"—and a malicious attitude is what you need to cultivate when looking for defects:

  - Attempt to force all error conditions you can think of, and attempt to see all error messages that can occur.

  - Exercise code paths that interact with other components or programs. If those other programs or components don't yet exist, write some scaffolding code yourself so that you can exercise the APIs, or populate shared memory or shared queues, and so on.

  - For every input field in a GUI, try various unacceptable inputs: too many characters, too few characters, numbers that are too large or too small, and many other such items. The goal is to try to single out the errors in this way and then, once the simple test cases pass, try combinations of unacceptable inputs.

  Try the following also: negative numbers (especially if you are expecting only positive numbers); cutting and pasting data and text into an input field (especially if you have written code to limit what the user can type into the field); combinations of text and numbers; uppercase-only text and lowercase-only text; repeating the same steps over and over and over and over and over and . . .; for arrays and buffers, adding $n$ data items to your array (or buffer) and then attempting to remove $n + 1$ items. There are obviously many more—these are offered only to whet your appetite for thinking maliciously.

This list is the result of a combination of years of experience in development and testing, extensive reading on the subject of testing (especially works by James Whittaker[16] and Boris Beizer[17]), and countless discussions with other developers and testers. It is by no means a comprehensive list; modify it as necessary according to your own imagination, creativity, and understanding of your own strengths and weaknesses.

### Scaffolding Code

*Scaffolding code simulates other parts of the code that have not yet been completed.*

Scaffolding code is the "throwaway" code you write to mimic or simulate other parts of the code that have not yet been completed (sometimes also referred to as "stubbing" your code). If you need to create it for your own use, don't throw it away; make sure you pass it on to the test team. It may be that the scaffolding code you provide will allow them to get an early jump on testing your code, or at least give them a better idea of what to expect when the other components are ready. It can also provide a solid basis for their test automation efforts.

If your product has protective security features, test those features carefully. Providing scaffolding code that can create the situation you are trying to prevent becomes very important: you must be able to create the very situations against which the system is attempting to protect itself.

Another simple example of "scaffolding code" is providing code to manipulate queues. If your product makes use of queues, imagine how easy it would be to have a tool that would allow you to add and delete items on the fly from the queue, corrupt the data within the queue (to ensure proper error handling), and so on.

### Test-Driven Development

*When a developer has finished writing the code, it has already been tested.*

Arising from within the agile/XP development community is an important technique known as test-driven development (TDD). While still falling in the realm of defensive testing techniques—but providing a solution from an almost opposite direction—the concept of TDD

---

16. Whittaker 2003.
17. Beizer 1995.

is that the developer *first* writes a test case and *then* writes code for that test case to run against. If the test case fails, the code is changed until the test case passes. And not until after the test case passes is new code written (other than the code necessary to make the next test case pass). The ideal of this methodology is that when a developer has finished writing his or her code, the code has already been tested, and a full suite of automated test cases exists that can be run by test teams, change teams, and even customers should the team so choose.

Kent Beck, the "Father of Extreme Programming," has written about TDD in *Test Driven Development: By Example,*[18] which provides an excellent introduction to TDD. A newer work by Dave Astels covers TDD more thoroughly and has received much acclaim.[19] Consider using TDD if you and your team have already implemented many of the techniques and practices discussed above and you are ready to take your improvement and development efforts to the next level.

### Source-Level Debuggers

The use of source-level debuggers is one key way in which thorough individual testing can be performed. For developers, being able to use debuggers is vital; the benefits of source-level debuggers far outweigh any learning curve, and we certainly encourage readers to make the effort to learn a debugger, and to learn it thoroughly. Here are just a *few* ways you can use source level debuggers to test your code:

*The benefits of source-level debuggers far outweigh any learning curve.*

- **Set breakpoints.** This allows you to stop execution of the code at a specified location and then "single step" through the code so that you can watch what each line of code does.
- **Manipulate data on the fly.** You can set a break point just as your code is entered and then reset the value of a parameter that is passed in to see if your code handles the (now) invalid parameter in the way it should. Using the debugger in this way saves the time and effort of trying to get that actual error condition to occur.

---

18. Beck 2003. Additionally, for a brief overview of TDD, see: http://www.agile-data.org/essays/tdd.html.
19. Astels 2003.

- **Set "watches" on variables.** Putting a "watch" on a variable sets a conditional break point that will be hit only if the value of a specified variable is being changed.
- **View the call stack.** This allows you to see which routines called your code, which is a tremendous aid in debugging defects.
- **"Trap" errors when they occur.** If you don't know exactly where a defect occurs, many source-level debuggers will automatically drop you into the debugger—at exactly the right location—when a system-level application error occurs (for example, an attempt to dereference a null pointer). Simply run your application under the debugger, without trying to step through the code and without setting breakpoints.

## Conclusion

As strongly implied at the outset of this practice, preventing defects from occurring is a significant step toward improving code quality and developer efficiency. Further, finding any defects that do get introduced as early as possible also significantly improves product quality and efficiency. One of the best parts of this practice is that the techniques described work independently of any development methodology (e.g., iterative, waterfall, agile/XP) and generally cost virtually nothing to adopt.

However, sometimes the use of such techniques seems counterintuitive: given the typical schedule and staff pressures cited in the introductory discussion of this practice, it is often tempting to sacrifice solid, strategic goals for tactical necessities. Projects and practitioners are often tempted to hit unrealistic or unreasonable schedules at the expense of using sound development techniques, but the implications are far-reaching and often affect many subsequent releases, not just the current one.

*The importance of establishing a culture cannot be overstated.* The ultimate benefits of considering these techniques thoroughly and implementing them intelligently and selectively in your organization will result in fewer defects in your code, fewer regressions, higher quality, and lower rework costs. But none of these benefits will occur unless the project leadership actively promotes an environment in which the adoption of these techniques will be welcomed, and even *expected*. The importance of establishing a culture that enables and encourages the adoption of techniques to prevent defects, or at least detect those that do make it into the code, as early as possible cannot be overstated. Without such a culture, much of what is discussed in this practice will likely fall on deaf ears.

## Other Methods

It is difficult to say this without appearing cynical or sarcastic, but the following comments are the result of objective observation: employing none of the techniques described in this practice—in other words, "doing nothing" (or almost nothing)—is the primary alternative method employed when writing code. The time and resource pressures that we have alluded to are not fictional; almost every developer knows what it is like to be constantly under the gun. Generally speaking, developers are a conscientious lot, with an appreciation for concerns such as quality and craftsmanship. But when hounded for a particular deliverable on an unreasonable schedule, it appears necessary to be satisfied with producing code that "works for me" rather than writing code using many of the techniques outlined in this practice. To return to our opening analogy, this is the equivalent of "offensive driving," that is, driving along in the hope that all the lights will be green, the speed limits are mere guidelines, and other drivers stationary. In such circumstances, a collision is inevitable. Similarly, in the end doing nothing almost certainly means longer schedules and lower quality, resulting in ever-increasing schedule pressures; it's a vicious cycle.

XP is very much a code-focused approach, and its techniques (including pair programming and test-driven development) are good approaches to improving code quality. Test-first design in particular ensures higher-quality code, because there is no opportunity for untested code. Pair programming, on the other hand, is somewhat more controversial. It adds a lot of value by ensuring that all code is looked at by two people, and it enables programmers to share their knowledge. Pair programming and test-first design are techniques that you should consider applying. The other techniques listed in this practice should also be considered. We believe that most development organizations will adopt a mix of techniques that work for them.

## Levels of Adoption

This practice can be adopted at three different levels:

- **Basic.** Coding guidelines and standards exist and are followed by developers.

  The creation and use of coding guidelines and standards ensure that the development team begins to think about "defensive coding" ideas while writing code. (Note that many of the techniques listed in the Defensive Coding Techniques section above provide a good foundation for creating coding guidelines and standards.) Informal peer reviews of written code take place. Designs are thoroughly assessed in order to prevent design defects from being introduced. Developers try to understand the environment that the code will run in so that any operating system and middleware dependencies can be addressed early—thus preventing defects arising from API changes, middleware updates, and so on. The goal is *defect prevention*.

- **Intermediate.** Developers actively test their own code. Discovering and fixing defects as early as possible will work only if developers test code thoroughly before a separate test team runs the code in a test lab. Code reviews take place systematically and consistently. A thorough understanding of customer environments and product usage contributes to defect prevention. Static code analysis is being accomplished, and the introduction of pair programming is showing positive results. Following the defensive testing techniques described above (plus any others that developers may wish to include) will help to shift defect discovery to earlier in the project lifecycle and likely shorten it.

- **Advanced.** More formal code inspections are performed and static, structural, and runtime code analysis tools are used extensively. Performance testing is a standard part of the development process. While performing code inspections and setting up an environment where tools can be run against the code certainly takes more effort, doing so will help teams discover more defects earlier than would otherwise be the case. Inspections and static, structural, and runtime analysis should not be viewed as replacements for coding standards or individual testing but as complementary to those efforts. Test-driven development is widespread.

## Related Practices

- *Practice 1: Manage Risk* discusses the key idea in risk management, which is not to wait passively until a risk materializes and becomes a problem, but rather to seek out and deal with risks.
- *Practice 6: Leverage Test Automation Appropriately* describes how automating appropriate amounts of the test effort can also realize improved product quality and shorter product development schedules.
- *Practice 7: Everyone Owns the Product!* addresses how to orient the responsibilities and mindset of team members to ensure that everybody takes ownership of the final quality of the product, broadens the scope of team responsibilities, and learns to collaborate more effectively within the team.

## Additional Information

## Information in the Unified Process

OpenUP/Basic covers basic informal reviews (optionally replaced by pair programming) and developer testing techniques. OpenUP/Basic assumes that programming guidelines exist and requires developers to follow those guidelines. OpenUP/Basic recommends that an architectural skeleton of the system be implemented early in development to address technical risks and identify defects.

RUP adds guidance on static, structural, and runtime code analysis, as well as defensive coding and advanced testing techniques. RUP also provides guidance on how to create project-specific guidelines and apply formal inspections.

## Additional Reading

For detailed books on software development, defensive coding and testing, and code inspections, we recommend the following:

David Astels. *Test-Driven Development: A Practical Guide*. Prentice Hall, 2003.

Kent Beck. *Test-Driven Development: By Example*. Addison-Wesley, 2003.

Alistair Cockburn and Laurie Williams. "The Costs and Benefits of Pair Programming." http://collaboration.csc.ncsu.edu/laurie/Papers/XPSardinia.PDF.

Steve McConnell. *Code Complete: A Practical Handbook of Software Construction, Second Edition*. Microsoft Press, 2004.

James Whittaker. *How to Break Software: A Practical Guide to Testing*. Addison-Wesley, 2003.

Karl Wiegers. *Peer Reviews in Software: A Practical Guide*, Addison-Wesley, 2002.

For books that provide you with an understanding of how writing code fits with other lifecycle activities, such as design, implementation and testing, see the following:

Boris Beizer. *Black Box Testing: Techniques for Functional Testing of Software and Systems*. John Wiley & Sons, 1995.

Michael Feathers. *Working Effectively with Legacy Code*. Prentice Hall, 2005.

# Leverage Test Automation Appropriately

by Ted Rivera and Scott Will

*Investing in test automation that is appropriate for your organization and project can bring significant quality improvements and time savings.*

## Problem

Pressure to get a product out the door quickly and never-ending staffing shortfalls are twin demons that torment the production of much software today.[20] These two problems have led many teams to consider automating aspects of their testing to help increase productivity and improve quality. The problem, though, is that test automation, if not approached thoughtfully, can actually be *detrimental* to both productivity and quality. Teams can wind up investing too much time in automation, or cobble something together that doesn't really help find the types of defects that test automation is good at finding. In short, too much or too little test automation can have potentially dramatic and negative implications. Furthermore, the initial investment is not always well understood, ongoing maintenance of an automation test suite is often not considered, and the long-term effectiveness of automated tests can wane over time as the code becomes "inoculated" against the specific tests being run.

This practice addresses some of the different types of test automation available to independent testers and test teams, suggests ways to think through an approach to test automation, and discusses some of the potential pitfalls to be avoided.

---

20. For a three-dimensional discussion of this topic, see Yourdon 2004.

## Background

In his landmark work, *The Mythical Man Month,* Fred Brooks long ago opined that there was no such thing as a silver bullet in software development, and it would be difficult to counter this assertion.[21] Although there have been numerous advances and refinements in software engineering, none of these has produced new standards of efficiency or quality—although many cherish this expectation, or at least hope, for test automation. And while some still search for that elusive silver bullet, others have sought more modest incremental improvements in order to reduce the effects of the ubiquitous schedule and staffing pressures while still increasing the overall quality of their products. The people with these more measured expectations are most likely to recognize that they can make real progress by deploying appropriate test automation.

The test profession is older, and testers are more experienced now, than when the concept of test automation first emerged.[22] Initially, it was quite common to hear that test cycles would soon be reduced from months to a matter of days, or even that test teams could be eliminated altogether, all on account of the exaggerated predictions regarding test automation.

Test automation in its various forms—for example, code unit tests, user interface tests, acceptance tests, and so on—does hold forth many promises to the teams that choose to pursue it; except in the simplest environments, however, automation is not a quick fix. Nevertheless, like urban legends, test automation myths die hard. Let's consider a few:

- Myth: Test automation will allow you to reduce the time required for product testing to a mere fraction of what it would take to accomplish the same testing manually.

---

21. Brooks 1995: pp 179–226: " 'No Silver Bullet' asserts and argues that no single software engineering development will produce an order-of-magnitude improvement in programming productivity within ten years. . . ."

22. Fewster 1999 provides a number of interesting historical perspectives.

- Myth: Test automation will easily eliminate the need for independent testers and, in larger organizations, test teams.
- Myth: Test automation can be conceived of as a substitute for an effective overall approach to software testing.
- Myth: Test automation works well in all cases.
- Fact: In some instances, automation is inappropriate, either because of a low return on investment or because it is not well suited to a particular situation. Test automation cannot, for example, replace intelligent and interactive exploratory testing aimed at improving quality, which might have to be done manually.

On the other hand, test automation *will* allow you to achieve ends that would otherwise be impossible. For example:

- Architectural issues that could not otherwise be realized might be uncovered early on through load testing.
- Overall regressions can be greatly reduced.
- Perhaps most profoundly, human beings who would have had to perform tests manually that are now automated can do other things that only humans can do.

With these comments in mind, it is our aim to provide you with a perspective that will help you succeed in implementing effective test automation and integrating automation into your larger test efforts. You can think of effective test automation as similar to regular maintenance on your car. Regular oil changes, tire rotations, belt adjustments, and the like ensure your vehicle's consistent long-term performance, so that it will run smoothly on your most important days, such as when you're driving to that critical job interview or to your daughter's wedding. In the same way, test automation is not glamorous, but it can ensure that the worst problems you might otherwise encounter are averted in the mad rush to get your product out the door (see Figure 3.2).

*Think of effective test automation as similar to regular maintenance on your car.*

**FIGURE 3.2 Appropriate Test Automation, like Car Maintenance, Is Not Glamorous, But Essential.** *Appropriate test automation will keep things running smoothly and help you find and prevent problems before they result in a disaster.*

## Applying the Practice

*The aim is not simply test automation but test automation done appropriately.*

Note the key word in the title of this chapter—our aim is not simply *test automation* but test automation done *appropriately*. And just what constitutes *appropriate* test automation? Every team is going to answer that question differently.

## Understand What Is Appropriate for You

Appropriate test automation is not a one-size-fits-all effort. What is ideal for one team is rarely ideal for another. To begin with, what is *appropriate* for you depends on the goals established for your project.

- Are you developing a stop-gap product that will undergo no future development once released?

- Are you working with existing software that has been around for some time and is now undergoing significant functional enhancements?

- Are you developing a brand-new, strategic product that is expected to be around for years to come?
- Have you decided to embrace the XP approach to software development, where 100 percent unit-test and acceptance-test automation is expected?
- What performance characteristics will be required for your product?
  - Is extensive regression testing likely, for example, owing to iterative development or to the likelihood of multiple releases?
  - Is the stability of the build process a point of concern, suggesting the need for an automated smoke test?

What is *appropriate* also depends on the skill level of your team:

- Is all of your testing done by "hired hands," either contractors or short-term employees?
- Does the project team comprise seasoned testers, albeit with little automation experience?
- Do the testers have significant programming experience even though they are new to a test role?
- Do you have an experienced group of testers with significant automation experience?

Finally, what is *appropriate* depends on items that are unique to your organization:

- Is there a budget available to invest in test automation tools?
- Will you have to "roll your own" automation tools?
- Do you plan to use open source tools?[23]
- Is your management team willing to make an investment in automation, knowing that it is likely that the initial costs will be more than recouped later, or are they still skeptical about the value automation can bring? If they are still skeptical, you may first have to convince them with several small successful automation efforts before tackling something more comprehensive.

---

23. For some appropriate cautions, see Dan Farber, "Six Barriers to Open Source Adoption," http://techupdate.zdnet.com/techupdate/stories/main/ Six_barriers_to_open_source_adoption.html.

These lists are by no means exhaustive; the best approach in formulating a plan for test automation for your team or project is to consider not only these questions but others as well. The following sections are intended to provide a useful starting point: gather your team together and brainstorm where you need to get to in regard to automation and in relation to where you are now. If you can understand, agree on, and prioritize the automation you need, you will stand a fighting chance of obtaining the support you need to accomplish your goal.

## What Should You Automate?

The areas in which test automation is most beneficial fall into four broad categories:

- Environmental
- Regression
- User interface
- Stress and performance

> **NOTE:** Generally, "environmental" elements and "regression" are the most important aspects of test automation, because of the relative time savings a test team can realize. There may be exceptions (for example, in instances where extensive performance testing is required), but this is a fair heuristic to keep in mind.

## Environmental Automation

*Environmental automation can be one of the most helpful forms of test automation.*

Surprisingly, environmental automation is often overlooked, and yet it can be one of the most helpful forms of automation to test teams. By *environmental* we mean the ability to provision machines quickly for use by the test team. For example:

- Are you still using CDs to install an operating system image on your lab machines? How about all the product prerequisites?
- What about security patches that may need to be applied?
- Is tuning necessary?
- Are there parameters that need to be routinely provided?

Think about how many times you need to "scrape a machine down to bare metal" in your testing and reinstall everything from the ground up just to make sure that someone else didn't leave anything hanging around that may adversely affect your testing. In some instances it could easily take an entire day (or longer!) for one person to get one machine ready to be used for testing. You can easily regain the significant amount of time wasted in such an effort by automating the provisioning of the test machines.

The ability to lay down a specific version of an OS quickly, with all fix-packs and security fixes, as well as all product prerequisites, should be one of the first items you look at when automating. Additionally, when such a capability is created, others can potentially pick it up, thus multiplying its benefit to the organization. Still further, the benefits of environmental automation are greatest when you want to test a product in many different environments.

## Automating Regression Testing

Regression testing is no more complicated a notion than running tests more than once. Automating regression testing means building a suite of tests that can be used, and reused, as needed. This becomes especially important when doing iterative development. Figure 3.3 shows how automation is incorporated when using an iterative approach.

*Automating regression is especially important when doing iterative development.*

Note that the test suite created to test the first iteration is still being used as part of the "Iteration 2" test suite. Hopefully, you can see why automating the first test suite would be beneficial: it will be run again during testing of the second, third, and fourth iterations. And the reason it is being run during each of these iterations is to ensure that code added during later iterations does not break anything that was previously working—hence the term *regression*. Note that the same holds true for those tests created specifically for code added during the second iteration—theywill be executed again during the third and fourth iterations, and the tests will be run the same way each time.

*Consistency is key when dealing with regression testing,* and it is also one of the strengths of automated testing. If tests are not run the same way

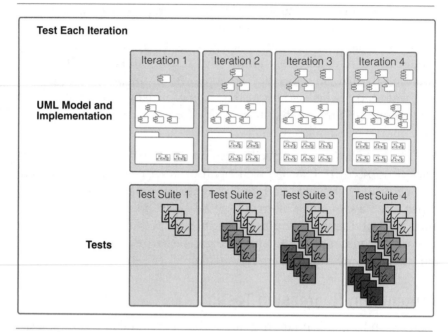

**FIGURE 3.3 Test Automation and Iterative Development.**

each time, how do you *know* that a defect has not been introduced between the time it was last executed and now?

The implications of testing are rarely considered as an organization begins to—rightly—adopt an iterative approach to development: they are too often an afterthought, or a worry. The reality of testing in an organization that employs true iterative development is that automation is less an *option* than a *necessity*—it is often physically impossible to test each build at each iteration with any degree of confidence, and test teams are consequently forced to "do the best they can." With an appropriate focus on automating a regression test suite, genuine forward progress can be maintained.

*Work closely with the development team in creating test automation.*

One way to not only maintain, but also accelerate, forward progress is to work closely with the development team in creating test automation. Often, developers will produce "test stubs" in order to do some testing on their code. With some forethought and planning, these test stubs can be designed to become the "seeds" from which testers can grow automated test suites. For those teams venturing into "test-driven development," this scenario is practically guaranteed.[24]

In sum, regression testing provides an assurance that regression errors have not been introduced, or at least helps ensure that any errors introduced will be caught. As such, it is especially important to the overall success of an iterative development approach. Additionally, regression testing is useful during the ongoing product maintenance, and for the same reasons: should a customer find a defect that requires a fix to be coded and then sent to that customer, the ability to execute a regression test suite prior to releasing the fix can help ensure that the fix will not break something else, thus providing greater assurance that the customer will not be further inconvenienced. Therefore, despite the real danger that your automation suite's apparent effectiveness will wane after the initial inoculation it provides, isn't this a better scenario than falling victim to the "disease" of defects? Still better, though, by maintaining your test automation suite you will continually find new defects and improve overall quality.

*Regression testing helps ensure that any errors introduced will be caught.*

> **NOTE:** To reiterate, environmental and regression test automation are generally the most important areas of automation to address, because they typically provide the most significant time and labor savings and the greatest overall likelihood of improving product quality.

## Automating User-Interface Testing

The next area that you should consider a good candidate for automation is the testing of the GUI code. It used to be that automated GUI code testing was nothing more than simple "record and play," which proved to be quite cumbersome in spite of the really cool demonstrations that accompanied the product "glossies." As soon as a programmer changed the GUI in any way (and this is the reality of the software development process), any previously recorded session became useless, and automation had to be started all over again. Add to this the fact that not much forethought was given to providing a

---

24. See Astels 2003 and Beck 2003.

structured approach to what was first "recorded" and then "played back," and test teams often found themselves with a mess on their hands.

*Appropriate GUI testing depends extensively on project goals and skills.*

Newer record-and-play tools, however, have overcome many of the initial shortcomings of this approach. While these tools are certainly the easiest way to start using automated GUI testing, tools that provide a programmatic interface allow for much more complex GUI testing. Being able to test each and every menu option, click on every button, and fill in every text entry field—all in much less time than it would take to do manually—is a great boon to independent testers and test teams. However, since you need a different set of skills to use programmatic interface tools than to operate the simple record-and-play tools, you should remember that *appropriate* GUI testing for your team depends extensively on the project goals, the type of product being developed, and the skill set of your test team.

The upside to user-interface testing is that it will help catch those defects that a customer will see, too often prominently displayed in living color. One of the potential downsides is that because most of the code written for your project is likely not user-interface code—automating user-interface tests may not be the highest priority—unit test tools are arguably easier to use and potentially provide a more easily demonstrable payback. As such, you should resist the urge to jump into automated GUI testing because it appears to be the easiest or most visible way to get started—if you choose to do so, make sure that it is part of an overall, well-conceived test automation plan.

## Automating Stress and Performance Testing

*Iterative development enables early stress and performance testing.*

One final area to consider is automating the *stress and performance* testing of the product.[25] In the traditional waterfall approach to software development, such testing usually cannot be accomplished until fairly late in the product development lifecycle. With many newer, iterative

---

25. There are other areas of automation possible as well, smoke testing being a notable example. Consider your automation project within the broader context of the "Full Lifecycle OO Testing" (FLOOT). See Ambler 2004.

development approaches, however, it is easier to perform stress and performance testing earlier in the lifecycle. For example, RUP suggests carrying out the first stress and performance testing during the elaboration phase, which focuses on getting the product architecture right. The ability to accomplish early testing here allows the project team to validate that the architecture is capable of supporting the specific performance requirements, thus mitigating risk. In later phases these automated tests are rerun to ensure that product performance and capabilities have not regressed in any way.

Stress testing is typically accomplished in two primary ways: (1) by running one test repeatedly and (2) by executing numerous instances of a given test at a particular time.

In the first situation, wrapping a single automated test with a script that loops back on itself is quite simple to create, but make sure that if you do so, it is because that is the way the product is going to be used; do not waste cycles automating this just because it is easy to do so.

In the second situation, you're simulating something like a number of users all logging onto a server at the same time, for example, when a bank branch office opens and all the bank tellers log on to the bank's main computer.

In performance testing, test cases can be "instrumented" to measure how long a given test takes to complete. Results can be recorded and then compared with previous results to see if the product performance is improving or declining. The ability to run performance tests repeatedly also provides the basis for creating capacity planning models, which can then be used to help customers understand the hardware required to achieve their desired performance levels.

Now that you are (hopefully) excited about the different possibilities that exist for test automation, it's time to look at one last issue you need to think through thoroughly before jumping in with both feet.

## Understanding the Costs of Test Automation

Many highly technical, intelligent engineers, and even many managers of technical engineers, fail to grasp the importance of finances in relation to the work they do. This problem is sometimes less critical in small shops, where there is a more obvious and immediate correlation between how efficiently the work is done and whether or not the shop remains in business. But whenever we as engineers or technical managers fail to connect the work we do with the bottom line, we run the very real risk of seeing all our hard work come to nothing. This is one reason why, for example, agile modeling emphasizes the principle "maximize shareholder investment." Automation projects are often scrutinized more closely than other projects for their return on investment, in large measure because of the inherent expectation that they will lead to demonstrable financial savings.

In any moderate to large automation effort, automation must be conceived of as similar to a development project. An automation blueprint (or design) must be developed. Prioritization of feature content, sizings, planning, staffing, and all the normal elements of software development should be considered. While it may be true that software used for internal purposes need not have the rigor of software produced for clients, an appropriate level of forethought and planning is still required if the results of test automation are to be effective. If, as a tester, you complain about the approach your partners take to development, it may be that you can use your test automation project to show a better way.

*Perhaps the biggest cost in test automation is the upkeep of automated tests.*

Perhaps the biggest cost in test automation, and one that is habitually overlooked, concerns the upkeep of automated tests. Any product design change will have a ripple effect on the corresponding automation test suite. To ensure continued usage of the test suites after product changes have taken place, someone has to update the automated tests that have been written. Sometimes the updates will be trivial and require only minimal effort to complete, whereas other times a significant design change can demand an equally significant change to the automated test suite. The extra work involved in the upkeep of the automated test suite must be recognized *and planned for* throughout the history of a product. When you build a schedule for testing that does not include time for automation *and* maintenance, you are accountable for your automation suite's decline.[26]

---

26. And more fundamentally, when you don't have input into the date on which a project ships, you have declared that you are content to "do the best you can" instead of "what needs to be done."

In spite of the costs, investing in test automation that is *appropriate* for your organization and project can be very beneficial, in terms of both time savings and quality improvements. Begin by acquiring experience, skills, and some initial "success stories" and then build on those from there—you'll be glad you did. To return to our car maintenance analogy, it is often easier to understand the cost of neglected car maintenance that results in tangible repair bills than to grasp the return on investment from routine maintenance that prevents problems in the first place. So also, with test automation, the return on investment is often undervalued. Actively communicate the value you are realizing from your investment in test automation.

*Test automation saves time and improves quality.*

## Other Methods

Aside from simply not testing at all, fundamentally, the only other option is to do testing *manually*. Even though there are significant benefits to appropriate levels of test automation, manual testing is still quite widespread. Manual testing does allow for certain levels of creativity and can be quite effective when the tester has a good intuitive feel for the product being tested—and that intuitive feel is not something that can be replicated by an automated test suite. However, adding test automation does overcome some of the many possible pitfalls of manual testing, notably:

- Lack of consistency (or repeatability).
- Lack of speed.
- Need for quick turnaround in a test cycle, for example, when late fixes by development and frequent builds during an iteration/release require such nimbleness.
- A certain "lack of control," such as in cases when a tester may forget the steps taken to get to the point where a defect was found, making it very difficult to perform defect analysis and provide a fix; with automated testing, the steps leading to defect discovery will be quite clear.
- Difficulty in understanding where progress is or isn't being made; automated testing lends itself easily to metrics gathering, especially "code coverage" metrics.

- The "factory" mindset; we are software engineers, not monkeys pounding on keyboards.

With these potential manual testing shortcomings in mind, it is easy to see why automated testing should be a regular part of your overall software testing strategy.

In XP, automated testing is mandatory. You simply can't perform test-driven development without automated tests, because rerunning the tests would just not be feasible. Automated testing is also a cornerstone of the Unified Process, since you cannot effectively grow a system iteratively without some form of automated regression testing. The Unified Process includes test-driven development as one recommended development approach, and goes beyond automated testing to include guidance on other forms of testing, such as exploratory testing and usability testing.

## Levels of Adoption

This practice can be adopted at three different levels:

- **Basic.** Environmental automation: provisioning of test machines and smoke tests are automated.

  What is one of the most repeated tasks in the test lab, one which is rarely factored into a test team's planning? It is quite likely the provisioning of test machines. The ability to rapidly reprovision a machine (or a set of machines) is something that can be done fairly easily, even by testers new to automation and provisioning. Also, smoke testing should also be accomplished at this basic level, especially on large or complex projects where build consistency or the core stability of the application is in question. These activities move you down and to the left on the process map.

- **Intermediate.** Create automated test suites corresponding to product development iterations that are subsequently used for regression testing of later iterations. Add user-interface testing to this mix.

  Part of adopting an iterative development approach to producing software requires the ability to create automated regression. Thus, having a team that understands the iterative approach, understands how to write solid automated test suites, and can also drive the GUI via GUI automation tools (especially those that provide a programmatic interface) takes on increasing importance. These are not skills that a new university recruit will likely have on day 1. But employing automated testing in conjunction with iterative development will move you down and to the left on the process map.

- **Advanced.** Automated tests are written to test the product at the limits (stress testing) and in order to provide the volume of data required to create capacity planning models.

Aside from the stress and performance testing done to help validate the performance and scalability goals of the product during early iterations, this advanced level of automated testing requires a deep understanding of software performance (and performance bottlenecks), software scalability issues, and numerical and data analysis, as well as the ability to create automated test suites that simulate both steady-state and maximum-effort use of the product.

Using the reams of information created through numerous runs of the automated test suites, and the resultant capacity planning models that are created from the data gathered by those tests, makes for very happy customers—customers who no longer have to guess at what hardware, software, and environment a particular product needs in order to function the way the customer expects. This level of adoption moves you down and to the right on the process map.

## Related Practices

- *Practice 1: Manage Risk* describes how to identify and deal with risks to your project. Automation can be used to mitigate risk but should also be reviewed in terms of the risk posed by an inadequate investment in automation.
- *Practice 2: Execute Your Project in Iterations* describes how to go about iterative development, and a key artifact in each iteration is an automated test suite that allows testing of new functionality, as well as regression-testing code written for previous iterations.

- *Practice 5: Test Your Own Code* details how developers can approach testing their own code holistically and includes techniques that will potentially be part of a broader test automation strategy.

## Additional Information

### Information in the Unified Process

OpenUP/Basic assumes that the basic development environment and tools already exist. Some level of test automation is assumed, in particular to support smoke tests and regression tests to ensure that builds remain stable.

RUP adds guidance on how to set up a test automation environment, from basic environmental automation to regression test suites. RUP also adds guidance on how to test larger systems of systems, which may include many levels and types of testing. Detailed guidance for specialized testing, such as globalization testing, performance testing, database testing, user interface testing, and so on, are covered by RUP and RUP plug-ins. RUP also includes guidance for using specific testing tools to perform automated testing.

### Additional Reading

For books, articles, and online sources referred to in this practice or related to it, consider the following:

David Astels. *Test-Driven Development: A Practical Guide*. Prentice Hall, 2003.

Frederick Brooks. *The Mythical Man Month*. Addison-Wesley, 1995.

Kent Beck. *Test-Driven Development: By Example*. Addison-Wesley, 2003.

Cem Kaner, James Bach, and Bret Pettichord. *Lessons Learned in Software Testing*. John Wiley & Sons, 2001.

Elfriede Dustin, Jeff Rashka, and John Paul. *Automated Software Testing: Introduction, Management, and Performance*. Addison-Wesley, 1999.

Mark Fewster and Dorothy Graham. *Software Test Automation*: *Effective Use of Test Execution Tools.* Addison-Wesley, 1999.

Edward Kit. "Integrated, Effective Test Design and Automation." *Software Development Magazine* (online version), February, 1999, and at http://www.sdmagazine.com/documents/s=761/sdm9902b/9902b.htm?temp=qHpycBTHQa.

Bret Pettichord. "Seven Steps to Test Automation Success." June 2001. http://www.io.com/~wazmo/papers/seven_steps.html.

Edward Yourdon. *Death March, Second Edition.* Prentice Hall, 2004.

# Everyone Owns the Product!

by Per Kroll

*Closer collaboration between team members and team ownership of the end product will result in a higher-quality product that better addresses the needs of the end users.*

## Problem

Many quality issues in software projects arise from items falling between the cracks. The gap often occurs because team members have too narrow a definition of what their job is or have difficulty transitioning work from one person to another. This is especially true with iterative development, where we move rapidly back and forth between requirements, design, implementation, and testing.

This practice describes how to orient the responsibilities and mindset of team members to ensure that everybody takes ownership of the quality of the end product, broadens the scope of their responsibilities, and learns to collaborate more effectively within the team

## Background

The other week, while waiting for a late-night flight, I was sitting in an airport restaurant. One of the servers was carrying a full load of dirty dishes back to the kitchen, and I was quite impressed that she could carry it all. Halfway to the kitchen a fork fell off one of the plates. Since her hands were full, she could not pick up the fork and continued to the kitchen. The fork remained on the floor.

Five yards behind came another server, empty-handed. I know she saw what happened, because she took an extra long step to avoid stepping on the fork. But she did not pick up the fork either; she just continued walking, although she appeared not to be in any kind of rush and the restaurant was half empty. It was not her job to pick up the fork, so the fork just lay there waiting for somebody to step on it.

One thing that differentiates an average eating establishment from a first-class restaurant is that in a first-class restaurant the entire staff are trained to consider it their job to give an extra hand to make sure that guests have a good experience. If a guest has an empty water glass, they offer to fill it up, even if it is not their table, or their job. If a guest seems to be looking for a server, they either inform the appropriate server or ask if they can be of assistance. They have learned that for the restaurant to continue to excel, all staff members must contribute what they can to create a great experience for their customers.

A couple of months back, I reviewed a troubled project. As I discussed various project problems and possible ways to address them with individual team members I consistently heard them say, "But that is not my job." Each team member seemed to have a very narrow definition of what his or her job was, and it was clear that a lot of responsibilities were not included in anybody's definition. Nobody felt responsible for detailing the requirements, ensuring that requirements and test cases were synchronized, or improving developer tests to ensure that code delivered to the test team was of sufficient quality.

To put it simply, the success of any project is everybody's responsibility, that is, everybody is responsible for doing whatever it takes to make the project succeed. This does not mean that you should not hold other team members responsible for doing their job, but when you see a task that needs to be done, either ensure that the responsible person does it, or do it yourself.

Many quality issues in software projects arise when new system representations are created based on our interpretation of an existing representation of the system, such as creating a design based on interpreting the requirements, or creating the code based on interpreting the design. In iterative development we transition very rapidly between different system representations to refine the requirements, design, implementation, and test specifications of a system (and not always in that order!). If we do not change our view of what our responsibility is, we would end up with a lot of discrepancies between our representations.

*Many quality issues arise when new system representations are created based on an existing representation of the system.*

## Applying the Practice[27]

This practice explains how the mindset of the team needs to be oriented to delivering a high-quality end product (see Table 3.1 for a summary). Responsibilities of each role have to adjust to the new mindset, and each person needs to take ownership of the end product. Let's have a look at how we need to orient the mindset of analysts, developers, architects, testers, managers, and customers in turn.

**TABLE 3.1 Summary of Required Mindset Orientation for Effective Iterative Development.** *Delivering a high-quality end product requires particularly close collaboration between analysts, developers, architects, testers, managers, and customers. This increased collaboration impacts responsibilities, means of communication, organization, and the way in which people see their role within the project team. In short, it creates new requirements for the mindset of each team member.*

| Old Mindset: "It's Not My Job!" | New Mindset: "We'll Get This Done!" |
|---|---|
| • Functional teams of either all analysts, all developers, or ... | • Cross-functional teams consisting of analysts, developers, testers, ... |
| • OK with low-bandwidth communication | • Must have high-bandwidth communication |
| • Communicate primarily through documents (requirements, design, . . .) | • Communicate through face-to-face meetings, evolving models, and tools |
| • Narrow specialists | • Generalists and specialists with bird's-eye perspective[a] |
| • Focus on the specification | • Focus on the intent of the specification |
| • "Not my job" | • "We are all responsible for the end result." |

a. See Ambler 2002.

27. This section is based on Kroll 2004.

## The Analyst's New Mindset

The mindset of an analyst needs to change from somebody who is "responsible for documenting requirements" to somebody who is responsible for making sure that the *right* requirements are documented, understood, and then properly reflected by developers and testers. This means that as an analyst, you need to do the following:

*An analyst is responsible for the right requirements being documented, understood, and properly reflected.*

- *Establish an ongoing dialogue with, and seek the participation of, the end user to ensure that the right system is developed.*[28] You need to do this not only to document the right requirements but also to ensure that end users appropriately see and use prototypes of the system as it is being developed. This approach helps you build the right system, since end users are frequently unable to understand the capabilities of an application based on reading a requirements specification, but they can understand prototypes. This dialogue also enables the end user to ask for the next logical set of enhancements, further increasing the business value of the application.

- *Encourage early implementation of key capabilities to understand what requirements will address business needs.* Even though the project manager,[29] with the help of the architect, is responsible for determining in what order to develop what capabilities, an analyst needs to understand what requirement areas may need early prototyping to ensure that the end users understand what capabilities will be delivered. This information needs to be communicated to the project manager.

- *Work with developers and testers to optimize requirements.* As developers and testers analyze the requirements and develop and test the application, they will make a lot of observations that may lead to requirements that are easier to implement and provide more value to the end users. The analyst needs to have an open and

---

28. Stakeholder participation is a key part of Unified Process, XP, and Agile Modeling.

29. In XP it is the role of the customer or customer's representative to prioritize requirements. In Scrum it is the role of the Product Owner, in RUP it is the role of the System Analyst, and in OpenUP/Basic it is the role of the Analyst.

ongoing dialogue with the developers and testers to ensure that their observations are properly reflected in the product.

- *Choose the right level of detail for requirements, based on the needs of your project and the phase you are in.*[30] As an analyst, you need to understand that more detailed requirements are not necessarily better. If requirements are too detailed, it will take too long to understand the most essential requirements and cost too much to keep them up to date. When the requirements reach a certain level of specificity, the cheapest way of refining them is not by making them more detailed but by writing code that reflects the improved understanding. Spending too much time on the requirements details up front distracts the team from mitigating key risks. On the other hand, if the requirements are too vague, a lot of time can be wasted in guesswork, which may have regulatory, contractual, or other effects.

## The Developer's New Mindset

*A developer is responsible for the development of a high-quality application that addresses the end user's needs.*

The mindset of a developer needs to change from somebody who is "just responsible for implementing the requirements" to somebody who is responsible for the development of a high-quality application that addresses the end user's needs. This shift means that as a developer you now need to do the following:

- *Broaden your responsibilities to include detailed design, implementation, and developer testing.* You want to minimize the number of handovers of information to different people to minimize potential errors and maximize efficiency. To minimize the number of handovers, make sure your team members take on as broad set of responsibilities as possible, so that you do not have one person doing the design and another doing the implementation. Make sure that whatever code you produce is of high quality; you need

---

30. See practices *Model with a Purpose* and *Maximize Stakeholder Investment* in Ambler 2002.

to test your own code and make sure that it works with the rest of the application.

- *Become part of the requirements effort: help find solutions for requirements.* As a developer, you often find ways to improve the application. You need to work with the analysts and the project manager to ensure that they understand any opportunities for improvements.

- *Become part of the test effort.* Modern best practices, such as test-first design, help you as a developer to focus on testing. With test-first design, you first specify what tests should be carried out and then build the software to pass the tests. This approach creates a strong focus on producing high-quality code and forces the team to concentrate on building high-quality applications. Also, advances in tool technology now allow Quality by Design,[31] making quality an integral part of the design process, allowing quality measurements to be made early in the design process, and enabling test drivers and test harnesses to be automatically generated from the design model. Quality by Design increases the quality and completeness of test code.

- *Make reuse of existing solutions a higher priority than building from scratch.* In the past, developers rightfully took pride in coming up with clever solutions to tricky problems. Unique solutions were produced from scratch to maximize system performance, minimize memory usage, or provide a good GUI. Of course, developers still need to come up with clever solutions, but the focus needs to move away from building solutions from scratch toward finding clever ways of tying reusable assets together into a workable solution through open source software, commercial-off-the-shelf (COTS) components, internally available components, and Web services. This shift away from custom-building assets to reusing existing solutions impacts not only the design and code but also the business, requirements, test, and management assets.

---

31. See Bryson 2001 for more information on Quality by Design.

## The Architect's New Mindset

*An architect is responsible for making high-level design decisions and ensuring that they are properly reflected in the final code.*

The mindset of an architect needs to change from somebody who does high-level design and then leaves the project to somebody who is responsible for making high-level design decisions, balancing the multitude of technical and project constraints; somebody who mentors the developers on the project vision; and somebody who stays throughout the project to ensure that the chosen design decisions are properly reflected in the final code. This approach means that as an architect you now need to do the following:

- *Be engaged in the project from start to finish.* Many projects suffer because architects come in early in the project, lay out the architecture, and then leave. One of the fundamental concepts in iterative development is the need to allow some flexibility for change, but changes that may impact the architecture should not be made without discussing them with an architect and the affected developers. Also, a paper architecture has limited value. Only when the architecture is implemented and tested does it provide significant value, and the architect needs to stay with the project until this goal is accomplished, as well as to handle change requests that may impact the architecture. In general, as an architect you should contribute some time in the inception phase, a lot in the elaboration and early construction phases, and less and less as you move toward the end of the construction and transition phases.

- *Prioritize and drive development of architecturally significant scenarios.* To validate the architecture, you need to implement those scenarios that are deemed architecturally significant (see *Practice 10: Prioritize Requirements for Implementation*). You need to determine which scenarios are architecturally significant and remain closely involved in their development, to ensure that the team makes and validates the right architectural decisions.

- *Ensure that all team members understand high-level design decisions.* As you make high-level design decisions, you need to ensure that all team members understand how to leverage those decisions. You may need to include training on available architectural patterns, such as patterns for interprocess communication or persistency and how to use them. You may also need to document and walk through the high-level architecture—what subsystems exist and their interfaces, how you will deal with change requests to the architecture, and how you will communicate with external systems.

- *Make sure that appropriate testing is done on the architecture.* As an architect, you need to make sure that the architecture not only works on paper but also does the job it is supposed to do. You must work with the testers to make sure that architectural qualities, such as performance, throughput, capacity, reliability, and scalability, are properly tested early in the project to avoid the need for major changes late in the project.

- *Coordinate discussions impacting high-level design decisions.* Throughout the project, there will be reasons to revisit architectural decisions, such as changing interfaces between various subsystems or responsibilities of subsystems. As an architect, you need to take an active role in these discussions to make sure that you understand and properly communicate any architectural changes to the affected team members.

## The Tester's New Mindset

The mindset of a tester needs to change from somebody who "injects quality at the very end" of a project to somebody who does testing from start to finish as well as becoming the test expert guiding other team members in regard to test-related issues. As a tester, therefore, you need to do the following:

*A tester does testing from start to finish and guides other team members in regard to test-related issues.*

- *Define a test strategy* that incorporates the stakeholders' definition of quality as well as the project team's priorities. All too often testers impose on the project their own predefined measure of quality, which not all stakeholders may agree on. Team members can succeed and correctly focus their efforts only if all share a view of what defines quality and project success.

- *Become the team's mentor on testing approaches and methodology.* Testers should share their expertise with the entire development team, for example, guiding management in test-related decisions, advising analysts on writing testable requirements, and helping developers conduct effective developer testing, in addition to actually performing much of the integration and acceptance testing.

- *Work with analysts and developers to ensure that requirements and design are testable.* Testers are trained to think about how to measure requirements satisfaction. Modern integrated test and development environments also constitute a major shift for both developers and testers by allowing continuous testing of work in progress using baselined code configurations. Testers need to provide feedback to the other team members so that they can make the appropriate improvements to the requirements, design, code, and other supporting artifacts.

- *Get involved in the test effort early in the project.* Iterative development involves testing in every iteration, which means that you need to shift the test workload from (primarily) the end of the project to a much more even distribution throughout the project. Testers need to work hand in hand with analysts and developers so that all understand what needs to be tested in each iteration. One way to ensure that this happens is through test-first design. Early in the project, testing will focus on finding "big issue" problems, such as major architectural concerns, that need to be addressed. Later in the project, testing will focus on validation and verification that the code is ready to be delivered to end users.

- *Focus on addressing defined test objectives.* Rather than trying to fix all defects—an often impossible task—understand what your objectives are with the test efforts. Determine the right level of quality and whether any specific aspects of the application need to be of a higher quality. Focus your test efforts accordingly.

- *Continuously automate testing of stable capabilities.* Iterative development means testing the most critical capabilities early in the project. You therefore need to test and retest these capabilities in successive iterations to ensure that problems considered solved do not recur. Full regression testing is impractical, and often impossible, without effective test automation, so automated tests should be developed continuously throughout the project. These tests should focus on what will be stable as the iterations proceed, so that they do not have to be radically changed in every iteration. This task requires collaboration with the rest of the development team (see *Practice 6: Leverage Test Automation Appropriately* for more information).

## The Manager's New Mindset

The focus of a manager needs to change from day-to-day management, secondary artifacts, and stable plans to leadership, results-based management, and team collaboration. As a manager, therefore, you now need to do the following:

*A manager focuses on leadership, results-based management, and team collaboration.*

- *Be a leader.*[32] As a leader, you need to make sure that the team understands and shares the vision of what is to be accomplished and is motivated to work together to reach the end goal. You need to establish shared values—what is acceptable and what is not acceptable—and continuously reinforce these values through actions. Rather than micromanaging, you need to continuously assess your position, determine the appropriate end point (and your view of the "right" end point will shift as you proceed through the project), and steer the team in the right direction. Finally, you need to help the team cope with the huge amount of uncertainty that always exists in software projects.

- *Empower your team.* Iterative development requires different skills and means of collaboration. As a leader, you need to make sure that your team has the knowledge and responsibilities they need to succeed. You need to create cross-disciplinary teams—that is, teams with analysts, developers, and testers—who can work together to achieve results. Support the changes in responsibilities and behavior described throughout this practice.

- *Be open about the risks the project is facing, continuously reassess risks, and use risks to prioritize project work.*[33] The most important distinction of the iterative development approach is to drive out major risks early in the lifecycle. It therefore requires openness and honesty about the risks faced by the project. Risk will help you determine what to focus on in the next iteration, and risks and their mitigation should be an important aspect of the status meeting discussions.

- *Assess status through demonstrable results rather than through completion of activities.* As a manager, your focus must now switch from

---

32. See Cantor 2001.
33. See Cantor 2001 and Highsmith 2004.

activities to demonstrable results. Completed activities are a poor measure of success, since the mere completion of an activity generally does not say anything about the quality of the end result. Rather, as a manager you should concentrate on assessing the results that have been achieved. Since the primary result is the software itself, the first measure of success should be delivered working software. This measure provides a more reliable assessment of the project's status than do secondary artifacts such as requirements and designs, because even though a requirements document has been "finished," it may later need major rework based on feedback from working prototypes.

- *Develop high-level plans for the entire project early on, but produce detailed plans only for the current and next iterations.* Traditionally, many managers spend a lot of time initially producing detailed project plans for the entire project. But in reality, so much uncertainty accompanies most projects that such plans merely serve to provide a false sense of assurance, suggesting fictional precision where none exists. Instead, managers should produce a high-level plan for the entire project that briefly describes the expected outcome of each iteration and detailed plans only for the current and following iterations.

- *Balance investments in requirements, architecture, design, implementation, and testing at any given time, to ensure that risks are being addressed.*[34] In the waterfall approach managers pay much attention to planning and requirements. In iterative development, managers at any given moment need to focus on balancing the investments in requirements, architecture, design, and implementation in order to address your risks. A manager should ask: "Which types of activities will best mitigate key risks right now?" Maybe it's only by prototyping a solution that you can address risks related to stakeholder buy-ins, or only by designing, implementing, and testing the architecture that you can address architectural risks.

---

34. Royce 1998.

## The Customer's New Mindset

The mindset of a customer needs to change from somebody who is external to the project to somebody who is an integral part of it. As a customer, therefore, you now need to do the following:

*A customer is an integral part of the project.*

- *Become an integral part of the development team.* Today, many customers expect minimal involvement in the development effort. They want to specify all their requirements up front, determine a fixed price, and then wait for delivery of the final system. Frequently, the result of this interaction model is a solution that does not address their true business needs and large discrepancies between what they were expecting and what was delivered, causing both the customer and the development team a great deal of pain. Instead, customers should seek to be active participants in the project.

- *Continuously provide feedback on capabilities that have been developed, such as working prototypes and user-interface designs.*[35] No matter how crisp the requirements are, they have a multitude of interpretations and possible implementations. Rather than investing in even more detailed requirements, it is often more effective to invest in more frequent interaction between developers and key stakeholders, including customers. As customers view the evolving application, they gain a better understanding of what it should do and can provide constructive feedback to improve the solution. Also, in many cases business needs evolve rapidly, and the requirements need to evolve in tandem with the changing business needs during the project duration.

- *Leverage progressive acquisition models in which an iterative approach to acquisition protects the interests of the buyer as well as the seller.* Contractual agreements also benefit from an iterative approach, or what is referred to as progressive acquisition. The idea behind progressive acquisition is to have an umbrella agreement for the entire project outlining the overall legal conditions that govern the business relationship between the two parties. The actual project

---

35. Feedback is an XP value; see Beck 2004.

is divided into two or more subcontracts. Earlier contracts are defined by time and materials, since neither party knows enough about the overall solution and costs to develop it to make up-front commitments. Later contracts are for a fixed price, minimizing risks on both sides of overruns or disagreements on what should be delivered.[36]

## Guidance for Larger Teams

The above guidelines point to a series of changes in the responsibilities of each team member. To avoid tasks falling between the cracks within a larger organization or project, you also need to consider additional changes:

*Produce precise documentation or models. Precise does not mean lengthy— quite the opposite.*

- **Produce precise documentation or models.** In previous discussions concerning this practice, we have emphasized collaboration as a means to reduce the chances that tasks will fall between the cracks. As teams grow, you need to support this collaborative approach with precise documentation to ensure that everybody is clear on what other people do. Note that "precise" does *not* mean lengthy. Quite the opposite, in fact; it is typically preferable to have a one-page UML diagram that is precise than ten pages of text.

- **Scalable collaboration infrastructure.** Establish an infrastructure that allows effective communication across geographies and teams. Examples of such an infrastructure include team-based tools for requirements management, management of reusable components and other assets, defect tracking, and configuration management. It also includes automation of status information, since updating this type of information can waste huge amounts of time as teams grow.

- **Enterprise architecture.** By having an enterprise architecture provide guidelines on how to architect individual applications, you increase the chances that various applications will work together and that you can share common components across applications. You should also have cross-team review boards perform architectural reviews.

---

36. Wideman 2003.

- **Program management**. Invest in program management to coordinate across teams. This coordination needs to take place across various functional areas, such as requirements, architecture, and testing.
- **Invest in organizational experts.** Many complex applications require the involvement of people with very deep skills. An individual project may not be able to acquire someone with these deep skills, nor take on a person, even part-time, with skills such as globalization or accessibility (dealing with how to make software accessible for people with disabilities).

## Other Methods

This practice is very well aligned with the broader agile community. The Crystal family of methods, XP, Scrum, Agile Modeling, Adaptive Development, and other methods all talk about the need to involve customers in the project, have the extended development team collaborate closely, and have all team members take ownership of the end result. The agile community has consistently promoted the softer issues around software development to reflect the reality that people issues are central to developing software.

*People issues are central to developing software.*

XP values associated with this practice include *communication, feedback, courage,* and *respect,* while XP practices associated with this practice include *sitting together, whole team,* and *test-first programming.* The practice of *whole team*[37] describes the importance of building cross-functional teams, the practice of *sitting together* deals with how to make people interact more throughout the day, and the practice of *test-first programming* deals with how to tie requirements, design, implementation, and testing efforts more closely together.

Another interesting area is involvement of experts. XP involves experts by moving them temporarily into a project as they are needed and out again as they are no longer required. XP points out the disadvantages of having people working in a project part-time, which typically makes them inefficient. XP also involves external experts as pair

---

37. Beck 2004.

programmers, allowing the team to learn from experts and to leverage their skills to develop more effective code. RUP is more open than XP to the notion that if certain types of expertise are in very short supply, you need to involve them on a part-time basis, maybe primarily as advisors or reviewers, especially in a large organization that can absorb the cost of building up deep expertise, even though the individual project cannot. Examples of such skills may include deep skills in globalization or accessibility.

Jeff Sutherland, one of the creators of Scrum, uses a metaphor of pigs and chickens when talking about managers and team members. The metaphor comes from a story about a pig and a chicken:

> *Chicken: Let's start a restaurant!*
> *Pig: What would we call it?*
> *Chicken: Ham n' Eggs!*
> *Pig: No thanks. I'd be committed, but you'd only be involved!*

This story reflects that it is the actual project members (pigs) who are committed to a project's success. As a team, we are responsible for the end product, and we should therefore have the authority to make decisions that have an impact on it. In Scrum, team members are allowed to make decisions for themselves within an iteration (sprint), without having managers or other external parties (chickens), who are only involved, second-guess what they should do. As an example, chickens are allowed to attend, but not to speak, during the daily scrum status meetings.

We authors salute the notion of self-managed teams and breaking down walls between team members, but we also feel that many people in the agile community assume that managers add little value and describe processes for managing around managers (as with the chicken and pig above). Even though some managers add only limited value to the execution of a project, our experience is that most add value through their daily work, and the team should seek to involve their managers more than only at iteration ends. We believe that rather than working around managers in general, we should instead assign them clear responsibilities, so that we can improve the behavior of poor managers, maximize the value of their contributions, and help make them into great leaders.

## Levels of Adoption

This practice can be adopted at three levels:

- **Basic.** Openly share information to encourage early discussion of ideas and evaluation of 10 percent complete materials. Avoiding guarding artifacts and code until they are perfect.

  The basic practice of information sharing should minimize the need for later rework, which should lead to a more relaxed process and shorter iterations.

- **Intermediate.** Assemble cross-functional teams, including the customer or customer's representative. Hold each team member responsible for the end product. Assess status primarily based on demonstrable progress. This approach forces the team to look at the complete product rather than just individual pieces, such as the requirements or the design. As issues are identified, the team identifies how to best resolve them, which typically involves cross-functional collaboration.

  The intermediate practice of cross-functional collaboration is crucial for effective iterative development and should in most cases also result in minimal bureaucracy. Note that this process will, however, make a manager's job more difficult, since it has more moving parts.

- **Advanced.** Adopt the practices described in the section Guidance for Larger Teams, including scalable platforms for collaboration, enterprise architectures, and organizational expertise.

  The advanced practice, which is primarily for larger organizations and teams, increases overhead associated with change and thus drives the project toward greater discipline and longer iterations.

  The exception is the practice of scalable platforms for collaboration, which requires a higher skill level but makes meaningful collaboration much easier, hence reducing the iteration length.

## Related Practices

- *Practice 12: Build High-Performance Teams* discusses what characterizes a high-performance team and how you can build a culture that nurtures those required characteristics. Finding the right team members and fostering the right culture in your team is crucial to instilling the right mindset.

## Additional Information

### Information in the Unified Process

OpenUP/Basic captures the guidance in this practice, with the exception of progressive acquisition and the guidance in the section Guidance for Larger Teams. RUP adds guidance for progressive acquisition, as well as in-depth guidance on how to collaborate effectively using more in-depth models and documentation and a variety of software development tools. RUP also provides guidance on cross-project coordination, such as program and portfolio management.

### Additional Reading

The following books capture guidelines around collaborative best practices and self-organized teams:

Kent Beck with Cynthia Andres. *Extreme Programming Explained: Embrace Change, Second Edition*. Addison-Wesley, 2004.

James A. Highsmith. *Adaptive Software Development: A Collaborative Approach to Managing Complex Systems*. Dorset House Publishing, 2000.

Scott Ambler and Ron Jeffries. *Agile Modeling: Effective Practices for Extreme Programming and the Unified Process*. John Wiley & Sons, 2002.

Alistair Cockburn. *Agile Software Development*. Addison-Wesley, 2002.

The following books describe best practices around people management, project organization, and project leadership:

Murray Cantor. *Software Leadership: A Guide to Successful Software Development*. Addison-Wesley, 2001.

Walker Royce. *Software Project Management: A Unified Framework*. Addison-Wesley, 1998.

# CHAPTER 4

# Balance Stakeholder Priorities

| | |
|---|---|
| ***Benefits*** | • Align applications with business and user needs.<br>• Reduce custom development.<br>• Optimize business value. |
| ***Patterns*** | 1. Define, understand, and prioritize business and user needs.<br>2. Prioritize projects and requirements and couple needs with software capabilities.<br>3. Understand what assets can be leveraged.<br>4. Balance asset reuse with user needs. |
| ***Anti-Patterns*** | • Achieve precise and thorough requirements before any project work begins.<br>• Document precise requirements at the outset of the project, driving the project toward a custom solution.<br>• Architect a system only to meet the needs of the most vocal stakeholders. |

The principle stated in this chapter's title articulates the importance of balancing often conflicting business and stakeholder needs, as well as balancing custom development versus asset reuse in order to meet these needs.

Most stakeholders would prefer having an application that does exactly what they want it to do, while minimizing the application's development cost and schedule time. Yet these priorities are often in conflict. As an example, if you leverage a packaged application to deliver a solution faster and at a lower price, you may have to trade off many requirements. If, however, you elect to build an application from scratch instead, you may be able to address every requirement on its wish list, but the budget and project completion date might both be pushed beyond their feasible limits as a result.

Rather than sending programming teams out to attack each element in a requirements list, you need to *understand and prioritize business and stakeholder needs*. This means capturing business processes and linking them to projects and software capabilities, so that you can prioritize projects and requirements effectively and then modify these priorities as you learn more about the application and stakeholder needs. It also means involving the customer or customer representative in the project to ensure that you understand what their needs are.

Second, *center development activities around stakeholder needs*. For example, by leveraging use-case-driven development and user-centered design, your development process can accommodate the evolution of stakeholder needs over the course of the project, as a function of changing business and your improved understanding of the capabilities that are truly important to the business and the end users.

Finally, understand what assets are available and *balance asset reuse with stakeholder needs*. Examples of assets include business models, legacy applications, services, reusable components, and patterns. Reuse of assets can in many cases lead to reduced project cost, and reusing proven assets often means higher quality in new applications (see Figure 4.1). The drawback is that in many cases you must trade off asset reuse against perfect satisfaction of user needs. Reusing a component may lower development costs for a feature by 80 percent but address only 75 percent of the requirements. Effective reuse thus requires con-

**FIGURE 4.1 Balance Asset Reuse with Stakeholder Needs.** *Using a component can radically reduce the cost and time to deliver a certain set of functionality. It may in many cases also require you to compromise on some functional or technical requirements, such as platform support, performance, or footprint (size of the application).*

stantly balancing reuse of assets with evolving stakeholder needs. Reusing an asset may also increase risk as a result of creating dependencies on external parties.

The anti-pattern to following this principle would be to document thoroughly the precise requirements at the outset of the project, force stakeholder acceptance of requirements, and then negotiate any changes to the requirements, each of which might increase the cost or duration of the project. By locking down requirements up front, you reduce the ability to leverage existing assets, which in turn drives you toward undertaking primarily custom development. Another anti-pattern would be to architect a system only to meet the needs of the most vocal stakeholders.

Let's have a look at some of the concrete practices that will help you balance the use of existing assets with evolving user needs:

- *Practice 8: Understand the Domain* shows how you can effectively communicate essential information about the problem domain to your project team.

- *Practice 9: Describe Requirements from the User Perspective* describes how use cases can help capture requirements so that end users and team members alike easily understand them.

- *Practice 10: Prioritize Requirements for Implementation* explains how to determine which requirements to address first in order to deliver customer value and mitigate key risks.

- *Practice 11: Leverage Legacy Systems* outlines how to leverage the many valuable assets you have in your organization.

# Understand the Domain

by Per Kroll

*A concise and shared understanding of the problem domain enhances communication and project effectiveness.*

## Problem

To develop an application, you often need to bring together people with very different backgrounds. You may have domain experts with limited technical expertise; developers, architects, and testers with limited domain expertise; and reviewers and other stakeholders with limited time to commit to the project and learn about the problem domain. These people often have an inconsistent or poor understanding of the problem domain in which you are building your software, such as how Company X signs up new insurance policies, or how Company Y deals with expense reports. This lack of understanding causes communication problems and increases the likelihood that they will build the wrong application. This practice shows you how to provide a concise and shared understanding of the problem domain.

## Background

For convenience, when communicating with each other we often leave out a lot of information, making assumptions about what should be evident to the recipient of the information. For example, if I tell you, "I want a house with one bedroom, one bathroom, and a large kitchen. And I want both a shower and a bathtub," you would most likely understand that I want the shower and bathtub in the bathroom, not in the kitchen or bedroom. However, if you had never been in a house, that information would not be obvious.

You have probably been in a meeting or discussion where everybody appears to be in agreement, only to discover later that each person came out of the meeting with a different understanding of what was agreed on. This is a common problem in software projects, where we are dealing with a lot of conceptual ideas and a problem domain that may be unfamiliar. Often, analysts write down requirements that are based on a misconceived notion of the problem domain; customers and other stakeholders do not understand what software requirements will address their business needs; and developers and testers do not sufficiently understand what problem the application is to address to build the right application. Obviously, such communication failures cause a lot of difficulties in software development.

So how do we deal with these problems in other areas of life? Let's say that you work in a bank and want to explain what account types are available to a potential customer. Pretty soon the multitude of options in terms of account types can become overwhelming. To make it easier to explain the various loan types, you present the customer with a list, such as the following:

- **Checking accounts.** Yield no interest, but provide a broad set of services at a low fee.

- **Money market deposit accounts.** Typically pay interest, but require a minimum balance, with fees charged for more than six withdrawals per month.

- **Savings accounts.** Reasonable interest, some fees.

- **Time deposits or CDs.** Often pay higher, fixed interest, but lock funds in for a predetermined period.

As you continue adding more details regarding which account types can be associated with an ATM card, credit cards, and direct deposit of paychecks, as well as which account types bear interest, you may find it easier to use graphics in addition to purely textual information to represent the many complex concepts and show how they are related (see Figure 4.2). We actually created this model when we first created a glossary and saw a need to model more complex relationships graphically through what we call a domain model. Domain models should be evolved as your understanding of the problem

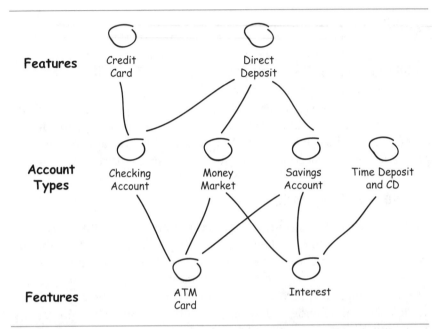

**Features** — Credit Card, Direct Deposit

**Account Types** — Checking Account, Money Market, Savings Account, Time Deposit and CD

**Features** — ATM Card, Interest

**FIGURE 4.2 Simple Domain Model.** *A domain model represents key concepts and their relationship to one another. This one shows different types of accounts and indicates which account type carries features, such as interest, ATM card, and credit card. This example provides you with a quick overview of the problem domain. It is important to include just the information required to explain the domain. Too much information clutters understanding and is too time-consuming for both the producer and consumer of information.*

domain evolves. This means that you should expect the domain model to evolve along with your requirements, design, implementation, and test assets.

In our daily life we present information through clear definitions and graphic depictions to offset some of the difficulties in communication caused by differences in perspectives and experiences. The practice described here extends these ideas even further in an organized and structured fashion.

*In our daily life we present information through graphic depictions.*

## Applying the Practice

To model the domain effectively, you first need to define key concepts within the domain, specify the key relationships between those concepts, and in some cases also detail the concepts in some depth. We will have a look at each of these activities and also provide some guidance on how to leverage key concepts most effectively in your development effort. Finally, we will discuss how you can capture business rules and use advanced practices such as business process modeling.

## Define Key Concepts

To make sure that you share a common understanding of the problem domain, first identify the key "items" the application deals with. For example, for a travel expense application, define what expense types you can submit, what type of approvers you may have, and so on. Also add a glossary of common terminology used in the domain that the team or stakeholders may not be familiar with. This glossary is often owned by the analyst but updated by all team members as appropriate. To avoid miscommunication and misunderstanding, participants should agree on a common terminology. Hopefully, some of your team members are knowledgeable about the domain and can use this opportunity to share that knowledge effectively with other team members. If all team members already have an excellent knowledge of the domain, you may not need to define many or any concepts. In many situations, however, although team members think that they all agree on key concepts, as you start to discuss and detail them, you notice discrepancies in different team members' views; you may want to sort these discrepancies out.

## Specify Relationships Between Key Concepts

*A domain model shows graphically how various concepts are related.*

Many of the items in the glossary are related to each other, and to understand the problem domain, you need to understand these relationships. For example, for a travel expense application you want to know the answers to questions such as the following: What types of expense items are there? Who needs to approve an expense report?

Can you automatically link an expense item to a transaction on your corporate credit card? What types of employee reimbursements are supported (direct deposit, checks)? This type of information can be captured in a glossary or domain model[1]. One of the benefits of a domain model is that it shows graphically how various concepts are related (see Figure 4.3).

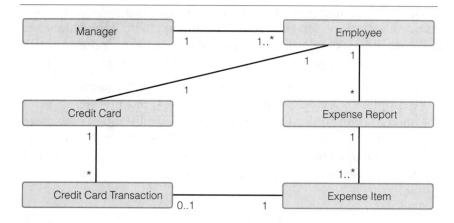

**FIGURE 4.3 Domain Model for a Travel Expense Application.** *A domain model represents key concepts and their relationship to one another. In this travel expense reporting system, each employee needs to have a manager and only one credit card recognized by the system. The model also shows that there seems to be a way to couple credit card transactions to expense items on an expense report.*

It is often a good idea to start by capturing a concept as a glossary item and then using the glossary as a source for identifying domain objects. If you know that a concept would be conveyed better graphically, you can capture it as a domain model directly. Another good starting point for the domain model is to ask a domain expert to use a pen and paper to draw you a picture showing an overview of the problem domain. As the expert graphically outlines the structure of key concepts, you often identify new concepts.

---

1. See Jacobson 1992 for more information on domain models.

Since many glossary items may have a corresponding domain object, information about the same concept may be stored in two places, which is undesirable. Instead, the glossary items should reference the domain object for a definition.

*Use UML to express the domain model.*

One of the purposes of the domain model is to provide an easily understood overview of the problem domain. We therefore use the standard language for software engineering, Unified Modeling Language (UML), to express the domain model.[2] To ensure that non–software experts understand your domain model, limit the number of different types of relationship you show between your domain objects. The most essential relationships to use include the following:

- **Association.** Associations show how instances of one concept (for example, a specific employee in Figure 4.4) relate to instances of another concept (for example, a specific expense report). An association may have a multiplicity. The multiplicity can, for example, specify that a specific employee can have any number of expense reports (denoted with a "*") but only one credit card (denoted with a "1").

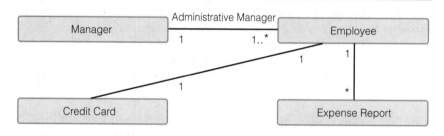

**FIGURE 4.4 Sample Association.** *An employee can file any number of expense reports (indicated by the "*" next to the expense report) but can have only one credit card on file in the system (indicated by the "1" next to the credit card) and only one manager. In reality, there may be many different managers (functional, administrative, and so on), but we can see from the role descriptor "Administrative Manager" that this system cares only about the administrative manager who has responsibility for approving expense reports.*

2. Many people also use data modeling notations to capture domain models.

- **Generalization.** Generalizations show a general concept and specializations of that concept, as shown in Figure 4.5.

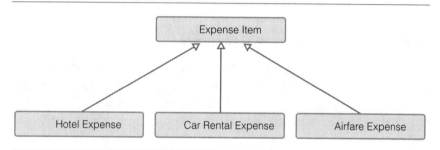

**FIGURE 4.5 Sample Generalization.** *There are three types of expense items: hotel, car rental, and airfare. These are all specializations of the general concept of expense items and thus share a number of common characteristics.*

- **Aggregation.** This relationship shows that one concept consists of, or is built up from, several other concepts (see Figure 4.6).

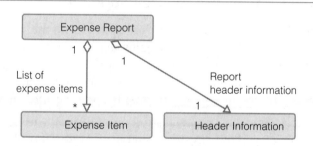

**FIGURE 4.6 Sample Aggregation.[3]** *This figure details some of the general information presented in Figure 4.3 by showing that an expense report is built up from header information specifying items such as purpose of trip and destination, along with a list of expense items. There is one set of header information, but there can be any number of expense items.*

---

3. UML allows you to show different types of aggregations, such as composition. It is outside the scope of this book to discuss these finer details, and you must always ask yourself whether additional specificity is required to explain the domain, or whether you are better off keeping things simple.

For domain models you should mostly use associations, and you may or may not use generalization or aggregations based on your needs and the audience. Role names are sometimes useful to clarify how one domain object relates to another.

## Detail Key Concepts as Required

You can also use a domain model to help everybody understand what critical information is typically captured for a domain object by capturing attributes. For example, a domain object *Credit Card Transaction* may have the attributes Transaction Amount, Transaction Date, and Transaction Establishment.

As you detail key concepts with additional attributes or associations, remember that one of the key principles in software development is to *travel light*. As Scott Ambler writes in *Agile Modeling*,[4] do *"just enough modeling and documentation to get by."* It is a common mistake to put too much information into your domain model. If you are not sure you need it, don't include it.

## Using Key Concepts in the Development Effort

When you describe requirements, for example in the form of use cases, reference domain objects and glossary items to make sure that your requirements specification uses clearly defined terminology. This step will, among other things, allow reviewers, stakeholders, testers, and others to understand the requirements and the problem domain.

*Domain objects are a great starting point for your design.*

Domain objects are also a great starting point for your design and will save you time later in the development effort. You will find that many domain objects map directly to a component, a set of components, an attribute within a component, and sometimes even a subsystem. In other cases you will find that a domain object has no corresponding representation in the design, since it captures a concept not managed by your application. Domain objects also provide you with a starting point for your data modeling effort, where many entities can be derived from your domain objects.[5]

---

4. Ambler 2002.

5. Ambler 2003.

## Document Business Rules

A business rule is a declaration of policy, heuristic, algorithm, or a condition that must be satisfied[6]; it is a requirement concerning how the business must operate. Business rules can be laws and regulations imposed on the business or guidelines for running the business effectively. Here are some examples of business rules:

*Business rules can be laws, regulations, or guidelines for running the business.*

- If an order is canceled, and not yet shipped, the order should be closed.
- A team must not have more than eight members.
- A rented car can be returned to a subsidiary company in another state. The renting subsidiary must ensure that the car has been returned by the end of the rental period. Ownership of the car will be transferred to the new subsidiary. Transfer of ownership must be initiated by the subsidiary that rented the car. The transfer value of the car should be decided according to fair estimate, as determined by corporate standard E-153.

Business rules are often captured in a separate document so that they can be referenced many times from different use cases, scenarios, or other requirements or design documentation but described only once. When writing use-case specifications or doing class designs, refer to applicable business rules in the same way that you would use glossary items. A document-based approach is useful when large numbers of business rules apply (for example, for financial products), or when there are lengthy textual descriptions for business rules (for example, for legislation). A disadvantage of this approach is that it captures business rules in a different artifact from the source where they apply.

Business rules can also be captured in models (see Figure 4.7), as code in business rule engines, or as tests. The advantage of this technique is that it captures and displays business rules at the source where they apply. The main disadvantage is that because business rules are scattered throughout the model, it is difficult to view related rules. Reports can be generated to provide an overview of all business rules in the model.

---

6. See the Glossary for the IBM Rational Unified Process.

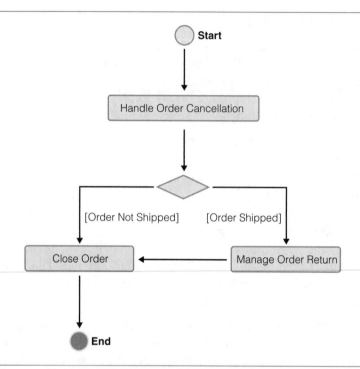

**FIGURE 4.7  A UML Activity Diagram Showing a Business Rule.** *This figure shows a UML activity diagram that represents the following business rule: "If an order is canceled, and not yet shipped, the order should be closed. If the order has been shipped, the Manage Order Return procedure should first be followed and the order then closed." (Adapted from "RUP Business Modeling Discipline," produced by Empulsys BV.)*

## Business Process Modeling

As software is increasingly crucial to how businesses are run, models of the business and of the software that supports it need to be closely coupled. To understand a particular business better, you can model "as is" or future business processes as a black box using business use cases, with textual description or activity diagrams providing detailed descriptions.

A variety of diagrams, including interaction diagrams and process models (see Figure 4.8), can also be used to produce white-box

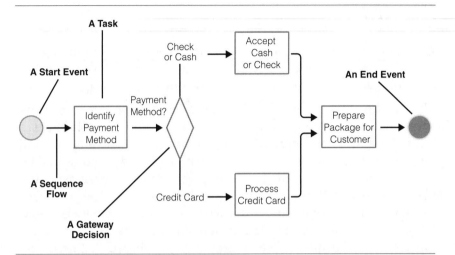

**FIGURE 4.8  A Process Model Using BPMN.** *This figure shows a process model that represents a business process. It uses an emerging OMG standard called Business Process Modeling Notation (BPMN), a language that allows you to graphically depict flows and decision nodes. The model can be used to simulate business processes. (Adapted from White 2005.)*

descriptions, or so-called business use-case realizations, so that you can understand how various people, organizations, or systems are collaborating to run the business process. Especially if you are modeling future business processes, you should simulate them using process models to understand whether the business process will work as planned.

A key aspect of business process modeling is to link the business process to existing or new software capabilities to ensure that the software you develop will enable you to run the business as expected. RUP refers to this approach as business-driven software development.[7]

*It is key to link the business process to existing or new software capabilities.*

---

7. Within the IBM Rational Method Compose product, see RUP Plug-Ins for Business Modeling, as well as SOA for the RUP approach to business-driven software development.

## Other Methods

All agile methods put a great deal of emphasis on understanding the domain, and a key aspect they all share is to involve the customer in the project team to ensure easy access to domain expertise.

*XP relies heavily on verbally communicating domain information.*

XP relies heavily on verbally communicating domain information by encouraging continuous communication within your team, thus creating and maintaining a minimum of requirements documentation and domain models. XP also leverages metaphors to aid communication. "A metaphor is a story that everyone—customers, developers, and managers—can tell about how the system works."[8] The metaphor concept has been criticized as insufficient and vague. If there is a need to clarify a certain aspect of the domain, you may capture some aspects of it as a model, preferably on a whiteboard. If this model needs to be communicated more broadly, you may take a photo of the whiteboard and place it on a Wiki Web site.

Scrum focuses primarily on management activities and does not provide specific guidance on domain modeling.

Agile modeling is, as the name indicates, more prone to do modeling and articulates the value of modeling the domain. A key principle is to create only the models you really need and not do too much modeling up front as you speculate about what functionality may be built. Agile modeling guides you in leveraging domain models to aid in your design and data modeling efforts.

*RUP puts greater value on documenting key aspects of your domain than do many other agile processes.*

RUP puts greater value on documenting key aspects of your domain than do many other agile processes, such as XP. The increased clarity of having a formal model can often save a lot of time by reducing the number of misunderstandings. RUP emphasizes only modeling the aspects of the domain that are relevant for the current project and developing a domain model iteratively, in conjunction with evolving the requirements, design, implementation, and testing. RUP does recognize that for certain projects, such as reengineering projects for which you have a very vague understanding of what type of system

---

8. Beck 2000.

you are dealing with, you first need to understand the domain enough to determine the correct next step. That analysis will help you understand what parts of a system you need to reengineer and whether you can leverage existing legacy systems, acquire packaged applications, or need to develop custom software to address your needs. It is, however, important to move as rapidly as possible toward partial implementations of the system in order to validate assumptions that you have made. RUP also emphasizes using tools built to allow you to collaborate easily on representations of your domain, versus, for example, using only whiteboards.

The agile community is increasingly focusing on how to couple the needs of the business closely with the software development effort by tightly integrating software development with business process design, and we should expect more guidance in this area over the next couple of years. Documentation on these topics can be found in RUP's Plug-In for Business Modeling[9] and Scott Ambler's *Enterprise Unified Process*.[10]

## Levels of Adoption

This practice can be adopted at three levels:

- **Basic.** Include somebody in the project team who understands the domain well, and also the customer if possible. Capture key concepts in a glossary.

  The basic practice of capturing key concepts keeps the process light, while making it easier to communicate what needs to be done within the team.

- **Intermediate.** Capture relevant concepts and their relationships as a set of class diagrams in a visual modeling tool. Reference glossary items as you document the system.

  The intermediate practice of capturing your domain model in visual modeling tools introduces some additional discipline, with an associated learning curve, but can also allow you to run the

---

9. See www.ibm.com/developer
10. Ambler 2005.

project more effectively, especially if it is a larger project. Changes can more rapidly and easily be communicated to the extended team, making it easier to support shorter iterations.

*   **Advanced.** Leverage business rules and business process modeling. This helps you to identify good components and services that map to how the business works. These components can be developed relatively independently, increasing your ability to deliver iteratively and improve the overall business over time.

The advanced practice of leveraging business rules and business process modeling adds additional discipline and an associated learning curve. It is a practice appropriate for more complex projects. Because you are now adding more documentation, it typically becomes more cumbersome to keep all the information consistent and up-to-date, all of which tends to drive you toward longer iterations.

## Related Practices

*   *Practice 9: Describe Requirements from the User Perspective* outlines how to document requirements in the form of use cases and support your requirements with storyboards and user-interface prototypes. It is desirable to model the domain in parallel with describing requirements.
*   *Practice 10: Prioritize Requirements for Implementation* shows how to determine which requirements to address in early iterations to drive the architecture and to mitigate key risks. Proper prioritization requires a good understanding of the domain.

## Additional Information

### Information in the Unified Process

OpenUP/Basic describes how to capture a glossary and how to depict key concepts graphically. RUP also provides guidelines and artifacts for domain object modeling and expands on that content to cover complete business modeling, including how to leverage business rules and how to simulate business processes.

## Additional Reading

The following books provide good insights into domain modeling and agile development:

Scott Ambler. *Agile Modeling: Effective Practices for Extreme Programming and the Unified Process.* John Wiley & Sons, 2002.

Eric Evans. *Domain-Driven Design: Tackling Complexity in the Heart of Software.* Addison-Wesley, 2004.

The following books provide a good insight into business rules and business modeling:

Ronald G. Ross. *Principles of the Business Rule Approach.* Addison-Wesley, 2003.

Ivar Jacobson, Maria Ericsson, and Agneta Jacobson. *The Object Advantage: Business Process Reengineering with Object Technology.* Addison-Wesley, 1997.

# Describe Requirements from the User Perspective

by Per Kroll

*Using use cases and scenarios makes the
system functionality easy to understand and
assists in developing, implementing, testing,
and documenting the system.*

## Problem

Many companies still document requirements as a list of declarative
statements, often referred to as "shall statements." Such a list is often
difficult for stakeholders to understand, since it requires end users to
read through and mentally translate the list into a visualization of
how they could interact with and use the system to do the work they
need to do. This approach tends to place unreasonable expectations
on the end users and causes them to have problems understanding
what functionality will be delivered. It also focuses the team on development of atomic functions or requirements, rather than on development of collaborating units that address a usage scenario. As a result,
applications developed in this way are often difficult to use and
require more time for integration and testing than applications developed using user-focused requirements.

This practice shows how to address the above problem by using scenarios and use cases to capture functional requirements. Nonfunctional requirements, such as performance, stability, or usability, can
still be captured using traditional techniques. The practice also discusses user stories and work items and explains how scenarios and
use cases are best developed in conjunction with, and used to drive,
other development activities—including user-interface design, design,
implementation, and testing.

## Background

I just got a new cellular phone, and I was quite impressed with how easily I could find relevant information in the manual. The manual included the following sections:

- Prepare your phone for use
- Get to know your phone
- Make and answer calls
- Use the phone book
- Use voice mail
- Work with the call log
- Customize your phone

When I pick up my phone, I am likely to want to take one of the actions described in the above list. The manual was thus organized around common usage models, or "use cases," to make it easy to find the necessary information. Good user manuals are often structured so that each chapter corresponds to a use case. However, the big difference between manuals and use cases is that manuals contain a lot of information about the user interface, whereas use cases purposely exclude user interface information because the user interface is the result of a large number of design decisions.

## Actors, Use Cases, and Scenarios

A use-case model describes a system's functional requirements in terms of actors and use cases. An *actor* represents a *type of user* of the system or *another system* that will interact with the system. A *use case* describes how each actor will interact with the system. It addresses how the system addresses a goal of the user[11] by capturing a complete service of measurable value to the actor.

Let's look at an example. On the way home from work you realize you are short of cash. You see an ATM and walk up to it. What is the service

---

11. See Cockburn 2001.

you would like the ATM to provide? Since you need cash, you would probably like the service *Withdraw Funds*. Other common services are *Transfer Funds* (from one account to another) and *Deposit Funds*. These are three examples of use cases. In each case the end result will be something that you want, something of measurable value. However, not every action is a use case. For example, *Validate Card* is not a use case by itself, since it has no measurable value to you to know that your card was validated. *Validate Card* is a means to an end, not an end in itself.

*Use cases describe how the end user will interact with our system.*

The way use cases work is that we describe the functional requirements by describing how the end user (or external system) will interact with our system to get the service provided through the use case. In the case of *Withdraw Funds,* we describe step by step how you interact with the system to withdraw money. You can look at it as writing a chapter in the user manual up front, but without mentioning any details about the user interface.

*A scenario is a description of a specific instance of a use case.*

It is essential to understand that a use case contains many *scenarios*. A scenario is a description of a specific instance of a use case. When you withdraw funds, you may do any of the following:

- Withdraw $100 from Checking, with a receipt being printed.
- Withdraw $40 from Savings, with no receipt being printed.
- Try to withdraw $30 dollars from Checking, only to be instructed that you need to withdraw a multiple of $20. You then try to withdraw $40, only to be informed that you do not have sufficient funds in your account.

Each of these sets of events constitutes a scenario, and as you can imagine, a specific use case can have many scenarios. Important scenarios should be tested, and later in the lifecycle will have a one-to-one mapping to a test case.

## Work Items and User Stories

Use cases and scenarios are also used to plan and track progress, and to determine what should go into a release. Smaller scenarios, which often take one to three weeks to implement, are used in iteration planning, allowing you to decide which scenarios to implement, and to track progress within an iteration. Scenarios that are too big to be included in an iteration are broken down into manageable units, either by slicing the scenario more thinly (for example, by implementing the scenario with a simplified persistency mechanism and fixed data to simulate user input) or by implementing only one segment of it, such as the first third of the scenario (see Figure 4.9).

The units that you are using for planning and tracking are called **work items.** Work items map to small scenarios, thin slices of scenarios, or segments of scenarios. Work items are, however, a generic concept that can also be used to plan and assign work not directly related to functional requirements, such as setting up a configuration management environment or delivering an internal training class. Work items are broken into more fine-grained work items as necessary.

*Work items are used to plan and assign work.*

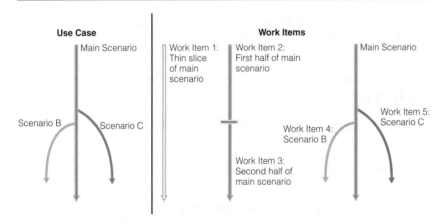

**FIGURE 4.9 Use Cases, Scenarios, and Work Items.** *A use case consists of a number of scenarios. As you determine which scenarios to implement in which iteration, you may need to divide them into thinner scenarios, or segments of scenarios. These scenarios, thin scenarios, or segments are called work items and are used to plan, estimate, and track work done within an iteration.*

A **user story**[12] is used by some in the agile community as an alternative to use cases and scenarios. A user story is used to briefly capture user requirements and to plan and track a project. As it should be possible

*A user story is used to briefly capture user requirements and to plan and track a project.*

---

12. Beck 2004.

to implement a user story within a single iteration, this effort should typically not take one person or a pair working together more than one to three weeks. If it requires more than three weeks of effort, the user story should be broken up into several smaller stories. In XP, user stories are written by users and should be no more than one or two sentences long. User stories are often loosely defined and typically map to a scenario, subsets of a scenario, or a supporting requirement, such as "the system should support Internet Explorer (on top of Firefox)"; see *Practice 10: Prioritize Requirements for Implementation.*

User stories are used in release planning meetings to determine what should be implemented in the next version of an application. They are also used in iteration planning meetings to determine what capabilities, that is, user stories, to implement in the next iteration. User stories can further be divided into developer tasks, and each user story should have associated test cases. During an iteration, track progress by identifying which stories have been implemented and tested.

## Applying the Practice

Capturing requirements from the user perspective requires you to do the following:

- Identify actors and use cases.
- Describe the use cases and scenarios.
- Produce user-interface prototypes or storyboards.
- Use user stories and enhancement requests appropriately.
- Evolve use cases and their implementations jointly.
- Plan, estimate, and track implementations of use cases and scenarios.
- Leverage use cases when writing user documentation.

Let's have a look at each of these activities in turn.

### Identify Actors and Use Cases

To identify actors and use cases, take the following iterative steps, preferably in a workshop involving relevant team members and stakeholders:

- **Step 1.** Identify as many actors (remember, actors represent both users and external systems with which the system interacts) as you can. Write a one-sentence description of each actor.

- **Step 2.** Associate each actor with use cases, capturing the actor's goals with using the system by providing a brief description of the use case. Provide a use-case diagram—a graphical depiction of your use cases and actors—to provide a simple overview of what the system is about and to act as a useful reference throughout the project.

- **Step 3.** For each use case, determine whether it requires interaction with other users or systems. This will help you identify additional actors. Continue to go back and forth between finding actors and use cases until you think you have identified enough to understand the scope of the system. You most likely have not gotten them all, but what you have should be good enough at this stage.

- **Step 4.** Write a sentence or two describing each actor,[13] and outline a couple of paragraphs for each use case. In this way you can avoid a situation in which each person has his or her own interpretation of what role the actor corresponds to and what the use case entails. Determine whether you need to come up with a few more use cases to cover all the functionality needed.

- **Step 5.** Create a *glossary* containing the key "items" dealt with in the application, or add items to a glossary if you already have one. Note that a glossary should ideally be organized by application family, so that all applications within a certain domain use the same one (for example, the domain of financial services, the domain of insurance). Review key items that the system is dealing with, that is, the business entities, and make sure that a use case describes how each business entity is created, maintained, and deleted.

  Example: For an insurance application dealing with policies: Do you have a use case that describes how to set up a policy? How to make changes to a policy? How to cancel a policy? This is a great way of discovering holes in your use-case model, and spending

---

13. For applications with a strong focus on usability, the description of an actor may later be evolved to a description of one or several personas; see Cooper 1999.

only 30 minutes on this activity often goes a long way. Note that you typically should *not* create a use case for each business entity; rather, you will often have a many-to-many relationship between business entities and use cases managing some aspect of that entity's lifecycle.

## Describe Use Cases and Scenarios

*When describing a use case, consider its two primary audiences: the stakeholders and the development team.*

When describing a use case, it is important to consider its two primary audiences: the stakeholders and the development team. Stakeholders leverage use cases to understand what services the system will provide to the users of the system. Use cases should therefore use a language that stakeholders easily understand and avoid drilling down to a level of detail that makes it hard for them to see which key capabilities are provided. The other key audience is the development team: developers and testers doing storyboards, design, implementation, testing, and user documentation. Use cases need to provide sufficient specificity and level of detail to be meaningful to the development team. It is also important to assess whether further detail is best expressed as additional text in a use case or is better expressed in the form of storyboard, test cases, or directly in the code.

It often takes just a few hours to produce a good draft of the most essential and typical use-case scenarios, though it generally takes considerably longer to complete the use case by detailing alternative flows of events within the use case. It is important to be clear on when it is sufficient to communicate requirements orally, versus also in writing. There is a cost to documenting: it takes time to write and to keep documents up-to-date. But there is often also a cost to not documenting: you may need to revisit decisions people have made and forgotten, or repeat what has already been discussed many times. A project may use several different strategies for detailing a use case.

1. **Strategy A: use for small-project, collocated teams, when the same person does requirements and development.** Briefly outline the steps within each scenario, and keep the description of each step to no more than one or two sentences.[14] Any additional

---

14. Cockburn 2001.

information is transferred through discussions and documented as storyboard, test cases, or code. This allows you to keep the use case to no more than two pages.

2. **Strategy B: use for larger, more complex projects, distributed teams**. Briefly outline the steps within each scenario, and keep the description of each step to no more than one or two sentences, as in strategy A. For many of the steps, you will have a lot of additional information to transfer to stakeholders, users, analysts, developers, testers, information developers, and so on.

   Document this additional information within the use-case description, but mark it as "transient" information, that is, information that does not need to be maintained. This can be done simply by setting transient information in italics or a distinct font or tagging it in some other way. Your use cases may grow to two to six pages, but they can be much longer for systems with complex sequencing, such as telecom systems, or much shorter when there are limited sequencing and few business rules to be applied, such as viewing—but not updating—a limited set of information. Once the use case has been implemented, the transient information is removed.

   This strategy is suitable for larger or more complex projects, or when you have a distributed team, or when team members cannot spend as much time face to face as is required with the previous strategy, perhaps because of different work schedules, constraints due to travel, or competing assignments.

3. **Strategy C: use for projects requiring high ceremony and documentation.** Use the same techniques as in strategy B, but maintain the additional information, rather than treating it as transient.

   This strategy is appropriate for projects requiring more ceremony, such as those concerned with compliance, contractual or other constraints, or building safety-critical systems.

You may find the following guidelines useful when documenting functional requirements in the form of a use case.

- Identify the steps in the flow of events for the most common scenario of the use case to which you are referring. These steps should capture the basic flow of events, or the "Happy Day" scenario—a scenario in which everything goes as expected. In the banking example above, that could be *Transfer Balance from Checking to Savings* when there are sufficient funds.

- Describe each of the steps for that scenario: (1) validate card, (2) select account to transfer from, (3) select account to transfer to, (4) select amount to transfer, (5) log transfer, and so on. Use the level of detail consistent with your team's chosen strategy (A, B, or C discussed above). Note that you may apply different strategies for different use cases, some of which may be more critical than others.

- For each of these steps, identify all the things that could go wrong, that is, all exceptions to the Happy Day scenario (see Figure 4.10). Document these alternative flows of events as "If XX, then YY..." and list them as sub-bullets under their respective steps.

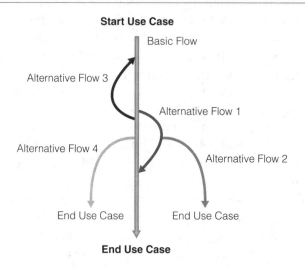

**FIGURE 4.10 Structuring of Flow of Events.** *The typical structure of a flow of events: the straight arrow represents the basic flow of events, and the curves represent alternative paths relative to "normal." Some alternative paths return to the basic flow of events, while others end the use case. A scenario is a combination of main and alternative flows from start to finish through a use case. (Reprinted from Kroll 2003.)*

- Continue to describe each alternative flow of events with the level of detail consistent with your chosen strategy. If the alternative flow of events becomes longer than a paragraph, place it in a separate section toward the end of the use-case description and reference it from the step in which it previously was described. This restructuring makes it easier to distinguish the Happy Day scenario, since the use-case description would otherwise be chopped into too many long parallel flows.

- If you have a lot of business rules, define these rules outside the use case in a separate requirements document. Within your use-case description, reference in each section the business rules that should be applied. This way of handling business rules is especially good if the same rules are referenced from many different use cases, or even applications.

  *If you have a lot of business rules, define these rules outside the use case.*

- Add preconditions and postconditions, that is, clarify what the use case expects and what it delivers, if not obvious from the use case steps. A precondition is the state of the system that is required before the use case can be started. A postcondition is the state the system is in after the use case has ended; see Bittner 2002 and Cockburn 2001.

## Using User Stories and Enhancement Requests

Some projects prefer user stories to use cases, because they provide less formalism. For small systems user stories work reasonably well, but they can easily become too numerous, especially for medium to large applications, and therefore hard to manage. In this case user stories end up providing you with a fragmented view of the application, as opposed to the goal-oriented view of a use-case model. If you use user stories for anything but very small systems, identify use cases and use them as a container for a number of related user stories. As appropriate, organize the stories in scenarios within the use cases. This approach will yield an end result that is somewhat similar to that described in the previous section, but using a less structured approach.

*User stories provide a fragmented view of medium to large applications.*

For existing application upgrades, you often get requests for support of additional user stories, that is, smaller extensions or improvements of current use cases and scenarios. RUP and OpenUP/Basic capture these as enhancement requests. As you decide to implement these enhancement requests, revise the use cases so that they are up-to-date. If you use strategy A or B above, you can do this quickly by adding one or two sentences to the use case impacted by each implemented enhancement request.

## Produce User-Interface Prototypes or Storyboards

*Consider complementing use cases with a user interface prototype or storyboard.*

Even though use cases should be easy to read for the casual user, you should consider complementing them with a user interface prototype or storyboard.[15] It is amazing how often users open up and provide a lot of useful feedback on the use case once they see a prototype. A picture often says more than a thousand words. . . .

It should, however, be emphasized that a use-case description is a functional requirements specification; you therefore do not want to include information about the user interface in the use-case description—which widgets to use, coloring, exact layouts of information—or about which design algorithm to use when implementing a capability, such as persistency or a list. If necessary, add references to user-interface prototypes, in case it is not obvious where to find them. Design decisions are better documented directly in the code, design, or user-interface prototypes. Putting design decisions in use cases makes these hard to read and rapidly obsolescent. Maintaining a clear separation between requirements and design also makes it easier to understand what are strict requirements and desires,[16] versus what are potential implementations of those requirements, so that you know when to go back to users to validate changes that are likely to be of interest to them.

---

15. See Kroll 2003.

16. Most "requirements" are not really requirements, that is, "something mandatory or obligatory," but rather something negotiable that it is desirable to implement; Beck 2004, p. 44.

## Plan, Estimate, and Track Implementations of Use Cases and Scenarios

We need to break down requirements into manageable chunks that we can use for iteration planning, for bottom-up estimation of how long time it will take to do a job, and to allow us to track progress. Based on team size and iteration length, among other things, you want chunks that represent an effort ranging from a couple of days to a couple of weeks. OpenUP/Basic and RUP call these chunks work items, which map to scenarios or parts of scenarios. XP calls them user stories (see the Background section at the beginning of this practice).

If you are using the Unified Process lifecycle, use cases and, to a lesser extent, scenarios are a primary vehicle used to scope the system in the Inception phase. Scenarios and work items drive development in earlier iterations, and as the application matures, the focus increasingly shifts to completing the use cases. Additional enhancements to existing use cases are captured as enhancement requests that are prioritized, and toward the end of the Construction phase they play an increasingly important role. For minor enhancement projects, enhancement requests take on a more important role throughout the project as a means of driving the work.

## Evolve Use Cases and Their Implementations Together

As always, keep the key principles in mind, especially *Demonstrate Value Iteratively*. It is easy to become too focused on perfecting the requirements, and many projects go under because the focus has turned to academic discussions on how to document requirements rather than on simply documenting the requirements *well enough* to enable successful implementation and testing of the system.

*It is easy to become too focused on perfecting the requirements.*

You need to evolve use-case descriptions in parallel with evolving storyboards, use-case realizations, the implementation of use cases, and the relevant test cases to validate the implementation of the use cases. Consider first documenting the obvious parts of a use-case description, creating an initial storyboard for the use cases, and then implementing and testing the most stable parts of the use cases. As you walk through the partial implementation, you are likely to get a lot of

*As you walk through partial implementations of a use case, you get invaluable feedback.*

invaluable feedback and hence a much better understanding of how to complete the use case.

## Leverage Use Cases When Writing User Documentation

*Write one user manual for each actor and one chapter for each use case.*

At the beginning of this practice we mentioned that a good manual should be structured along use cases. Typically, one user manual should be written for each actor and one chapter for each use case. This strategy ensures that the manual is structured according to major usage scenarios. For online help, you should make sure that the use cases correspond to major topics that are easy to find in the Table of Contents.

## Other Methods

All agile methods emphasize the user perspective, but they achieve this objective in different ways. A key aspect that they all have in common is including the customer in the project team.

XP documents the requirements in the form of user stories. These user stories are written down, preferably on an index card, using only a one- or two-sentence description. XP then relies on verbal communication between the customer and other team members to ensure that detailed information about the user stories is understood. Test cases for the user stories will provide more guidance on the user story and how it should be tested. The advantage of user stories is that they are easy to understand and to prioritize. They can be implemented rapidly, and daily progress against a set of user stories is easy to measure. The disadvantage of this approach is that you can be overwhelmed by too many user stories and easily lose track of the big picture.

Scrum does not prescribe how requirements are to be documented, but it is specific about organizing all requirements, change requests, and defects into one list called the Product Backlog. This list is prioritized and drives development in each iteration.

RUP and OpenUP/Basic leverage Scrum's concept of the product backlog and also recommend the documentation of requirements as use cases and scenarios. Scenarios and use cases focus on what the user wants to accomplish, which can easily be missed when focusing too much on user stories. Many similar scenarios can be organized into one use case, and by using alternative flows you can minimize the overall amount of text in a use case relative to having many scenarios. Scenarios, or parts of scenarios, are mapped to work items, similar to a user story, which are used as a planning, estimation, and tracking unit. Scenarios and work items drive development in earlier iterations, and as the application matures, the focus is increasingly on completing use cases.

## Levels of Adoption

This practice can be adopted at three different levels:

- **Basic.** Identify scenarios and use them to plan, estimate, and track iterations. Optionally, group scenarios under folders representing use cases.

  The basic practice of capturing scenarios keeps the process light, while making it easier to prioritize what should be done in which iteration.

- **Intermediate.** Describe and capture use cases textually. Identify key scenarios, but in the context of use cases. Capture alternative flows of events and failure scenarios using strategy B (see the section Describe Use Cases and Scenarios on page 176), that is, using one or two sentences to describe each step in the flow of events and marking additional information as transient. As appropriate, place detailed information in user-interface specification, designs, code, or test cases rather than in use cases.

  As long as you remember to document "just enough" information to allow rapid progress while clarifying how the system should work, the intermediate practice will take you down on the process map. Capturing the key capabilities that are to be implemented makes it easier to iterate, since you can more easily carve out small chunks of capabilities to implement and test within an iteration. The team will, however, need more knowledge and discipline to manage more structured use cases effectively.

- **Advanced.** Describe and capture use cases in clearly defined testable chunks (scenarios, alternative flows of events, or pieces thereof called user stories), each as a separate requirement. For each requirement, track attributes, such as an estimate of how long it will take to implement the requirement, who will implement it, traceability to test cases, and so on.

The agile community often recommends storing these requirements (user stories) on index cards for easy access and sorting. This method has the additional advantage of discouraging spending too much time on each requirement, but it may also lead to time being wasted on oral explanations (and repeat explanations) of what is meant by each requirement by not providing a sufficient level of detail. Our experience is that requirements management tools built to manage database records are more effective for projects that demand more than a few staff months of effort. This method also allows you to view individual requirements in the form of complete scenarios and use cases.

The advanced practice of dividing a use case into small, testable requirements adds ceremony. Add only the most essential attributes and information, and leverage the most suitable technology to minimize the level of ceremony. Assuming that you avoid dragging along a lot of irrelevant information, this detailed information should have no material impact on iteration length.

## Related Practices

- *Practice 8: Understand the Domain* describes how to document key aspects of the problem domain to minimize communication issues and to increase every team member's understanding of the problem domain. A good understanding of the domain is crucial to achieve concurrence on the requirements.

- *Practice 10: Prioritize Requirements for Implementation* shows how to determine which requirements should be addressed in early iterations to drive the architecture and to mitigate key risks.

## Additional Information

### Information in the Unified Process

The requirements discipline in OpenUP/Basic provides guidance on work items, scenarios, and use cases. RUP's requirements discipline adds guidance on more types of requirements, including stakeholder requests and supplementary requirements, as well as on using more disciplined approaches leveraging requirements attributes, requirements plans, and requirements management tools.

### Additional Reading

For detailed books on use cases, we recommend the following:

> Kurt Bittner and Ian Spence. *Use Case Modeling*. Addison-Wesley, 2002.
>
> Geri Schneider and Jason P. Winters. *Applying Use Cases: A Practical Approach, Second Edition*. Addison-Wesley, 2001.
>
> Alistair Cockburn, *Writing Effective Use Cases*, Addison-Wesley, 2001.

For books that provide you with an understanding of how use cases fit with other lifecycle activities, such as design, implementation, and testing, see the following:

> Per Kroll and Philippe Kruchten. *The Rational Unified Process Made Easy: A Practitioner's Guide to the RUP*. Addison-Wesley, 2003.
>
> Ivar Jacobson, Grady Booch, and James Rumbaugh. *The Unified Software Development Process*. Addison-Wesley, 1999.
>
> Peter Eeles, Kelli Houston, and Wojtek Kozaczynski. *Building J2EE™ Applications with the Rational Unified Process*. Addison-Wesley, 2003.

# Prioritize Requirements for Implementation

by Bruce MacIsaac

*Prioritize requirements to deliver value and drive down risks.*

## Problem

How do you decide what requirements to develop next? The right choices help you to maximize value to stakeholders and the business while balancing technical and business needs. Poor choices can lead you to deliver capabilities that aren't used or to identify problems late in the project that result in delays and even project failure.

This practice describes how to make choices that deliver value and drive down risks, while building a system that can evolve.

**FIGURE 4.11 Decide What to Build First.** *Poor choices can result in delays and even project failure.*

## Background

To identify and prioritize requirements for development, you should understand how requirements are classified.

## Classifying Requirements

Classifying requirements into different categories helps developers and analysts to reason about requirements. One popular classification scheme is called FURPS+,[17] an acronym for *functionality*, *usability*, *reliability*, *performance*, and *supportability*, with the "plus" referring to design, implementation, interface, physical, and other constraints (see Figure 4.12).

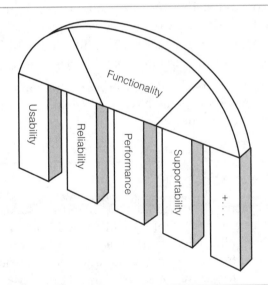

**FIGURE 4.12 FURPS+ Classification Scheme.** *People think mainly about the functional requirements. Recognizing the kinds of supporting requirements helps to identify and prioritize requirements.*

---

17. Grady 1997.

Here are some examples of different kinds of requirements for an automated banking machine:

- Functionality: A customer shall be able to withdraw cash.
- Usability: 95 percent of customers shall be able to use the machine successfully without help or training.
- Reliability: Average system down time shall be under 1 hour per week.
- Performance: No system action shall take longer than 3 seconds to complete.
- Supportability: The software shall be upgradeable remotely.
- Design constraint: The software shall use a relational database.
- Implementation constraint: The software shall be implemented in Java.
- Interface constraint: The software shall interface to the credit processing system using the existing message queues.
- Physical constraint: The software shall require no more than 100MB of memory and no more than 10GB of disk space.

Analysts and developers use these categories to help ensure that all different kinds of requirements have been considered, and to prioritize categories of requirements.

## Applying the Practice

To apply this practice, you should understand the stakeholders and project dynamics and assign roles to advocate for key goals, such as business value, quality, and technical feasibility. As you identify and clarify requirements, you can capture requirements attributes. These in turn help you to identify and prioritize scenarios and to group them into deliverable increments.

## Understand Stakeholders and Project Dynamics

Before you can prioritize requirements, you need to understand the goals of your stakeholders and how they measure success.

## Project Sponsors

Usually, one or more project sponsors pay the bills. What a sponsor values can differ from project to project. Sometimes the greatest value is placed on delivering usable functionality as early as possible, even if this means significant rework downstream. Other times, reducing overall long-term costs, or delivering high quality, are given higher priority. One sponsor may be interested in generating market interest by demonstrating prototypes of "sexy" features, while another may want to drive down key technical risks, such as performance and throughput.

When stakeholders have competing priorities, it is the project sponsor's overall goals that determine which take precedence. The project sponsor is thus the most important stakeholder. Nevertheless, he or she is usually driven by the needs of other stakeholders.

*The project sponsor's overall goals determine which requirements take precedence.*

## Customers

The customer is the key stakeholder that the project sponsor needs to satisfy (and may even *be* the project sponsor). A customer is someone involved in the decision to acquire a product. A successful product must have customers, so customer needs are paramount. While some customers may be users, others are decision makers in management or procurement departments.

## Users

The user is the key stakeholder that customers need to satisfy (and frequently is the customer). Customers frequently define success in terms of user success.

## Other Stakeholders

There are many other stakeholders, including testers, trainers, installers, and so on in both customer and development organizations. Understanding the goals of these stakeholders helps you to understand the value of each requirement and to communicate that value to project sponsors.

*Understand stakeholder goals to determine the value of requirements.*

Taking the time to identify each of the stakeholders, their goals, and their success criteria for the project provides the context for prioritizing requirements.

## Assign Roles to Advocate for Key Goals

Usually the sponsor wants everything—early delivery of high-value, "sexy" features, minimum overall costs and risks, and high quality. The key is to achieve the right balance.

One way to achieve balance is to ensure that each goal in a project has an advocate. The legal system achieves balance by having a prosecutor and a defense attorney. On a software project, you achieve balance by ensuring that you have advocates for customer and business value (a customer or analyst), driving down technical risk (an architect), and ensuring quality (testers). A project manager can then balance the inputs from these advocates and manage the project on a daily basis in accordance with the goals of the project sponsors.

**FIGURE 4.13 Balance Priorities.** *The project manager balances inputs from key advocates to decide on prioritization.*

## Identify and Clarify Requirements

Before prioritizing requirements, you must first understand them, clarify those that are poorly understood, and challenge those that are risky.

### Identify Key Functionality

*Showing, rather than telling, ensures understanding.*

A solid understanding of key functionality is needed to build a system that meets user needs. So how do you achieve such an understanding? *Practice 9: Describe Requirements from the User Perspective is* important, because it helps you identify the use cases and scenarios. The relative value of each use case can be assessed to identify core capabilities. Whenever possible, involve real users to ensure that prioritization reflects their needs. Iterative development is also key; it allows you to implement key parts of the working system and ask, "Is this what you meant?" rather than spending vast amounts of time creating ever thicker and more detailed specifications. Showing, rather than telling, ensures understanding.

### Identify Supporting Requirements

So far the focus has been on the core functionality. You also want to ensure that you have identified all the other requirements that are important—the URPS+ in FURPS+.

You can use categories and examples of supporting requirements (sometimes called technical, nonfunctional, quality, or supplemental requirements[18]) as a checklist to verify if you have a requirement in a particular category.

But how do you come up with a complete set of candidate-supporting requirements? RUP's template and examples of "Supplementary Specifications" are a good starting point. Here are some other sources:

- Eeles 2004 provides a questionnaire that lists a large number of requirements types, along with questions for determining their applicability.
- The Software Engineering Institute has created a catalogue of "general scenarios"—expressions of quality attribute requirements—which can be reused across many different kinds of systems to define quality requirements.[19]

---

18. Supporting requirement is a broader term than nonfunctional requirement. Many supporting requirements, such as requirements for logging and accessibility, are functional requirements that support major use cases, but are typically not themselves expressed as use cases.

19. See Bass 2003 and http://www.sei.cmu.edu/publications/documents/01.reports/01tr014.html.

## Clarify and Stabilize Significant Requirements

Significant requirements that are poorly understood or likely to change should be prioritized for clarification and stabilization. This step is particularly important if those requirements affect core functionality, are architecturally significant, or have a major impact on effort estimates. In some cases it means that you should conduct further requirements analysis before implementing the requirement. In other cases some form of prototyping may work best.

## Challenge Risky Requirements

I recall a project with a performance requirement to display radar data within a fixed response time. When the software was completed, measurements showed that the response time was almost 10 times the specified limit. The money was spent, and the project was supposedly complete, but an essential requirement had not been achieved. The project manager had few options. He directed the developers to fix the problem, and after much effort and expense, the response time was improved to about twice the required amount. No further improvement was possible, and the project manager prepared for a tense meeting with the prime contractor. Luckily, there was a happy ending: the prime contractor admitted having overstated the requirement, and the achieved performance level was better than actually required.

But there could easily have been a less nail-biting ending. The infeasibility of this requirement could have been demonstrated early in the project, before all the money was spent and the project manager had so few options. More important, someone could have challenged the requirement itself up front by asking, "Why is such a tight response time required?" Far less effort and expense would then have been spent on unnecessary optimization.

## Identify and Prioritize Scenarios

Earlier we described the importance of identifying and prioritizing key functionality, best expressed as use cases. However, a complete use case often contains a lot of functionality. To demonstrate value, drive down risk, and get early feedback, you should typically deliver a subset of functionality, rather than complete use cases. The best way to express this subset is as a scenario, that is, a single path through one or more use cases, or sometimes even a subset of a scenario; see *Practice 9: Describe the Requirements from the User Perspective* for more information.

The basic scenarios of core functionality are a good place to start. Start with the basic "happy path," the most straightforward set of steps when everything goes right, while deferring alternative flows, variations of user input, and error condition checking until later. These will typically require many fundamental components and uncover patterns, because end-to-end scenarios usually involve all layers of the system—including user interface, business logic components, and infrastructure mechanisms such as data persistency and interprocess communication. These can often be used to assess nonfunctional requirements. For example, once a basic scenario has been implemented, measuring the performance of that scenario can identify problems or build confidence in the system's performance. And of course, core functionality is useful for getting early user feedback.

Take the air traffic control system use case "File a flight plan." A flight plan identifies an aircraft, when it is leaving, where it is leaving from, where it is going, and the trajectory it plans to follow. There are many kinds and formats of flight plans and countless types of trajectory, including blocking out chunks of airspace, formations with other aircraft, use of various kinds of distance and bearing beacons, and even uncontrolled ("I'm going to fly around and have fun"). Implementing this use case is a huge effort. So what should you focus on first?

The answer is to start with the simplest, most essential scenario and build up from there. In this case the simplest scenario is to file a flight plan direct from point A to point B, specified as latitude and longitude. This scenario represents a fraction of the required logic for the use case, but by implementing it you achieve certain goals:

*Start with the simplest, most essential scenario and build up from there.*

- You demonstrate the process by which flight plans are created and enable early user feedback on this process.
- You design and implement key elements of the system:
  - Trajectories and points on the earth's surface
  - Flight plans

- User interface forms and dialogs
- Supporting infrastructure (mechanisms such as interprocess communications, data distribution, and so on)

- You can measure system loading and response times for this scenario and determine if the architecture is likely to scale to meet these and other supporting requirements.

*Additional scenarios are implemented based on stakeholder priorities.*

Such a basic scenario is suitable for a first iteration. Additional scenarios are implemented based on stakeholder priorities. The following could be some competing priorities:

- Time to market of key features.
- Minimum overall cost and risk.
- Demonstration of "sexy" technical features to attract early adopters or keep sponsors interested.

If your main goal is to minimize cost and risk, you would typically add scenarios that establish the architecture—in particular, scenarios that demonstrate component integration, key patterns, and quality attributes. For example:

- Implementing the main path of the most commonly executed use case is often enough to test system performance under expected load conditions.
- Establishing a pattern for using a logging mechanism is more important than completing functionality to produce nicely formatted log reports.
- Implementing a skeleton of the user interface for a few key scenarios may be enough to validate that the system is sufficiently usable.
- Risks with using a new technology can be addressed by building a part of the system that uses that technology.

## Capture Requirement Attributes

At the most basic level, you could simply compile the use cases and nonfunctional requirements into a list and use that as a basis for planning. You could then describe what will be implemented in each iteration and supplement this with text detailing how much of each use case is to be implemented and what risks are to be mitigated.

In larger projects, trade-offs are facilitated by recording and reviewing requirements attributes. A spreadsheet, database, or requirements management tool can be used for this purpose.

We have found the following requirements attributes useful for prioritization.

*In larger projects, trade-offs are facilitated by recording and reviewing requirements attributes.*

- **Benefit:** Importance to stakeholders. Any ordered rating system will work. However, you should reserve the highest benefit rating for critical requirements, that is, those that are the reason the system is being developed, and without which the system serves no useful purpose. Lower ratings are relative to one another and are used (with other attributes) to decide which requirements should be considered for de-scoping.

- **Effort:** Estimated effort. You can use a numeric rating such as "effort days" or categories, for example: Low = < 5 days, Medium = 5–20 days, High = >20 days. In defining effort, you should decide which overheads (management effort, test effort, requirements effort, and so on) are included in the estimate.

- **Architectural impact:** Indicates how this requirement will impact the software architecture, for example:
  - **None.** Fits within the existing architecture.
  - **Extends.** Requires extension of the existing architecture.
  - **Modifies.** Requires changes to the existing architecture to accommodate the requirement.

- **Stability:** Likelihood that this requirement will remain unchanged and that the development teams' understanding of the requirement will also remain unchanged. You can use a similar categorization system: Low = <10%, Medium = 10–50%, High = >50%.

- **Risk:** Percentage likelihood that implementation of the requirement will encounter significant undesirable events such as schedule slippage, cost overrun, or cancellation. Again, you could use categories: Low = <10%, Medium = 10–50%, High = >50%.

  Alternatively, you can fold risk into the "architectural impact" described earlier, marking risky requirements as potentially extending the architecture.

These attributes help you to make good decisions about prioritizing requirements. To drive down risks, you prioritize high-risk requirements that affect the architecture, stabilizing unstable requirements as needed. To deliver value, you prioritize high-benefit, low-effort requirements and de-scope low-benefit use cases with high effort or high risk.

The most difficult decisions you have to make are when prioritizing high-benefit requirements against lower-benefit requirements that have high risk or that affect the architecture. Prioritization is ultimately a business decision, so if delivering early value is paramount (such as when showing off features to generate customer interest), you may choose to prioritize high-benefit requirements. If minimizing overall cost and risk is paramount, then you may implement architectural and risky requirements first.

One balanced approach is to prioritize architectural and risky requirements that are critical for a minimal release, ignoring requirements that could be deferred or dropped. This approach avoids investing in requirements that may not be needed or may change and speeds up completion of a minimal release, which in turn allows earlier user feedback. The architect should still consider likely changes (as described in *Practice 16: Architect with Components and Services*) to guide the selection of architectural choices, but implementation is limited to what is needed.

### Additional Notes

There may be two use cases that use the same components and address similar risks. If you implement A first, B is no longer architecturally significant. If you implement B first, A is no longer architecturally significant. Similarly, the effort to implement a requirement depends on how much supporting infrastructure is in place. In general, therefore, the requirements attributes can depend on the iteration order and should be reevaluated when the ordering changes, as well as when the requirements themselves change.

Managing attributes of every statement within a use case is time-consuming. Instead, start with attributes at the use-case level, and if more than just the "happy path" is critical, add a note to explain what is critical. Notes don't scale, so for complex use cases you may wish to be specific about which parts of the use case (alternative flows, conditions, or special requirements) are critical and architecturally significant. You can do this by adding attributes to requirements within the use case and prioritizing accordingly. This level of management works best if supported by a requirements management tool.

## Identify and Prioritize Deliverable Increments

In larger systems the number of scenarios can become large, and the interdependencies can be hard to follow. When planning iterations, it is best to think in terms of increments of deliverable functionality. Start by identifying the minimum functionality for a first usable release. Then identify additional minimum chunks of functionality that are worth delivering in a subsequent release. This sequence of releasable functionality provides a framework around which you can plan your iterations.

*Start with the minimum functionality for a first usable release; then add functionality for subsequent releases.*

Denne 2004 describes deliverable chunks as Minimum Marketable Features (MMFs). "Marketable" implies that the chunk of functionality stands on its own, delivering significant value to the customer, whereas "minimum" ensures that you focus on the minimum functionality that delivers that value.

Identifying MMFs can be done "top down" from the features described in the initial project vision or "bottom up" by grouping individual scenarios or subscenarios. Once requirements have been grouped into MMFs, you can prioritize and manage each MMF, rather than the individual scenarios or subscenarios it comprises. This can simplify requirements management and project planning. However, when the MMF spans iterations, as is often the case in early iterations while the architecture is being established, you will still have to prioritize parts of the MMF to implement in each iteration.

Denne 2004 also recommends separately identifying and prioritizing elements of the architecture, based on which MMFs require which elements. This can make it easier to reason about the priority and value provided by underlying architecture elements.

## Other Methods

Traditional waterfall development details all the requirements, and then all the design, before implementing and testing. It is difficult to deliver a valuable subset of functionality, and there is no opportunity to improve the requirements and design based on experience gained from implementation and testing.

Unified Process and other iterative methods value incremental delivery of functionality, based on prioritized requirements. There are some differences in how prioritization is done, however. XP recommends that developers identify and communicate risks, but that the Customer decides which user stories are built first.[20] In Scrum the Product Owner represents project stakeholders and prioritizes requirements.[21] In RUP the System Analyst prioritizes by customer and business value, the Software Architect prioritizes by architectural value, and the Project Manager balances competing concerns and makes business decisions to satisfy the project sponsors.

In practice, if there is good communication between the team and customer representatives, the same result is achieved. However, in RUP and OpenUP/Basic, the architect explicitly works out a proposed order of implementation to drive down technical risk. When scaled up for larger projects, Scrum includes an architectural prioritization approach similar to the Unified Process.[22] In contrast to both the Unified Process and Scrum, XP is much looser—there is no explicit architectural prioritization.

Note that architectural prioritization need not compete with customer prioritization. The customer (or customer advocate) typically defines a minimum set of requirements for a first release. Supporting that minimum set takes a few iterations and requires much of the architecture. The role of the architect in this case is typically to prioritize work further for iterations leading up to that first usable release. If the architect wishes to add other work to drive down risk, then the project manager works with the various stakeholders to reach the right business decision.

---

20. Beck 2001.

21. Schwaber 2004.

22. Schwaber (2004) refers to this process as "staging."

## Levels of Adoption

This practice can be adopted at different levels:

- **Basic.** Prioritize essential functionality for implementation.

  This allows early delivery of useful functionality and early user feedback, and generally speeds development.

- **Intermediate.** Balance priorities of architecturally significant requirements and requirements with high business and customer value.

  Establishing the architecture early allows developers to work in parallel in successive iterations, fleshing out the skeleton already established. Parallel work enables shorter iterations.

- **Advanced.** Systematically capture all relevant categories of requirements and the various attributes that contribute to prioritizing requirements.

  Managing a large set of requirements systematically requires time, effort, and discipline. Such investments are usually associated with larger projects, and the additional work usually requires longer iterations.

## Related Practices

- *Practice 1: Manage Risk* emphasizes that risks are a major factor in selecting scenarios for implementation and recommends implementing the riskiest scenarios first.
- *Practice 2: Execute Your Project in Iterations* allows you to use iterative development to implement key parts of the working system, based on prioritized requirements.
- *Practice 9: Describe Requirements from the User Perspective* is key to developing an understanding of core functionality because of its focus on providing significant value. The use cases developed with this practice are the basis for the scenarios that demonstrate the architecture, in particular those that demonstrate key patterns and component interactions.

## Additional Information

### Information in the Unified Process

OpenUP/Basic describes a basic requirements prioritization approach suited to small projects, similar to that described in this practice. RUP adds additional guidance needed for larger and more specialized projects, including traceability and requirements management guidance. This additional guidance becomes particularly important when requirements involve more than one team or organization—for example, when subprojects, reuse, product line engineering, and subcontracting are involved.

### Additional Reading

For guidance on managing requirements, see the following:

> Dean Leffingwell and Don Widrig. *Managing Software Requirements: A Unified Approach.* Addison-Wesley, 2000.
>
> Kurt Bittner and Ian Spence. *Use Case Modeling.* Addison-Wesley, 2002.

For guidance on scheduling functional increments using business value, see the following:

> Mark Denne and Jane Cleland-Huang. *Software by Numbers.* Prentice Hall, 2004.

For more on architectural requirements, see the following:

> Len Bass, Paul Clements, and Rick Kazman. *Software Architecture in Practice, Second Edition.* Addison-Wesley, 2003.
>
> Peter Eeles. "Capturing Architectural Requirements." *The Rational Edge,* April 2004. http://www.ibm.com/developerworks/rational/library/4706.html.

# Leverage Legacy Systems

by Bruce MacIsaac

*Maximize the value you get from legacy systems
by ensuring that short-term changes are part
of a longer-term plan.*

## Problem

Software evolves to meet changing needs. As it evolves, it often becomes increasingly difficult to understand and change—the original developers leave, the documentation becomes outdated, and the code often degrades as a result of suboptimal changes over time.

This practice describes how to balance the needs of stakeholders against the cost of change and how to maximize the value derived from legacy systems.

## Background

Systems often outlive the assumptions of their original designers. The millennium bug is a classic example. Assuming that the software would be replaced by 1999, early designers used two-digit dates; that assumption cost billions to correct. My own grandmother was the victim of a similar false assumption. When my grandfather passed away in the 1970s, she bought a dual headstone, precarved with her name and "19__." At the age of 112, Mary MacIsaac, like many legacy systems, continues to outlive the designer's expectations.

As needs change and design assumptions prove false, systems need to evolve. One way to evolve is to patch as you go. The heiress to the Winchester family fortune took this approach when she began extending the family mansion in 1884 and continued building extensions to the house until the day she died in 1922. The result (Figure 4.14) is the oddest patchwork of a house you can imagine: 160 rooms, and a maze

**FIGURE 4.14 Winchester Mystery House.** *(Photo courtesy of Winchester Mystery House, San Jose, California.)*

of stairs and passages that end up in the strangest places, or go nowhere at all.

*As software is extended, it can become increasingly difficult to understand and change.*

As software is extended over time to serve new requirements never anticipated by the original designers, it can take on a similar patchwork style, becoming increasingly difficult to understand and change. But before diving into the details of solving this problem, let's start by defining legacy systems and what it means to evolve them.

## What Is a Legacy System?

While some have defined a **legacy system** as "any production-enabled software,"[23] the focus of this practice is mature systems that serve ongoing needs. Usually these are old, monolithic systems, built using older design approaches and older technologies.

---

23. Ulrich 2002.

## What Does It Mean to "Evolve" a Legacy System?

Evolving a legacy system means updating it to meet changing needs. Some categories of evolution are listed below:[24]

- Maintenance—fixing bugs and incrementally adding small amounts of functionality or features over time. This approach frequently leads to a system that is increasingly difficult to understand and modify.
- Adaptation—adding new capabilities by integrating the existing system with other systems. This approach includes cosmetic makeovers, whereby the underlying functionality remains relatively unchanged but is wrapped in a new user interface or system interface, and migration, whereby the system is adapted to a new platform.
- Redevelopment—building a system with the same or similar functionality to replace an existing system. The existing system defines key requirements for the new system. Some software from the existing system may be reused.
- Combination—combinations of the above.

## Applying the Practice

Legacy evolution projects can be run much like any other project, with some important differences. Some of the differences and opportunities unique to legacy evolution projects are discussed in these practice guidelines:

- Improve the code gradually with refactoring and unit testing.
- Define a vision.
- Evaluate the business case.
- Balance stakeholder needs against the impact to the asset.
- Reuse requirements.

---

24. These categories, and inspiration for much of this practice, come from Kruchten 2001 "Using the RUP to Evolve a Legacy System."

- Reuse architecture, design, and implementation.
- Reuse other artifacts (test, user documentation, and so on).
- Apply modern practices.
- Take an enterprise perspective.

## Improve the Code Gradually with Refactoring and Unit Testing

In the 1970s, Marty Lehman captured his "laws of software evolution," among which is the trend for software to decline in quality and increase in complexity unless the tendency is actively prevented. This still holds true today.[25]

*Short-term fixes are like credit card debt: if ignored, they add up and cost more in the long term.*

The natural inclination when working in a large code base is to avoid areas of code that are not well understood. Changes are hacked into places where they do not belong, because to make the change "correctly" would take longer and might introduce new defects. In the short term this method appears to save time, but over time it creates code that is confusing and even harder to modify further. A great analogy is credit card debt: if you don't pay off your debt monthly, it costs a lot more in the long run.[26]

It is possible to create legacy code that improves, rather than degrades, over time. But doing so requires a team that treats each change as an opportunity to improve the code base and has a willingness to invest in that improvement.

*Use unit testing and refactoring to improve code with each change.*

A major challenge is avoiding errors when modifying poorly understood code, that is, preserving the behavior that isn't supposed to change. Before changing any legacy code, first ensure that there are sufficient unit tests to preserve the existing behavior. You can then add changes and refactor, and run the unit tests to confirm that there are no unintended changes in behavior.

In many cases it is difficult to add unit tests, because the code is composed of monolithic or highly coupled units. See Feathers 2005 for

---

25. Lehman 2000.

26. Kerievsky (2005) has a good description of this "design debt" metaphor, originally attributed to Ward Cunningham.

solutions to these challenges, in particular, guidance on breaking dependencies between units so that they can be independently tested.

## Define a Vision

When making significant changes to a legacy system, it is important to have a vision. The advantage of a legacy system is that the original problem it was designed to address is already solved. So the vision needs to address how the problem has changed. Here are some specific questions to consider in relation to legacy evolution:

- Why is a change needed?
- Who are the changes for?
- What is the value of the existing system?
- Is its basic design still usable? Can requirements be reused (does it still do what users need)? Are there algorithms, business rules, or data that can be reused? Does the design encapsulate functionality that would serve as a good component in an enterprise architecture?
- What kind of evolution is needed (maintenance, adaptation, redevelopment, or combination)?

## Evaluate the Business Case

Legacy software is paid for, and it works, so it's often an asset worth keeping. But a good business case must consider both short-term and long-term objectives in order to decide how and if existing systems should evolve or be replaced, and over what period of time.

A business case often has to consider more than just direct costs. It must also address the following questions:

- Is the aging system causing inefficiencies that should be addressed?
- Does the aging system carry administrative or other hidden costs?
- Can the system be maintained over the long term, or are there growing concerns over quality or lost knowledge due to staff attrition?
- Are there other risks associated with "business as usual"? For example, are key business needs being shelved, or are opportunities being lost because they are not supportable with the existing system?

## Balance Stakeholder Needs Against the Impact to the Asset

As with any project, there are often conflicting priorities. There is often pressure to make quick fixes that do not consider longer-term impact. Creating and documenting a vision and business case help ensure that broader concerns, such as maintainability, are addressed.

Evaluation of the business case involves more than just assessing the cost of each individual change. As noted above, individual changes can be individually simple, but over time they can seriously degrade the software. When evaluating the business case, consider the cost of doing the changes "right," not just the cost of the quick fix.

*Business decisions should balance value to stakeholders against both short-term and long-term costs.*

If the system was never designed for certain changes, the "right" fix may be prohibitively expensive, forcing you to choose a suboptimal solution. But just because you can make a change to a legacy system doesn't always mean you should. Users can often work around limitations in legacy software, just as we all must do with commercial software. Ultimately, the right choice is a business decision, and you may choose short-term gain over long-term cost. However, before making such a compromise, identify the true impact of doing so, and make a conscious decision that balances the value to stakeholders against both the short-term and long-term costs. See *Practice 10: Prioritize Requirements for Implementation* for more on dealing with conflicting priorities.

## Reuse Requirements

Establishing a baseline is about capturing the valuable aspects of the existing system. The most valuable aspect of an existing system may be its current functional behavior: business rules, how to handle edge conditions, and so on. It's also valuable to know what existing users dislike about the existing system, so that you know what needs to be changed and how.

*Take advantage of what exists already, and reference it rather than recreate it.*

Should you apply use cases? When redeveloping a poorly documented system, creating use cases is a good way to capture how the system is currently used and how it should work in the future. However, most systems have user manuals and other supporting documentation that captures the behavior, and there is little value in converting such descriptions into some other format. In such cases it is more efficient simply to identify the use cases and reference the existing documentation for the details. Identifying the use cases is still important, because, rather than listing features, use cases focus on how the system provides value to its users, ensuring that system updates continue to provide real value.

## Reuse Architecture, Design, and Implementation

It is becoming increasingly important to integrate legacy applications with other applications to provide greater capabilities and seamless operation, both within a business and between businesses. Services are a key enabler for this integration, because they provide flexibility and minimize coupling. Part or all of a legacy application is often wrapped as a **service** in an overall service-oriented architecture.[27]

In the simplest case, the legacy system is reasonably isolated. Integration focuses on the externally visible behavior and dependencies,[28] as described in *Practice 16: Architect with Components and Services*. Integration is much more challenging when there is coupling across systems. Functionality and data are often redundant across systems, or split in a way that creates complex interdependencies. In this case you may need to explore the inner workings of these systems to understand existing limitations and evaluate strategies for improvement.

In either case some understanding of the existing system is needed. As with requirements documentation, it is usually not a good idea to create a whole new set of design documentation. Instead, take advantage of what exists already, and reference it rather than recreate it. Aging documentation is often out of date, so proceed with caution. Balance the need for the documentation against the effort to do the updates.

*Balance the need for documentation against the effort to create it.*

Here are some suggestions for documentation:

- Ensure that there is a description of the major components, their interfaces, and how they interact to provide externally visible

---

27. Krafzig 2005 provides guidance on transforming legacy applications into services.
28. Ambler 2002 discusses this in terms of "contract models."

behavior. Identify and document redundancies and assumptions across components, both in terms of functions and data. Creating a "Software Architecture Document" is a good way to do this.

- Don't document the entire detailed design. Instead, document detailed design as needed to understand which pieces of the software will be evolved and how those pieces need to change. Tools to reverse engineer "design information" may be helpful, but they require an experienced developer to pick out the important elements and make sense of them.

- Identify the data sources, and determine what data will need to be migrated.

## Reuse Other Artifacts

Follow the general principle that all existing system artifacts should be considered an asset and kept if still useful. For example, tests for the existing system are often applicable to the evolved system; user documentation may be a good starting point for documenting the evolved system, and so on.

## Apply Modern Practices

So far we have focused on reuse to ensure that existing system assets are used effectively. However, when reuse is not possible, modern practices can be directly applied: new requirements can be described in terms of use cases, and new design can leverage visual modeling and patterns.

Practices that apply to running the project—including tackling risks, developing iteratively and incrementally, prioritizing requirements, and empowering teams—can always be applied.

*Improve processes and tools incrementally.*

Also, a general caution: making too many changes at once can lead to failure. Usually, the best approach is to improve processes and tools incrementally, because you get a quicker return on investment and can learn from each increment how to be more effective in the next increment.

## Take an Enterprise Perspective

Legacy systems are usually part of a larger enterprise architecture that serves critical business interests. The problem with legacy systems often lies not in the individual systems but rather in the intertwining of multiple systems, as well as in the variety of groups within the organization that have a stake in each of those systems. Solving these issues requires a high level of understanding of how the business functions, an evolution strategy for the enterprise architecture, and coordination across projects to ensure that all the pieces continue to fit.

At this enterprise level, problems are similar to those on a small project but larger in scope.

These enterprise process topics are beyond the scope of this book. See the Additional Information section for recommendations on how to explore them in more detail.

## Other Methods

Most maintenance projects have little in the way of methodology. Defects and small enhancements are scheduled and implemented without consideration of, or investment in, long-term sustainability, resulting in long-term system degradation.

The approach of improving legacy code through extensive unit testing and refactoring[29] derives from the test-first design and refactoring principles found in XP.

For more significant changes, Unified Process recommends reusing other artifacts (requirements, architecture, and so on) and capturing essential aspects of the architecture (description of major components, their interfaces, and how they interact). Principles for "agile modeling"[30] can be helpful here.

In terms of deciding what changes to make, Unified Process takes a business-driven approach balancing the needs of stakeholders against

---

29. Feathers 2005.
30. Ambler 2002.

short- and long-term costs and objectives. This approach is covered in more detail in *Practice 10: Prioritize requirements for Implementation*.

## Levels of Adoption

Legacy evolution projects can be relatively simple or very complex. Moving from basic to more advanced levels of this practice will improve your capacity to handle more complex legacy projects.

- **Basic.** For systems remaining in *maintenance*, minimize degradation by ensuring that fixes are done cleanly and correctly.

  For systems undergoing *adaptation* or *redevelopment*, reuse what you can, document just what you need, and apply newer methods sparingly.

  The basic practices of clean fixes and minimal overheads keep the process light.

- **Intermediate.** Create a vision and business case for legacy systems to ensure that they get adequate attention and funding. Adopt an incremental improvement approach that includes automated testing and refactoring.

  Incremental improvement requires relatively little ceremony to be effective, but does require commitment from the team and management.

  Establishing a vision and a business case are additional investments that require more management.

- **Advanced.** Develop an understanding of how the overall business functions, and create a long-term business vision. Define a strategy for evolving the enterprise architecture to meet that vision, and coordinate across projects to make it happen.

  Establishing enterprise-level processes are additional investments that require more management.

## Related Practices

- *Practice 8: Understand the Domain* shows how an overall strategy for evolving legacy systems requires a good understanding of business needs.
- *Practice 16: Architect with Components and Services* explains how legacy applications are frequently wrapped as a service in an overall enterprise architecture.

Most of the other practices also apply, and how they apply has been the subject of much of this practice. In summary, best practices apply, with the caution that reverse engineering design and requirements artifacts may not be worth the effort—reusing what already exists is often more practical.

## Additional Information

## Information in the Unified Process

OpenUP/Basic describes basic practices applicable to most small projects. As such, OpenUP/Basic includes practices for creating a vision, business case, and architecture, as well as practices for continuous improvement through refactoring and iterative development.

However, legacy evolution is also an enterprise concern, including business planning and defining a strategy for legacy architecture transformation. The *Business Modeling* and *Legacy Evolution* plug-ins to RUP partly address these topics, and other enterprise process plug-ins are planned. For specialized guidance on integrating legacy systems into a service-oriented architecture, see the *Service-Oriented Architecture* plug-in to RUP.

## Additional Reading

Legacy evolution concepts and approaches:

William M. Ulrich. *Legacy Systems Transformation Strategies*. Prentice Hall, 2002.

Robert S. Arnold. *Software Reengineering (IEEE Computer Society Press Tutorial)*. Institute of Electrical & Electronics Engineers, 1993.

Improving legacy code through refactoring:

Michael C. Feathers. *Working Effectively with Legacy Code*. Prentice Hall, 2005.

Joshua Kerievsky. *Refactoring to Patterns*. Addison-Wesley, 2005.

Integrating with existing legacy systems and data:

Dirk Krafzig, Karl Banke, and Dirk Slama. *Enterprise SOA Service Oriented Architecture Best Practices*. Prentice Hall, 2005.

Gregor Hohpe and Bobby Woolf. *Enterprise Integration Patterns*. Addison-Wesley 2004.

Scott Ambler. *Agile Database Techniques: Effective Strategies for the Agile Software Developer*. John Wiley & Sons, 2003.

# CHAPTER 5

# Collaborate Across Teams

| | |
|---|---|
| ***Benefits*** | • Team productivity.<br>• Better coupling between business needs and the development and operations of software systems. |
| ***Patterns*** | 1. Motivate people to perform at their best.<br>2. Encourage cross-functional collaboration (e.g., analysts, developers, testers).<br>3. Provide effective collaborative environments.<br>4. Integrate business, software, and operation teams. |
| ***Anti-Patterns*** | • Nurture heroic developers willing to work extremely long hours, including weekends.<br>• Have highly specialized people equipped with powerful tools for doing their jobs, with limited collaboration among different team members and limited integration of different tools. The assumption is that if everybody just does his or her job, the end result will be good. |

The principle of collaboration across teams stresses the importance of fostering optimal communication. This goal is achieved through proper people management and the setting up of effective collaborative environments.

Software is produced by talented and motivated people collaborating closely. Many complex systems require the collaboration of a number of stakeholders with varying skills, and the largest projects often span geographical and temporal boundaries, further adding complexity to the development process. This is why people issues and collaboration—what some have referred to as the "soft" element of software development—have been a primary focus in the agile development community. Following this principle requires answering many questions, such as the following:

- How do we motivate people to perform at their best?
- How do we collaborate within a collocated versus a distributed software team?
- How do we collaborate across teams responsible for the business, software development, and IT operations?

The first imperative in effective collaboration is to *motivate individuals on the team to perform at their best*. The notion of self-managed teams, which has gained popularity in the agile community, is based on making a team commit to what they should deliver and then providing that team with the authority to decide on all the issues that directly influence the result.[1] When people feel that they are truly responsible for the end result, they are much more motivated to do a good job. As one of the principles behind the agile manifesto states, "Build projects around motivated individuals. Give them the environment and support they need, and trust them to get the job done."

The second imperative is to *encourage cross-functional collaboration*. As Walker Royce says, "software development is a team sport."[2] An iterative approach increases the need for working closely as a team. We need to break down the walls that often exist between analysts, devel-

---

1. Schwaber 2002.
2. Royce 1998.

opers, and testers and broaden the responsibilities of these roles to ensure effective collaboration in an environment with fast churn. Each team member must understand the mission and vision of the project.

As teams grow, we need to provide them with *effective collaborative environments*. These environments facilitate and automate metrics collection, status reporting, and build management, as well as bookkeeping around configuration management. This efficiency reduces the need for meetings, which frees up team members to spend more time on more productive and creative activities. These environments should also enable more effective collaboration by simplifying communication, bridging gaps in place and time between various team members. Examples of such environments range from shared project rooms and whiteboards to networked or Web-based solutions such as Wikis, or integrated development environments and configuration and change management environments.

Our fourth imperative under this principle is *integration across business, software, and operation teams*. As software becomes increasingly critical to how we run our business, we need to create close collaboration among (1) the teams deciding how to run our current and future business, (2) the teams developing the supporting software systems, and (3) the teams running our IT operations. In most companies, these three groups have poor communication (see Figure 5.1).

The anti-pattern to following this principle would be to nurture heroic developers who are willing to work extremely long hours, including weekends. Another anti-pattern would be to have highly specialized people equipped with power tools for doing their jobs, with limited collaboration among different team members and limited integration of different tools. The assumption is that if everybody just does his or her job, the end result will be good.

Let's have a look at some of the practices that will help you achieve the above goals:

- *Practice 12: Build High-Performance Teams* discusses what characterizes a high-performing team and how you can build a culture that breeds high-performance teams.
- *Practice 13: Organize Around the Architecture* explains how you can organize your team to minimize stepping on each other's toes.

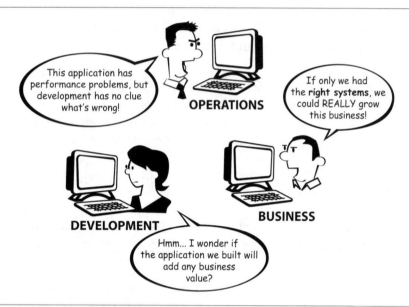

**FIGURE 5.1 Collaborate Across Business, Development, and Operations Teams.**
*As software becomes more critical to how we run our business, we need to collaborate more closely around teams responsible for how to run the business, how to develop applications, and how to run the applications. In most companies these three groups have poor communication.*

- *Practice 14: Manage Versions* offers guidance on how to effectively manage changes to the hundreds, if not thousands, of artifacts a project will have.

# Build High-Performance Teams

by Per Kroll

*Build high-performance teams by defining a set of values
and nurturing those values through everything you do.*

## Problem

As Walker Royce observed, "Software development is a team sport." To develop software, you need people with different functional responsibilities: analysts, architects, developers, testers, configuration managers, project managers, and so on. Further complicating matters, you may have people at different locations with different cultural backgrounds and different personal objectives. All of these variables make it harder to build cohesive teams.

This practice looks at what it means to have a high-performance team and how you can create one. A high-performance team is a cohesive team that collaborates effectively to accomplish agreed-on goals within provided parameters.

It should be noted that this practice may not be appropriate for all cultures or all companies. Your team should adopt a culture only if it is compatible with the overall culture within your company and society. Consequently, it may not be possible to implement all the guidelines in this practice within your team.

## Background

Before we dive into the specifics of building a high-performance team, let's look at the importance of influencing the culture for your team and then elaborate on the differences between a team and a family.

217

## Influence Your Team Culture

Each organization has a different culture, and you need to live within that culture. But you can often fine-tune or extend that culture in one or two areas, as long as your modifications do not go against the core values of your company. Let's look at one area that it is critical to address if you aim to build high-performance teams.

Some organizations are content with average people. They may build a culture in which all employees keep their jobs, no matter how poorly they perform. In such an environment the needs of the individual are always considered more important than the needs of the team. Such organizations will have some great teams, some bad teams, and some mediocre teams, but most teams will be mediocre or poor. Still, this may be a winning strategy for some organizations. A combination of lifelong employment resulting in low turnover and correspondingly low rehiring costs, relatively low salaries, and slow and steady project performance may lead to business success—especially if software development is a noncritical business aspect of the organization.

Other organizations focus on employing only superstars. Superstars are put in the spotlight and given all the rewards. The culture of such organizations emphasizes individual performance over team performance. When forced to make difficult choices between team cohesion and star performers, management will decide in favor of the star performers. This strategy can be very successful, especially in a highly dynamic industry focused on explosive short-term results rather than solid long-term performance. Those of us living in Silicon Valley saw this model become extremely popular during the Internet bubble of the late 1990s, only to decline somewhat after the bubble burst.

This practice will discuss a third type of culture. Looking at how to build a high-performance team that can sustain solid results over an extended period of time, we explain how to build a culture that nurtures both individual and team growth, in which the needs of the team are balanced against the needs of the individual and turnover is low because team members feel that they make a difference and are appreciated for their contribution.

## A Team Is Not a Family

Sometimes people try to make a project team feel like a family. That may be the right thing for your company and the teams you try to build, but it is not consistent with building a high-performance culture. So what is the difference between a team and a family?

The greatest thing about your family is that they are always there for you. They encourage you to succeed and support you in all your endeavors. No matter how badly you fail, your family is there to help you out, even when you do not deserve it. Ideally, a family is willing to do whatever it takes to help other family members, no matter what the situation.

Imagine you are a member of a successful sports team. When you practice, you all try to help each other to become better players. You know that your team will only win if everybody is at his or her best. A player who is not good enough when the season starts is left off the team. And if a player is extremely skilled but does not get along well with the other team members, you try to find a way to integrate that player into the team. If nothing helps, you have no alternative but to remove the high-performing, but disruptive, team member.

If, in the middle of a game, you notice that one of your team members is not performing, other team members will step in to try to help. Maybe the player is tired, and just needs a few minutes to rest before returning to optimal performance. You always try to do whatever it takes to get the person back to being a high performer. But if the poor performance continues for some time, you will replace the person with another player, either during the game or at least before the next game. Similarly, in a software team, team members do whatever they can to help other team members be at their best, but if they still cannot reach a certain standard, the team has to let them go.

The previous discussion demonstrates how important it is that you should *not* think of a team as a family when it comes to building high-performance teams. Let everybody in the team know where the bar is, do whatever you can to help people rise above the bar, and keep only the people who can perform to your standards.

Such an environment may sound unpleasant to work in ("Will I be laid off tomorrow?"), but it is not, at least not for high performers. People who are temporarily not performing will be given plenty of warning, and plenty of help, since you want them to succeed. You may change people's positions to find them a job where they can not only succeed but excel. However, team members unwilling to put in the energy it takes to succeed or unable to perform above the bar because they just do not have what it takes will have to leave the team. That is part of the deal.

Low performers will not like this type of workplace. They will not seek a job in such an environment, and they will often leave such an organization voluntarily rather than wait to be fired. This self-selection is a good thing, because it means that once you have established such a high-performance culture, the forces in place make it easier to maintain a high-performance team.

*A family is based on unconditional love and support.*

*A team is based on effective collaboration to achieve common objectives.*

The bottom line is that whereas a family is based on unconditional love and support, and as such does not push out or abandon other family members who are less capable, a team is based on effective collaboration to achieve common objectives. If certain team members cannot or will not be valuable contributors, you should first seek to improve their performance; but if that approach does not work, you must remove those team members from the team.

## Applying the Practice

Building high-performance teams is difficult. It may be possible in situations of turmoil to achieve results quickly by hiring a lot of new people, but you have to change the culture more slowly when managing teams in stable environments. Building high-performance teams is an ongoing effort; you are never "done." You must instill the appropriate values and provide organizational clarity. You must hire the right people onto the team. You need to build trust among team members to ensure that they work well together, and you must help them establish the right means of communication. Finally, you need to get people excited about being on your team, that is, you must be able to "create a winning team." Let's have a look at each of these topics.

## Instill the Right Values

To build an effective team, you need to have shared values that provide a set of explicit and implicit rules to live by.[3] These values provide a foundation for the interactions among team members, guiding your team in what is desirable and accepted behavior and what is not. The values constitute a manual against which you can assess alternatives in your decision-making process. Lack of adherence to a set of values will likely cause friction among your team members and make it more difficult for them to make appropriate decisions in their daily work. But how do you establish a set of values that can guide your team and help build team cohesion?

First, focus on a small set of critical values. Many values are potentially desirable: honesty, breakthrough thinking, customer focus, quality, fairness, devotion, customer success, revenue focus, fiscal responsibility, community involvement, integrity, ethics, teamwork, and so on. Identify a small set of values that can be used to differentiate between a good and an excellent performer in your organization. Look around you. Pick out your star performers, and identify the values they demonstrate that the average performers do not.

*Identify the values star performers demonstrate.*

Second, values need to be continuously communicated. Over the last few years, value posters have become common in the corporate world. You see posters extolling the importance of teamwork, integrity, and so on, but these posters risk being laughed at if they become the primary way of communicating values. Discuss the values of your team when you recruit new team members or when you start a new project. Does each team member understand the values, and are they committed to adhering to them in their work? In team meetings, make sure that the values of the organization come across as you discuss your work. If one of your values is customer focus, explain to your team how a new feature being added relates to that value. As you praise people for the work they have done, explain how they showcased the values of your team.

*Values need to be continuously communicated.*

---

3. Lencioni 2000.

*Adherence to values must be an essential part of the standard performance evaluations.*

Another important communication vehicle is that of rewards, which leads us to our third important way to establish a set of values. Your reward system can support adherence to your organization's values in many ways. You may institute special rewards, such as being able to attend more conferences or courses, or having greater input into what projects to work on. If you want to promote teamwork, also make sure that some of the rewards are given to the team when they meet their collective targets, not just to individuals when they meet their individual targets. Adherence to values must be an essential part of the standard performance evaluations that determine bonuses, raises, and promotions. The best way to make people abide by a set of values is to ensure that such behavior really pays off and is truly valued by managers at all levels of the organization.

As an example, in my organization we do rankings every six months. During the ranking sessions we discuss how each person has performed relative to our established values, ensuring that both the management team and the employees truly understand and live by the values of the organization. To excel, therefore, you need to reach out to the extended team, drive collaboration between your team and other teams, show that you can effectively mentor other team members, and help the extended team to improve their performance. You cannot just do a great job on your individual tasks. When you use ranking sessions, it becomes obvious that the organization really lives by its values. If you want to get promoted, if you want to receive bonuses, you need to leave your ego at home and focus on team performance, innovation, and respect in all your relationships, in addition to customer success.

## Provide Organizational Clarity

For your team to work effectively, all team members need to understand and agree on the answers to some basic questions, including the following:

- What is the mission of your team?
- What is the vision of the application to be delivered?
- How will you measure team success?

- Who are your project stakeholders?
- How will you measure project success?
- Who is responsible for what?
- What procedures should you follow to carry out the work?

Providing clarity around these issues is essential for effective team-work. In a RUP project you find this type of information in the Vision Document, Software Development Plan, and Development Case.

## Hire the Right People

Hiring is your most important decision. We cannot overemphasize the importance of getting the right people onto your team.[4] Obviously you need to ensure that the person you hire has the right skills, but there are also other considerations.

- **Does the person share the values of your organization?** Will this person fully adopt and live by the value system of your organization? The answers to those questions are not typically found by asking straight out whether the potential team member "wants to work in a high-performance team" or "respects and trusts their team members." The appropriate answer is obvious, and few people would answer no. Instead, when recruiting you should pose *behavioral* questions, asking the interviewee to recall his or her behavior in a particular situation, thereby revealing attitudes that the answer to an abstract, theoretical question would not. For example, you could find out whether or not a candidate trusts/respects the people he or she has worked with in the past by asking, "Tell me about a time you exercised leadership in a situation where you knew not everyone in your work group was supportive of your idea." As the interviewee spins out a tale to answer your question, he or she is much more likely to give you useful information than if you had asked simply, "What is leadership?" or "How do you get along with other people?"

*Ask the interviewee to recall his or her behavior in a particular situation.*

---

4. See Rothmann 2004.

- **Do other team members respect and support the person joining the team?** It is a good idea to have eight to ten people in your team interview any new people, even when you know that they are qualified. It helps the team gel, and team members cannot then say that they were never asked for an opinion. Sure, not everybody in a larger team can interview every new team member, but to the extent possible, you should make sure that people are (1) aware of who is about to be employed and (2) have a chance to give their opinion. Sometimes you need to go against the advice of some people on your team, but even in those cases, you can have a clear dialogue explaining why you disagree and why you still plan to recruit the person.

- **Does the person have a feel for your team and project?** By having the new person interview with a large cross-section of your team, she or he will hopefully know ahead of time what the team environment is like. Each team member will hopefully communicate some of the team values, and if there is a mismatch, the new person may choose not to join the team.

## Build Trust

*Trusting your peers means trusting that they will not try to harm you.*

Many people think that trusting your peers means not questioning the quality or correctness of their work. Nothing could be more wrong.[5] Trusting your peers mean trusting that they will not try to harm you, and that they will consider only what is best for the project. When you trust your peers to this degree, you will be glad when they (constructively) provide feedback on your work to help you improve, question your conclusions, or ask you to improve the quality of your work. You know that they are just trying to help you to be a better team performer.

*If your team meetings are boring, you probably do not have a high-trust environment.*

A team built on trust is a team that has a lively and healthy debate about issues and project risk. If your team meetings are boring, you probably do not have a high-trust environment. During team meetings in a high-trust environment team members engage in heated discussions on how to solve various problems your project is facing and

---

5. Lencioni 2002.

often challenge the way the project is currently being executed. At the same time, people respect each other. They let people finish making their point rather than interrupting them. They admit when they were wrong, and they give credit to whoever came up with great ideas. They attack the issue, not the person. They believe in challenging each other and being open to new ideas, not bringing down other team members.

It is sometimes difficult to encourage healthy feedback and lively debate in projects. As Patrick Lencioni points out in his admirable *Five Dysfunctions of a Team*, "It is only when team members are truly comfortable being exposed to each other that they begin to act without concern for protecting themselves. As a result, they can focus their energy and attention completely on the job at hand, rather than being strategically disingenuous or political with each other."

Often, cultural differences get in the way, and in many cultures (including some parts of the United States) people are very careful not to say anything that can be construed as direct criticism of another team member. Also, in some cases certain team members are elevated to a "super hero" status, making it virtually impossible to challenge their judgment. In those situations you must continually push for a more open and direct form of communication, stepping in if necessary by asking pointed questions when you feel that other team members are too vague or indirect to open up a challenging discussion.

## Establish Rules of Communication

With all of today's communication technology, you might think that communication is no longer a big issue. Wrong. Although we have the tools we need for effective communication—cellular phones, telephone conferences, instant messaging, videoconferences, team rooms, and discussion technology—these technologies are often used inappropriately and in fact even get in the way of effective face-to-face communication.

*Tools for effective communication are often used inappropriately.*

Especially when you have distributed teams, it becomes essential to establish some rules of communication to maximize effectiveness and team cohesion. You may want to consider some of the following rules:[6]

- **Encourage face-to-face communication whenever possible.** For example, if you have to have a telephone conference with participants at other sites, have all participants at your site get together in the same conference room, rather than having them call in from their individual desks.

- **Use phone discussion or face-to-face meetings to resolve e-mail debates.** An e-mail debate that has led to two series of responses (B responds to A, A responds back to B) must be followed by a phone call or face-to-face meeting between A and B to minimize confrontation and endless e-mail discussion. The resolution coming from the phone conversation can be summarized in an e-mail to all participants.

- **Consider forcing all team members in a distributed team to use instant messaging.** The ability to see which team members are at their desks makes it easy to resolve minor issues quickly through instant messaging or over the phone. Some teams working in multilingual environments find that instant messaging actually works better than a phone call, since some team members may have problems communicating orally with other team members.

- **Strongly encourage joint lunches or other get-togethers that are not directly related to work.** This tactic strengthens team cohesion and allows a lot of work issues to be resolved in their infancy while team members enjoy each other's company. Often, new ideas are brought to birth that would otherwise not be voiced. The increasingly common practice of eating lunch at one's desk while trying to work is in fact highly inefficient. It leads to a loss of productivity and reduced team cohesion.

- **Consider using team room capabilities, allowing you to have one place for all team-related activities and artifacts.** Provide repository-based tools, making it easy for all team members to reach current requirements, defects, and other relevant information. Leverage a common version control system for versioned artifacts.

---

6. Also see Cockburn 2002 and Ambler 2002.

- **Place team members in close proximity to each other.** To facilitate osmosis of information, whenever possible place team members in the same room or in close proximity to each other. Make sure that you use the same water fountain and soda machine, and that you constantly run into each other.

## Create a Winning Team

Winning is fun. We all love to win. It certainly beats losing. By ensuring that yours is a winning team, you will attract talented people, and people working for your project will be more enthusiastic and willing to put in the extra effort needed to reach your next milestone, whether it is a weekly build, a monthly iteration, or a twelve-month project. But how do you go about creating a winning team? Here are some guidelines:

*Winning is fun. It certainly beats losing.*

- **Succeed with the first iteration.** If you do iterative development, make sure you succeed with your first iteration. Many teams try to accomplish too much in the first iteration, and as a result the project starts off with a failed iteration. *Try to take on less than you expect you can manage—early iterations often take longer than you expect.*
- **Limit commitments.** Try to limit the number of commitments your team makes, but ensure that you do a great job delivering on those commitments. By pushing back on the number of requests you get, you create an environment where the workload is manageable enough for the team to have a chance of succeeding.
- **Just do it!** Instill a "just do it" attitude. Many teams and people waste too much time preparing, discussing, and thinking about how to do something and too little time just doing it. Iterative development is, among other things, about instilling a "just do it" attitude on a larger scale, and you should bring that mindset to smaller tasks too.
- **Let team members assign and estimate tasks.** Have team members sign up for tasks and do their own estimates. They are more inclined to enjoy a task that they chose and more likely to be committed to an estimate they made themselves.[7]

---

7. See Beck 2004, principle *Accepted Authority.*

- **Positive attitude.** Instill a positive attitude. Attitude has a huge impact on our well-being and that of the people around us. A positive attitude allows the team to put in the extra effort it takes to succeed.

## Other Methods

All the agile methods offer a great deal of guidance in the areas of building effective teams and the softer issues concerning team collaboration. For example, XP gives explicit values for effectively developing software: *communication, simplicity, feedback, courage,* and *respect.* The principles and practices in XP are there to support these values and their effective implementation.

Enterprise Unified Process[8] provides guidance in some of the areas related to people management covered here, such as how to obtain and keep highly qualified staff.

Scrum and XP both focus on self-organized teams, meaning that the teams are responsible for how to do the work. As an example, in Scrum teams have the freedom to execute upon an iteration (Sprint) using whatever approach they like, as long as they meet the Sprint goal. They can, for example, hire a consultant, change working hours, and change what requirements to implement, as long as they stay within budget and overall corporate guidelines. By providing developers with the responsibility for delivering a quality end product, and the associated ability to take the necessary action, you motivate teams to perform at their best. At the same time, management can have its say at the end of the Sprint, which is never more than thirty days away, so the risk for management in letting the team loose is limited.

RUP and OpenUP/Basic provide organizational clarity by clearly defining roles and responsibilities, as well as providing guidance on how to capture project stakeholders, realize the project vision, and measure project success. RUP and OpenUP/Basic also incorporate

---

8. See Ambler 2005.

many of the techniques listed in this section, many of which are derived from Scrum, XP, and other agile processes. Both RUP and OpenUP/Basic currently focus on including this set of "soft" techniques.

A key message for agile processes is that all team members have equal value as human beings.[9] Many people in the agile community cry out against measuring individual performance. For example, some reviewers of this book pointed out that ranking is inconsistent with agile values, but we believe that part of respecting people is being clear about what they are doing well and where they can improve, in line with the agile values of feedback and courage. We believe that as long as ranking and individual performance measurement are carried out in an honest and open fashion, with clear communication about values and which delivered results lead to a certain ranking, they align very closely with agile principles. Scrum is very clear about the need to weed out team members who consistently fail to perform.

## Levels of Adoption

This practice can be adopted at three levels:

- **Basic.** Ensure that you provide organizational clarity through clear communication of project vision and project responsibilities. Make each team member responsible for overall project success.

    The basic practice of clear communication should minimize bureaucracy and thus allow you to have shorter iterations.

- **Intermediate.** Establish and live by the values of your organization. Agree on how you will deal with team communication issues. Even when many problems in a project are known, people do not want to talk openly about them. Establish trust, and encourage constructive feedback and open communication so that you can discuss issues and resolve them.

    The intermediate practice of trust and constructive feedback is crucial for any team doing iterative development; it allows you to minimize bureaucracy and thus have shorter iterations.

---

9. See, for example, Beck 2004, value *Respect*.

- **Advanced.** Use a performance evaluation system that effectively evaluates adherence to established values.

The advanced practice of coupling your performance evaluation system to your values should allow you to instill the right values effectively in your organization. Done correctly, this should not cause a lot of extra overhead but should instead allow you to minimize bureaucracy and thus have shorter iterations.

## Related Practices

- *Practice 7: Everyone Owns the Product!* addresses how all team members need to orient their mindset and the way they collaborate within the team to enable effective teamwork. This is a key aspect of creating a high-performance team.
- *Practice 19: Rightsize Your Process* shows how to work more effectively by focusing only on the activities in your process for which the benefit of doing the activity is greater than the cost, thus creating higher-performing teams.

## Additional Information

## Information in the Unified Process

OpenUP/Basic and RUP provide guidance on clear communication of the vision to the team and team organization and apply many of the techniques listed in this practice. OpenUP/Basic and RUP currently stay away from topics related to team culture, but we propose to add guidance from this book and other sources to provide more coverage in this domain.

## Additional Reading

For books that cover people aspects of software projects, see the following:

Murray Cantor, *Software Leadership: A Guide to Successful Software Development*, Addison-Wesley, 2001.

Walker Royce, *Software Project Management: A Unified Framework*, Addison-Wesley, 1998.

Scott Ambler, John Nalbone, and Michael Vizdos, *The Enterprise Unified Process: Extending the Rational Unified Process*, Prentice Hall, 2005.

Alistair Cockburn, *Agile Software Development*, Addison-Wesley, 2002.

Sanjiv Augustine, *Managing Agile Projects*, Addison-Wesley, 2005.

For nonsoftware books that deal with teamwork, productive and less productive behavior, and people skills in general, see the following:

Patrick Lencioni, *The Five Dysfunctions of a Team*, Jossey-Bass, 2002.

Patrick Lencioni, *The Four Obsessions of an Extraordinary Executive*, Jossey-Bass, 2000.

John R. Katzenbach and Douglas K. Smith, *The Wisdom of Teams: Creating the High-Performance Organization*, HarperBusiness, 2003.

Dale Carnegie, *How to Win Friends and Influence People*, Pocket Books, 1990.

Johanna Rothman, *Hiring the Best Knowledge Workers, Techies & Nerds: The Secrets & Science of Hiring Technical People*, Dorset House, 2004.

**Organize Around the Architecture**

by Per Kroll

*Organizing large projects around the architecture
enables more effective communication and collaboration.*

## Problem

As projects grow in size, communication among team members becomes increasingly complex. The cost of communication increases, and it is hard for team members to know enough about the overall system not to step on each other's toes and overlap their work. One solution would be to have project members to talk to most other project members to make sure they know enough to do a good job. This process soon becomes burdensome, however, and results in reduced efficiency.

This practice describes how you can address that problem by organizing your teams in such a way that you minimize the need for project members to talk to large groups of people to do their job. By organizing around the architecture, you can significantly reduce the number of project members who need to talk to each other.

## Background

Say there are fifty people who will work on a major landscaping project. They will install a deck, a swimming pool, a rose garden, a front lawn, a back lawn, and a children's playhouse. As a project manager, how would you organize those fifty people? To make sure that the whole project fits together, you need somebody to "own" the overall architecture and somebody else to own each of the major components—deck, pool, rose garden, and so on—to ensure the coordinated execution of each of these major items. In addition to giving you and the architect a single point of contact for each major component, this strategy makes it unnecessary for each of the fifty project members to know what each other project member is doing. If you are on the pool team, you clearly need to know mainly the specifics of the pool. However, to ensure that everything will adhere to the style of, say, a classical English country estate, you may also have to understand some of the project's overall themes. Now let's see how this example relates to running a software project.

One of the many benefits of a robust software architecture is that it clearly divides the system responsibilities into well-defined subsystems with well-defined interfaces. The architect or architecture team worries about the architecture and how it all ties together. Individual developers still need to understand the overall system, but they can focus primarily on a subset of a system, that is, one or several subsystems assigned to them. Organizing around the architecture reduces the risk of people stepping on each other's toes and duplicating work.

Organizing around the architecture also improves communication.[10] Generally, face-to-face communication is most effective, except in the case of large projects, which have too many communication paths. The upper half of Figure 5.2 shows how many possible communication paths there are among all team members: note that it grows geometrically with the size of the team. For a team of size $n$, the number of communication paths = $n * (n-1)/2$. This means that a two-person team has 1 communication path, a three-person team has 3 communication paths, but a six-person team has 15 communication paths.

An increase in communication paths destroys project team efficiency, and you need to find a better method than having everybody communicating with everybody else. You can solve the problem by making one team responsible for the architecture and several small teams each responsible for one or several subsystems. Communication among these few teams is channeled through the architecture team to resolve issues around the overall solution and interfaces between subsystems. As you can see from the lower half of Figure 5.2, this approach leads to simplified and effective communication even in large projects. You

---

10. Kroll 2003.

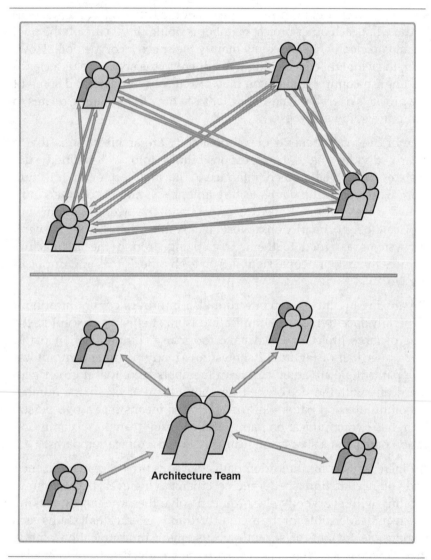

**FIGURE 5.2 Organizing Around Architecture Minimizes Communication Overload.** *The number of possible communication paths among team members grows geometrically with the team size. Organizing around the architecture radically reduces the number of communication paths within a team. Issues regarding subsystem interaction are resolved by the architecture team, which owns the interfaces between subsystems. (Reprinted from Kroll 2003.)*

typically also need to facilitate other types of communication by having coordinating teams deal with issues related to testing, scheduling, resources, process, and requirements.

Also note that iterative development, with its continuous integration and testing, is the best means of exposing issues to the extended team. If various pieces of your system do not fit well together, the integration and testing will point out what issues you are facing, allowing the relevant people to collaborate to fix them. Following this practice depends on the use of effective configuration and change management environments.

## Applying the Practice

As your team grows, you need to find smart ways to divide the work among subteams. In this section we discuss the responsibilities of the architecture team and suggest a few alternative team structures for development teams, based on the overall architecture and size of project. Next we look at the responsibilities of teams owning various subsystems. We then offer guidance on collective code ownership and show how your decisions around who can change what code impact how you do use-case-driven development. Finally, we take a quick look at other teams that are typically not organized around the architecture. Let's have a look at each of these items in turn.

## The Architecture Team

Early in the project, you should designate a person or team to be responsible for the overall architecture. The architecture team must not work in isolation from the rest of the development team. Instead, architects should work with the entire project team to drive the architecture work, including identification of required subsystems. Architects should also make sure to detail the requirements that will have a fundamental impact on the architecture and design, implement, and test the aspects of the system that constitutes the architecture.[11] If you

*Early in the project, designate responsibility for the overall architecture.*

---

11. See Ambler 2002.

are using the Unified Process lifecycle, the architecturally significant aspects of your system should be implemented and tested by the end of the Elaboration phase.[12]

Later in the project, the architecture team will ensure that each subsystem is developed according to the agreed-upon architecture, that is, that subsystem interfaces are not changed without discussions with the architecture team and other affected teams; that architectural patterns are properly leveraged and not compromised; and that architectural constraints, such as requirements around stability, load, and performance, are adhered to.

As you develop various subsystems, you will need to modify the architecture. As an example, subsystem interfaces may need to change. The architecture team is responsible for understanding the impact such a change will have on other subsystems and for bringing concerned parties together to discuss the impact and resolution of issues. You may also need additional or modified architectural mechanisms,[13] such as an additional mechanism for dealing with persistency. The architecture team needs to assess the need for an additional mechanism; determine whether it can be resolved by modifying an existing mechanism; and, if not, ensure that all team members understand the availability of the new mechanism and when it should be used.

In summary, the architecture team will be active throughout the project to ensure that the appropriate team members are involved in decision making, that architectural risks are mitigated, and that changes to the architecture are communicated to all concerned parties.

## Structure of Development Teams

There are many different ways in which you can divide a large application into subsystems. The right subsystem structure for your project will depend, among other things, on the type and size of system you are building.

---

12. Kroll 2003.

13. A mechanism is a standard software capability that is needed by the system, such as mechanisms for persistency, interprocess communication, message routing, or security.

Smaller systems may have an architecture consisting of a number of subsystems, without any clear organizational structure between one and another. An alternative would be to organize subsystems around major business functions, in what is often referred to as vertical organization, or organization around feature sets (see Figure 5.3).

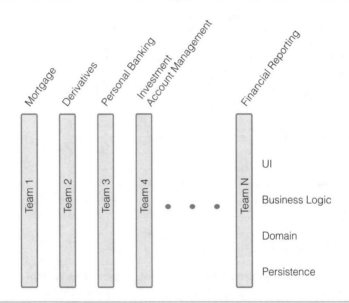

**FIGURE 5.3 Teams Organized Around Vertical Business Functions or Feature Sets.** *Smaller teams may choose to organize around vertical business functions or feature sets, such as the mortgage or derivatives in this example. Each team would build the user interface, business logic, domain, and persistency capabilities it needs.*

As systems grow and become more complex, you may use a third method, namely, organizing subsystems in distinct layers, in which the lower layers deal with infrastructure, such as subsystems for persistency, reusable user-interface components, distributed computing, and so on. On top of these, you may have a layer providing domain-specific components, such as components for the financial domain. On top of these, functional subsystems provide the business functions

*As systems grow, organize subsystems in distinct layers.*

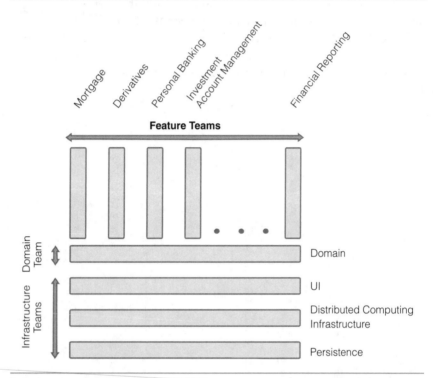

**FIGURE 5.4 Teams Organized Around Horizontal Layers and Vertical Business Functions.** *When building large and complex systems, it is often advisable to organize around horizontal layers for infrastructure and domain-specific layers, while making separate feature teams responsible for vertical business functions.*

required by end users, such as mortgage, derivatives, personal banking, financial reporting, or investment account management (see Figure 5.4).

## Subsystem Teams

*Each major subsystem should have a team responsible for it.*

Each major subsystem should have a team responsible for it. Depending on the size of each subsystem, one team may be responsible for several. A team responsible for the persistency layer may, for example, have several subsystems handling the interfaces to each of the supported databases. Subsystem teams are responsible for understanding the architectural constraints they have to live within, the subsystem interfaces, permissible technology choices, architectural patterns to adhere to, architectural requirements, and so on.

As mentioned above, subsystem teams typically need to make changes to the architecture, that is, the interfaces or behavior to their subsystem or other subsystem(s), so that they can implement their subsystem in a reasonable way. They should then work with the architecture team to ensure that the changes they want to make are acceptable, and that the architecture team and impacted subsystem teams fully understand what changes need to be made. The appropriate subsystem team(s) then implement the changes and properly communicate them to all project members. This process of managing the subsystem interfaces is what Grady Booch refers to as "managing by the seams."[14]

It is important to point out that although some people in your team will be responsible for the architecture and others will own a subsystem, this division does not excuse working in isolation from other teams. All team members have a continuous responsibility to do what it takes to build a successful product—see *Practice 7: Everyone Owns the Product!* As an architect or a developer responsible for a subsystem, you should help out wherever necessary and always look at the bigger picture: are you building an application that will address your business needs? Having responsibility for a certain subsystem, however, means that you are expected to be the primary point person for discussions and resolution of issues related to that subsystem, and you own the integrity of that subsystem.

## Can Anybody Change Any Code?

XP[15] and Agile Modeling[16] both promote collective ownership, that is, the notion that anybody should be able to change any code or model.

---

14. Booch 1996.
15. Beck 2004. Corollary practice *Shared Code.*
16. Ambler 2002. Core practice *Collective Ownership.*

We believe that such a practice works primarily for small projects with limited system complexity, for which team members can easily communicate with each other to understand what changes have been made, and why; or for slightly larger teams with very skilled team members. If, for example, you are organized in vertical teams as in Figure 5.3, several vertical teams may be changing shared domain components. This way of working is typically fast and effective if effective configuration management practices are used.

*For large projects, team members implement changes to their own subsystem.*

For larger projects, at a minimum you need to make sure that the responsible subsystem team is notified of any changes, so that they can review and approve the change. Otherwise, you run a big risk of having code changes introduce unexpected problems, and you can waste a lot of time trying to find defects introduced by somebody who had only limited appreciation for the complexity and interdependencies of the code within a subsystem. In our experience, the best approach for large projects is to have subsystem team members implement changes to their own subsystem.

## Use-Case-Driven Development

We recommend using use-case-driven development,[17] that is, identifying requirements in the form of use cases and scenarios,[18] making somebody responsible for the design and implementation of each use case and scenario, and also designating somebody to test each one. (Note that for the rest of this section, all discussions about use cases also apply to scenarios.)

When designing each use case, describe how various components interact to provide the functionality of the use case. Typically, a use case will leverage capabilities in several different subsystems. It is a good idea to have somebody responsible for each use case who will work with the people involved to ensure that the functionality captured in the use case is delivered.

---

17. Jacobson 1992.

18. See *Practice 9: Describe Requirements from the User Perspective* for more information.

For smaller systems with collective ownership of the code, the person responsible for a use case also implements it. For larger systems, the person responsible for a use case works with the developers responsible for individual components to specify jointly which capabilities various components are to deliver, and the developers responsible for each component then implement and unit-test the agreed-on capabilities.

*For smaller systems, the person responsible for a use case also implements it.*

For extremely large systems, use cases may cut across several major subsystems, and the person responsible for a use case distributes only the different chunks of a use case among the involved subsystems; this is called "requirements flowdown."[19] The subsystem team agrees to implement a certain aspect of a use case, and the team then needs to design and implement how that should be done.

## Is Everybody in the Team Organized Around the Architecture?

So, will everybody on the team belong either to the architecture team or to a subsystem team? No. Larger projects usually have many other teams that you may consider including in your project:

- A team owning system-level requirements.
- A team owning integration/builds.
- A team owning system-level testing.
- Various teams with functional specialties, such as a user-centered design team, or teams responsible for standards compliance, such as accessibility (to ensure that applications can be used by people with disability).

## Other Methods

There are at least two essential differences between our application of iterative development and what XP suggests. The first difference con-

---

19. See the RUP product for more information, especially the plug-in for Systems Engineering.

cerns whether to focus on architecture early on. XP explicitly states that you should develop only for what you need today. According to this method, therefore, you should not expend any effort predicting what architecture you need to support capabilities you plan to develop later in the project, or in future projects. If you find that you need to change the architecture later in the project, you do it through refactoring. By keeping the code simple and using test-first design, refactoring can be done at a reasonable cost. Our experience is that later rework of the architecture is often costly, especially when teams expand and applications become more complex. Another reason RUP, OpenUP/Basic, and Agile Modeling recommend that you focus on architecture early on is to enable you to align the organization of a larger project with the architecture. To do that, however, you need to baseline a stable architecture early on. This practice may hence be difficult to leverage when using XP.

The second major difference is that XP emphasizes shared code; anybody can change any code, and nobody should own subsystems or major components. We believe, on the other hand, that you need to make somebody responsible for each subsystem and major component, but that people can make updates to other team members' subsystems and components as long as they keep the owner up to date with the work done.

Scrum provides guidance for scaling development teams. For smaller teams (up to twelve people) have a daily short meeting with all team members, a so-called "scrum." As your team grows, have a representative from each of the subteams meet daily to understand what each team is doing, to resolve issues, and to ensure smooth collaboration across subteams ("scrum-of-scrums"). Scrums and scrum-of-scrums are great complements to the above suggestions on how to organize your teams. It is, however, important that this cross-team coordination not only involve scrum masters but also require similar coordination with those who are dealing with testing, requirements coordination, and common infrastructure.

## Levels of Adoption

This practice can be adopted at three levels:

- **Basic.** The team is organized around feature sets or vertical business functions, as in Figure 5.3. You assign owners to the vertical subsystems/feature sets and apply collective code ownership. An architect oversees the architecture and makes sure that architectural issues are resolved as necessary. Tight communication among all developers minimizes overhead.

  The basic practice of organizing around feature sets with collective code ownership is appropriate for small teams. It provides a minimum of ceremony and allows you to have short iterations.

- **Intermediate.** The project is organized around a combination of vertical and horizontal teams, as in Figure 5.2. Changes to the architecture take place after the architecture team agrees on proposed changes.

  The intermediate practice of having a combination of vertical and horizontal teams is appropriate for medium-size teams. You are now adding more complexity in communications and should consider using scrum-of-scrums. The added complexity tends to drive you toward longer iterations.

- **Advanced.** Same as intermediate, but change requests are formalized toward the latter part of the project. You need to formally document a suggestion to change the architecture, and an Architecture Control Board (the architecture team with representatives from various subsystem teams) needs to approve the request. You then communicate the decision on supporting material to all concerned teams.

  The advanced practice of formal handling of changes to architecture is appropriate for large development teams. It adds a lot of ceremony, and you need to consider whether that approach is right for your project and, if so, when it is appropriate to add this level of ceremony. If you are using the Unified Process lifecycle, you should not introduce this level of formality until some time in the Construction phase.

## Related Practices

- *Practice 7: Everyone Owns the Product!* discusses how to collaborate across the entire team to develop a high-quality product and to avoid having issues fall between the cracks. Achieving the right collaboration is a key parameter to consider when organizing your team.
- *Practice 16: Architect with Components and Services* describes the benefits of developing with components and explains how to develop a component-based architecture. A component-based architecture provides clean interfaces between subsystems, making it easier to organize around the architecture.

## Additional Information

## Information in the Unified Process

OpenUP/Basic describes how an architect coordinates many of the technical issues that need to be resolved. These issues often center on the architecture. RUP adds guidance on layered and other architectural paradigms, how to organize the team around different architectural paradigms, and how to evolve the team structure as you progress through the project phases.

## Additional Reading

Philippe Kruchten. "The Software Architect and the Software Architecture Team." In *Software Architecture*, P. Donohue, ed. Kluwer Academic Publishers, 1999.

Kent Beck with Cynthia Andres. *Extreme Programming Explained: Embrace Change, Second Edition.* Addison-Wesley, 2004.

Scott Ambler, John Nalbone, and Michael Vizdos. *The Enterprise Unified Process: Extending the Rational Unified Process.* Prentice Hall, 2005.

Ken Schwaber and M. Beedle. *Agile Software Development with SCRUM.* Prentice Hall, 2002.

Walker Royce. *Software Project Management: A Unified Framework.* Addison-Wesley, 1998.

# Manage Versions

by Bruce MacIsaac

*Effective version management is critical to managing complex software and its changes over time.*

## Problem

Many software development efforts involve multiple people and multiple teams, often geographically separated, working in parallel on interdependent software, developed over multiple iterations and targeted at multiple products, releases, and platforms. It is easy to lose track of what has changed and why, and how the pieces fit together. The results can have a serious impact on cost, schedule, and quality.

This practice describes how to manage versions of files, components, and products while keeping chaos at bay.

## Background

My wife's family loves to solve jigsaw puzzles, and I have spent many a Christmas puzzling with them. They are very good at it. However, whereas I, as a novice, may pick a piece out of the pile and spend ages trying to make it fit, they purposefully group similar pieces, connect them into meaningful chunks, and then deliver those chunks to the evolving puzzle.

Version management is similar. If you treat each change to a file separately, you can easily lose track of where it fits into the bigger picture. If instead you organize changes into meaningful sets and deliver them into stable environments, you can work much more effectively.

*Organize changes into meaningful sets and deliver them into stable environments.*

Software developers working in parallel need stable workspaces into which changes can be incorporated. Integrators need to pull the right

**FIGURE 5.5  Delivering Meaningful Sets of Changes.**  *To manage change effectively, identify meaningful sets of changes, and deliver them into stable environments.*

versions of software together in order to make them work together. Testers and final product delivery need to make sure that they are testing and delivering builds composed of the right pieces.

Change management is becoming increasingly difficult for the following reasons:

- Iterative development approaches mean constantly evolving components.
- Shared components across products means that a single component may have many variants, each evolving in parallel.
- Increasingly dynamic component and service-oriented architectures mean more ways in which components, services, and legacy systems can be combined to serve new purposes.

These challenges demand that teams evolve from managing change at the individual file level to delivering meaningful sets of changes into stable workspace environments.

## Applying the Practice

Effective version control requires secure storage, balance of control and access, and a logical approach to managing sets of changes at all levels.

## Store Artifacts Securely

Most software projects today use some kind of version control system to track versions of individual files in a repository. This is a good fundamental practice, as it allows multiple developers to work on a file without losing each other's changes. It also allows developers to recover from data losses; easily back out changes to individual files; and track the history of changes, for example, to determine when a defect was introduced.

Version control is not limited to source code. Other artifacts, including documents, data, models, and executables, should be placed under version control whenever you wish to avoid loss, recover earlier versions, and track history.

The repository stores all versions of your files and so must be fault-tolerant, reliable, and backed up with appropriate disaster recovery procedures. In addition, you may need it to be scalable and distributed to support larger distributed teams.

## Balance Control and Freedom of Access

In some development environments people fear that unauthorized persons will introduce defects, and so impose many controls to prevent such changes. In other environments developers are encouraged to make changes wherever they see something that can be improved. Which is the right approach?

I consider the following to be a balanced approach: allow anyone to make changes, but require such changes to be codeveloped or reviewed by someone intimately familiar with the element being changed. For large projects, permissions should be organized around the team structure, as described in *Practice 13: Organize Around the Architecture*.

*Allow anyone to make changes, but require changes to be codeveloped or reviewed by an expert.*

Freedom to make changes encourages collaboration in the software development, enabling improvements to be incorporated quickly, while involving an expert ensures that naïve developers don't introduce problems as they add "improvements."

## Use Version Control for Components and Component Configurations

Version control shouldn't be limited to individual files. Of increasing importance is version control of components and configurations:

*It is easier to assemble consistent systems from consistent component baselines than from multitudes of individual files.*

- It is easier to assemble consistent systems from consistent component baselines than from multitudes of individual files.

- Components and configurations can be tested and documented as having reached a specified quality level, making it easier for clients to decide when to migrate to a newer version.

Whether your project is producing an entire system or a component in a larger system, you should create a baseline of that product at each major milestone. In an iterative development approach you should create a baseline at least once at the end of each iteration. Baselines allow you to track progress between iterations and reproduce earlier versions. This can be helpful in identifying when and how defects were introduced, generating release notes, and gathering progress measures.

More than just the source code should be baselined. Instructions for how to build the executable software and dependencies such as compiler version, operating system version, and command line options should also be baselined, to ensure that builds can be reproduced. This step becomes particularly important when a baseline is released to customers, as the ability to recreate a customer's build is important to providing system support and maintenance.

## Provide Controlled Workspaces

There is a practical joke that works as follows: first you buy several sizes of a hat and give the one that fits to a friend as a gift. Then you periodically switch that hat with a larger or smaller one. Your friend will be convinced that his or her head is changing size.

It is very difficult to reason in an unstable environment. A developer needs a workspace in which to make changes and test them without being impacted by unexpected changes other developers have made. The answer to the problem is to ensure that each developer has a private workspace where he or she can periodically recreate a baseline to pick up changes made by other developers in a controlled manner. It is important to pick up a consistent set of changes that completely implement a capability or fix a bug. And it helps to know what has changed—not just the details of what changed in each file, but what are the new capabilities and what bugs have been fixed—so that the impacts can be identified.

*Workspaces let developers make changes without being impacted by others.*

Similarly, testers and integrators need controlled workspaces that allow them to pick up complete sets of changes and know what has changed.

## Organize Consistent Sets of Changes with Activities

When accepting changes into a controlled workspace, the first question you should ask is, "What changed?" The changes are easiest to understand if all those that serve a single purpose are identified and managed as a set. Let's call this set an "activity change set,"[20] because it is the result of performing a complete activity such as fixing a defect or adding a feature.

The simplest way to define a change set is to work on one activity at a time and then deliver the completed changes to the integration environment. This method works well, provided you have a single code stream and have no need to back out or track changes.

*An "activity change set" is the result of performing a complete activity, such as fixing a defect or adding a feature.*

If you want to deliver activity change sets to multiple code streams, or track changes at the activity level, you want tool environment support. Ideally, your version control environment allows you to indicate the activity you are working on (such as a feature or a defect); the environment then tracks your changes until you finish or until you

---

20. IBM Rational Clearcase refers to this set of changes as an "activity." Other tools use other terms; for example, Bitkeeper calls it "change set," while Perforce uses the term "change list."

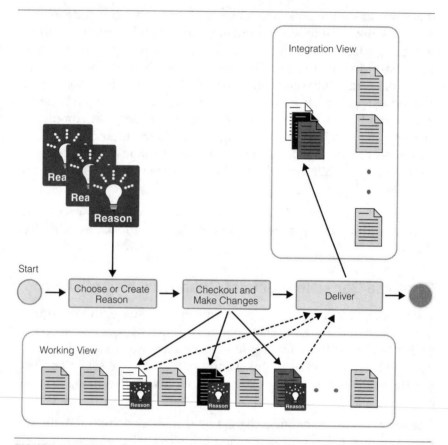

**FIGURE 5.6 Making Changes Associated with an Activity.** *All the changes asso-ciated with the activity (reason for the change) are delivered as a consistent whole.*

switch to another activity. Figure 5.6 shows a typical flow for this way of working.

Since all changes are associated with an activity, they can be delivered and accepted into other workspaces as a consistent whole (see Figure 5.6). It thus becomes possible to generate reports of how two baselines differ, not just as a list of files but as a list of activities that have been performed. This approach aids in creating release notes, assists testers in determining appropriate tests, and so on.

## Enable Parallel Development with Streams

As you deliver changes into a workspace, that workspace evolves. A logical workspace, consisting of a baselined set of versioned files plus activities that describe what has changed since the baseline, is called a "stream." Figure 5.7 shows a typical set of streams for parallel development.

Other stream variations are possible. For example, you can create a separate stream to stabilize each build and then, once the build is stable, deliver the changes back into the integration stream[21] (see Figure 5.8).

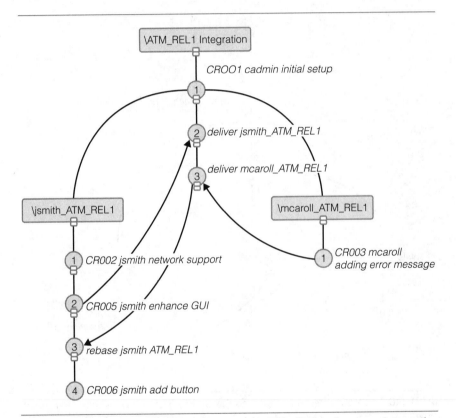

**FIGURE 5.7 Streams for Parallel Development.** *This figure shows an integration stream and the streams of two developers, jsmith and mcarroll. Jsmith completes two changes, CR002 and CR005, and then delivers them for integration, as shown by the arrow. Mcarroll does CR003 in parallel and delivers it for integration as well. Jsmith recreates a baseline and then continues work. (Adapted from Bellagio 2004.)*

---

21. See Berczuk 2002 for detailed guidance on using streams to manage integration.

*Streams and activities make parallel development easier, since changes can be delivered as sets into parallel streams.*

Parallel development is much easier with streams and activities. Developers can work in different streams, and as they complete activities, their changes can be selectively delivered into integration and other streams. Maintaining each stream as a controlled environment, and each activity change set as an evolution of that environment, helps you to understand exactly which changes have been applied, and where.

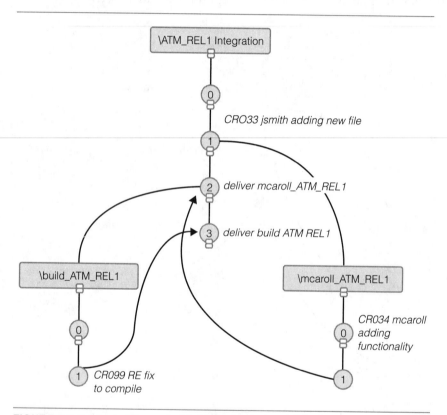

**FIGURE 5.8 Separate Stream to Stabilize the Build.** *This figure shows changes delivered by a developer (mcarroll) to an integration stream, stabilized in a separate build stream, and then returned to the integration stream. (Adapted from Bellagio 2004.)*

## Use Activities and Streams to Manage Variants

Ideally, a software component is developed and then evolves over time. However, it is sometimes necessary to create more than one variant of the same component, for a number of reasons:

- Functionality may be required to support variations in user needs.
- A single product may be targeted at different hardware and software platforms or a different country, culture, or language.
- Older versions of a product may need to be maintained to support an existing customer base.

Activities and streams can make it easier to manage multiple variants being developed in parallel.

Let's consider an example in which a company has a product line with three variants of a particular product—let's call them A, B, and C. A defect in the installer component for version A has been found. The component has been fixed for A and a baseline recreated. What do we do with products B and C?

- Product B uses the same version of the installer (prior to the fix). The integrator for product B picks up the new baseline for the component. Tests for B may need to be updated. Tests for B are rerun to ensure that nothing has broken.
- Product C uses a different version of the component. The activity change set can be applied to C's product stream and the changes merged, as shown in Figure 5.9. A good merging facility can in most cases merge changes and prompt when there are conflicts, such as if the defect corrects code that does not exist in C. Because a fix has been merged into a different version of the component, inspection and testing are critical to ensure that this alternative version of the fix works.

Maintaining different evolutionary paths of a component is more expensive in the long run, as each change needs to be evaluated for applicability to the different versions and may need adjustment and specialized testing in those different versions. In general, it is better to

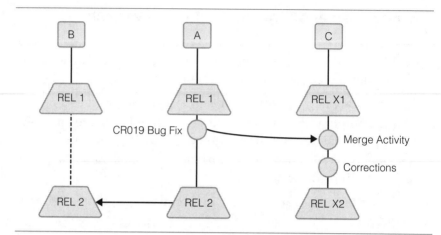

**FIGURE 5.9 Merging a Fix into Different Product Streams.** *This figure shows three product streams using a common installer component. A fix in A is picked up by B. C is using a different version of the component, making a merge necessary.*

use an architecture that isolates those elements that can change, using components that are easy to swap out or otherwise configure. For example, one telecommunications company had a large catalog of telephone switches, but underneath the hood, the software was exactly the same—the cheaper version simply had some of the features disabled. During development, some components would temporarily evolve independently, but the changes were always pulled back into the base. Figure 5.10 shows how this can be done, with a "main" stream used as the basis for two project streams, REL1 and REL2.

*Activities let you manage streams in terms of the bug fixes and features that differentiate them, rather than getting lost in the complexity of individual file differences.*

As these examples show, dealing with multiple streams is complicated, even with the advantages that activities provide. With activities, you can manage streams at a high level—the bug fixes and features that differentiate the streams. But without activities, you have to deal with all the individual file differences, an explosion of complexity that can be impossible to manage.

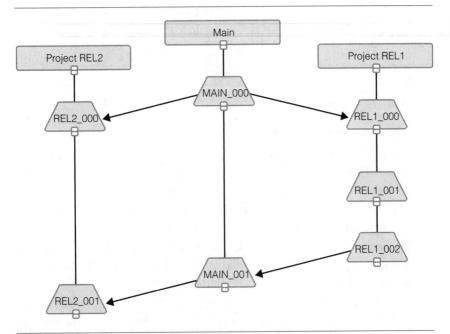

**FIGURE 5.10  Parallel Projects.** *This figure shows integration streams for two parallel projects, REL1 and REL2. REL1 initially diverges, but changes in REL1 are then delivered back to a "main" stream and later incorporated into the REL2 project. (Adapted from Bellagio 2004.)*

## Other Methods

Agile methods, such as Scrum and XP, generally focus on the needs of smaller teams. XP in particular recommends a single code stream and "continuous integration," in which every few hours changes are incorporated and tested in the integration environment. This simple approach ensures continuous improvement.

Unified Process similarly recommends that integration be as continuous as possible and change management as simple as possible. However, the need to track changes increases with product and organizational complexity. RUP's guidance for configuration and change management extends to cover the needs of larger projects, multiple product lines, standards compliance, enterprise reuse, and enterprise architectures. These challenges increasingly demand that teams organize and deliver changes as meaningful "activity" sets.

## Levels of Adoption

This practice can be adopted at different levels:

- **Basic.** Version control of files and builds allows the history of individual files and builds to be tracked. Changes for a specific purpose are collected and integrated as a set.

  This fits with the agile practice of continuous integration and requires little in terms of tools or training.

- **Intermediate.** Isolated workspaces reduce interference among team members working in parallel. Activity-based control and delivery of change sets help to manage changes.

  A good version control tool can help you keep track of your work and so increase your ability to work in an iterative development environment. Some overheads with tooling and training exist, but they are not a significant barrier for most projects, even most small projects.

- **Advanced.** Shared components are managed across different product lines.

  Managing components shared across different product lines requires disciplined change management. Such efforts are usually associated with large projects, or enterprise-level reuse and architecture efforts.

## Related Practices

- *Practice 2: Execute Your Project in Iterations* describes the importance of growing systems in increments that are continuously integrated. Incremental change and continuous integration are facilitated by the ability to deliver meaningful sets of changes.

- *Practice 13: Organize Around the Architecture* describes how teams are organized around the components in the architecture. Team interactions are facilitated by effective version control of those components.

## Additional Information

### Information in the Unified Process

OpenUP/Basic describes a basic activity-based configuration and change management process suited to a typical small project. OpenUP/Basic assumes that the project has the tools and environment in place, and thus focuses on execution of the project, not on plans and setup.

RUP adds guidance to address tool selection, environment setup, configuration management plans, audits, multiple product lines, standards compliance, enterprise reuse, and enterprise architectures.

## Additional Reading

For additional guidance on version control and change management, see the following:

David Bellagio and Tom Milligan. *Software Configuration Management Strategies and IBM Rational ClearCase: A Practical Introduction, Second Edition*. IBM Press, 2005.

S. Berczuk and B. Appleton. *Software Configuration Management Patterns: Effective Teamwork, Practical Integration*. Addison-Wesley, 2002.

Jason Leonard. "Simplifying Product Line Development Using UCM Streams." *The Rational Edge*, http://www.ibm.com/developerworks/rational/library/1748.html.

# CHAPTER 6

# Elevate the Level of Abstraction

| | |
|---|---|
| ***Benefits*** | • Improved productivity.<br>• Reduced complexity. |
| ***Patterns*** | 1. Reuse existing assets.<br>2. Use higher-level tools and languages to reduce the amount of documentation produced.<br>3. Focus on architecture. |
| ***Anti-Patterns*** | • Go directly from vague, high-level requirements to custom-crafted code. |

Complexity is a central issue in software development. Elevating the level of abstraction helps reduce complexity and the amount of documentation required by the project, while facilitating communication. You can achieve this elevation through reuse, the use of high-level modeling tools, refactoring, and stabilizing the architecture early.

One effective approach for reducing complexity is to *reuse existing assets*, such as reusable components, legacy systems, existing business processes, patterns, or open source software. Two great examples of reuse that have had a major impact on the software industry over the last decade are reuse of middleware—such as databases, Web servers, and portals—and, more recently, open source software, which provides many smaller and larger components that can be leveraged. Moving forward, Web services will likely have a major impact on reuse, since they provide simple ways of reusing major chunks of functionality across disparate platforms and with loose coupling between the consumer and provider of a service (see Figure 6.1). As a result, you can more easily leverage different combinations of services to address your business needs. Reuse is also facilitated by open standards, such as Simple Object Access Protocol (SOAP), Web Services Definition Language (WSDL), Reusable Asset Specification (RAS), Universal Description, Discovery, and Integration (UDDI), and eXtensible Markup Language (XML).

Another approach to reducing complexity and improving communication consists of *leveraging higher-level tools, frameworks, and languages*. Standard languages such as Unified Modeling Language (UML) and rapid application languages such as Enterprise Generation Language (EGL) provide the ability to express high-level constructs, such as business processes and service components, to facilitate collaboration around high-level constructs while hiding unnecessary details. Design and construction tools can automate moving from high-level constructs to working code by providing wizards to automate design, construction, and test tasks; by applying patterns, generating code and enabling usage of code snippets; and by making integration and testing seamless development tasks through integrated development, build, and test environments. Another example is project and portfolio management tools, which allow you to manage financial and other aspects of multiple projects as one entity versus a set of separate entities.

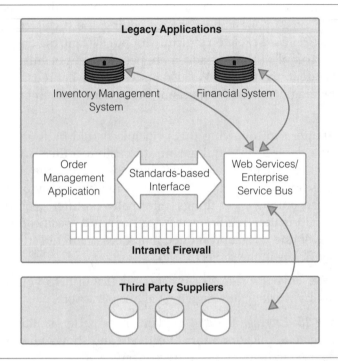

**FIGURE 6.1 Reuse Existing Assets Through Service-Oriented Architectures.**
*One of the problems with reuse is that two components need to know about each other's existence at development time. Service-oriented architectures alleviate that problem by providing what is called loose coupling; a consumer of a service can dynamically find a provider of a service. You can hence wrap existing components or legacy systems into services, allowing other components or applications dynamic access to their capabilities through a standards-based interface, independent of the platform and implementation technology used to develop the various components.*

A third approach to managing complexity is to *focus on architecture*, no matter whether you are trying to define a business or develop a system or application. In software development we aim to get the architecture designed, implemented, and tested early in the project. Consequently, early in the project we define the high-level building blocks and the most important components, their responsibilities, and their interfaces. We define and implement the architectural mechanisms, that is, ready-made solutions to common problems, such as how to deal with persistency or garbage collection. By getting the architecture right early on, we define a skeleton structure for our system, making it easier to manage complexity as we add more people, components, capabilities, and code to the project. We also understand what reusable assets we can leverage and what aspects of the system need to be custom-built.

The anti-pattern to following this principle would be to go directly from vague, high-level requirements to custom-crafted code. Since few abstractions are used, a lot of the discussions are made at the code level versus a more conceptual level, thus missing many opportunities for reuse, among other things. Informally captured requirements and other information require many decisions and specifications to be revisited over and over, and limited emphasis on architecture causes major rework late in the project.

This chapter covers a series of practices that will help you manage complexity by working at a higher level of abstraction:

- *Practice 15: Leverage Patterns* explains how patterns allow you to produce an application more effectively and shows how patterns can be used to help enforce the architecture.
- *Practice 16: Architect with Components and Services* describes the benefits of developing with components and demonstrates how to go about developing a component-based architecture.
- *Practice 17: Actively Promote Reuse* provides guidelines for how to enable and promote reuse of assets.
- *Practice 18: Model Key Perspectives* discusses how models can help you understand, communicate, and accelerate development.

Let's have a look at these practices in turn.

# Leverage Patterns

by Bruce MacIsaac

*Leverage patterns to solve problems and
to capture and communicate solutions.*

## Problem

Broad experience is a quality in short supply, and even experts should
not be inventing new solutions if there are proven solutions that work.
**Patterns** offer "distilled experience" with the following benefits:

- Patterns can help users solve problems faster by providing tried
  and true solutions.
- Systemwide patterns ensure that problems are solved once and
  that solutions are applied consistently across the system.
- Experts in short supply can be leveraged more effectively by capturing their experience in patterns that can be applied over and
  over again.

This practice describes how to use patterns to solve problems and capture and communicate solutions.

## Background

Let's start with a few key definitions.

### Pattern: A General Definition

Before giving a definition, let's start with a simple example. "Divide
and conquer" is a time-honored strategy in war, government, and
computing science. The strategy can be described as follows:

- *Name:* Divide and conquer
- *Problem:* The opposing army is large and imposing. Or, in mathematics or computing terms, the problem is large and intractable.

- *Solution:* The divide-and-conquer strategy consists of weakening an enemy by dividing its forces. This military solution has a long history, going back at least to Sun Tzu's *Art of War* 2,400 years ago. The Romans also used it to build their empire, making treaties with one state so that they could attack its neighbor.
  In mathematics and computing science, the strategy is applied by dividing a large problem into several smaller problems that are easier to solve and can be combined to solve the larger problem.

- *Applicability:* This pattern fails if the opposing armies refuse to be divided. American revolutionary forces in 1776 successfully applied the counter-pattern "united we stand."[1]

**FIGURE 6.2 Divide and Conquer.** *A pattern, such as "divide and conquer," applies to many different situations.*

---

1. Oddly enough, "divide and conquer" can also fail in mathematics. Reference "Simpson's Paradox" at http://en.wikipedia.org/wiki/Simpson's_paradox.

This simple example demonstrates the defining characteristics of a pattern:

- The memorable and descriptive name makes it easy to remember and apply. You don't need to describe the technique every time it is applied.
- The pattern solves a recurring problem.
- It is not a complete solution, but rather a strategy that can apply in different circumstances (sometimes as different as war and computing science).
- The pattern doesn't apply in all circumstances. A good pattern description indicates when the pattern should be applied.

## Benefits of Patterns

Whether developing a new system or integrating or upgrading an existing system, basic problems recur that have already been solved. When the solution is distilled and captured as a pattern, it can be reused, which saves time. But more important, using proven solutions reduces risk and so increases the likelihood of success.

*Patterns are proven solutions to common problems.*

Patterns are also useful as a means to understand and document existing systems. Like an archaeologist, you can excavate the patterns used by the original software designers and use patterns to document that architecture.

Learning standard patterns provides developers with a rich vocabulary for communicating design alternatives and offers a toolkit full of proven solutions that can be applied as needed. Developers thus become more effective and efficient. One caution: overuse of patterns can complicate a design. It is generally best to apply new patterns in their simplest form until you have gained experience.[2]

*Overuse of patterns can complicate a design.*

## Software Design Patterns

Software design patterns are patterns that solve software design problems. In addition to providing a name and description, design patterns

---

2. The Agile Modeling practice is to "apply patterns gently"; see Ambler 2004.

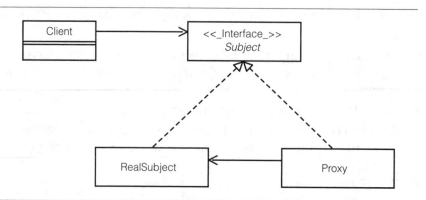

**FIGURE 6.3 Structure of the "Proxy" Design Pattern.** *The client uses an interface. Both the Proxy and RealSubject implement that interface, but the Proxy just redirects calls to the RealSubject.*

can often be enhanced by diagrams. Figure 6.3 shows an example of the "Proxy" design pattern,[3] expressed in UML.[4]

Figure 6.4 shows the behavior (how invoking the proxy results in a delegated call to the RealSubject).

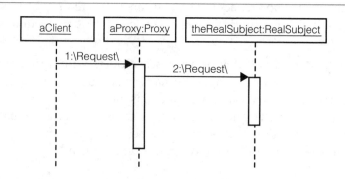

**FIGURE 6.4 Behavior of the Proxy Pattern.** *Calls to the proxy are redirected to a class that provides the real implementation.*

---

3. For a detailed description of the problems solved by this pattern, see Gamma 1994.

4. See *Practice 18: Model Key Perspectives* for more on using UML.

Note the following characteristics of the notation used in this pattern:

- It does not identify actual classes; rather, it describes generic roles to describe characteristics of pattern participants.
- The real classes could be anything, from an online auction querying a credit card system to a ground station talking to a satellite.
- The use of roles allows the pattern to be applied in many different kinds of software systems, with many different classes.

## Software Architecture Patterns

A software architecture pattern is a design pattern that has a wide impact on the overall system. Because of the wide range of problems encountered in software development, architecture patterns (and more generally design patterns) are typically organized into categories of the problems they solve, such as the following:[5]

- Structural patterns: how to organize software into manageable units for development.
- Distribution patterns: how to distribute processing across multiple processors.
- Concurrency patterns: how to deal with parallel processing.
- Persistency patterns: how to store data in files and databases.
- Presentation patterns: how to design software for user interfaces.

The pattern categories above closely relate to the architectural views described in RUP.[6] Considering each view and pattern category helps ensure that the key aspects of the architecture are addressed.

A reference architecture is a collection of patterns that define a basic architecture for a system. Using a reference architecture is easier than picking and choosing individual patterns, but offers less flexibility.

*Using a reference architecture is easier than picking individual patterns.*

---

5. The Pattern-Oriented Software Architecture Series (Buschmann 1996, Schmidt 2000, and Kircher 2004), and Fowler 2003 are excellent references for architectural patterns.

6. RUP uses the architecture views described in Kruchten 1995.

## Applying the Practice

Learning to apply patterns is a skill that takes time and practice to cultivate. The following section provides guidance for getting started with patterns and introduces more advanced applications of patterns.

## Increase Your Knowledge of Relevant Patterns

*Developers should be familiar with key patterns.*

It is important for developers to be familiar with key patterns relevant to their field and to use them as basic tools for solving problems and communicating solutions. The section Additional Information at the end of this practice lists some good places to start.

## Use Reference Architectures

There may be existing documented architectures within your organization, or in literature, that fit closely with the system that you are trying to build. A good "reference architecture" is a collection of related patterns that fit a particular business and technical context and should include examples and other artifacts to enable their use. One such set of reference architectures is IBM's Patterns for e-Business.[7] The IBM Patterns for e-Business Web site provides more than a simple list. It includes a wizard that helps you progress from identifying the business problem that you are trying to solve to choosing the specific architecture that meets your needs.

*Reference architectures are patterns proven to work together.*

Reference architectures are a good way to start looking at patterns. The set of patterns is predefined, which saves you picking and choosing patterns yourself. Reference architectures are also less risky, since the selected patterns have been proven to work together.

## Identify Patterns for Cross-Cutting Concerns

Solving common problems the same way keeps an architecture consistent and understandable. Architectural patterns for structure, distribution, concurrency, persistency, and presentation generally impact

---

7. Accessible at http://www.ibm.com/developerworks.

multiple components of the system. Requirements to support global-ization, security, redundancy, error reporting, and so on typically also affect multiple components.

There are two aspects to addressing most cross-cutting concerns: (1) identifying software that provides common services (sometimes referred to as "mechanisms") and (2) describing how those mechanisms are to be used by the client software (patterns).

In early analysis, these mechanisms are described textually, as a place-holder for one or more components yet to be selected or designed. Classes are mapped to mechanisms as shown in Figure 6.5.

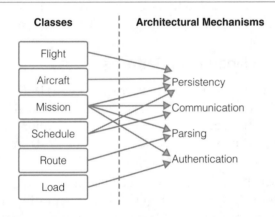

**FIGURE 6.5 Mapping Design Elements to Analysis Mechanisms.** *Classes and sub-systems are mapped onto the identified analysis mechanisms: the arrows indicate that the class uses the mechanism. A client class often uses several mechanisms.*

As analysis and design proceed, analysis mechanisms, such as "persis-tency," are narrowed to specific design mechanisms, such as "relational database persistency" and patterns of use. This relationship is then further refined to specific implementations such as "Cloudscape data-base," and patterns of use can be demonstrated with working examples.

As the system evolves, you may find similar code appearing in sev-eral places, or different code being used to solve similar problems. Such discoveries frequently signal a need to define and refactor to a common pattern.

*Multiple solu-tions to similar problems indicate a need for patterns.*

## Document Patterns Used in Your Project

*Applying systemwide patterns improves consistency and simplicity.*

Architectural patterns are solutions to key technical challenges, many of which have systemwide implications. If there are no guiding systemwide patterns, developers may come up with different solutions to similar problems, causing additional effort and unnecessary complexity. Consciously applying patterns throughout the system generally leads to more consistency and simplicity.

To ensure that the architecture doesn't degrade, architectural patterns need to be documented and enforced. Enforcement here simply means that the architecture should not be allowed to degrade through sloppiness; developers and reviewers should defend standard patterns and avoid deviations whenever possible. The simplest way to do this is to create good examples early in the project for others to follow.

## Using UML to Document Patterns

An intermediate application of patterns is to use UML to document the patterns in your software, as shown in the previous "Proxy" example. UML provides a rich standard visual notation for capturing both structure and behavior. The advantages of UML are further discussed in *Practice 18: Model Key Perspectives.*

*Document patterns precisely and compactly with UML.*

Your main goal should be to document the problem and to describe when the pattern applies and when it does not apply. Diagrams, UML or otherwise, can help you create compact and precise descriptions.

## Automated Pattern Application

Tools[8] are available that not only document patterns using UML but can also apply and enforce patterns in a model. As an example, you might decide to apply the "Proxy" pattern (described earlier) to a particular client and subject class. A wizard can automate applying the pattern—generating the interface and proxy class from the subject

---

8. For a list of UML tools, with varying levels of support for patterns, visit http://www.uml.org.

class, revising the original client to invoke the proxy, and generating calls from the proxy to the real-subject class.

Note that since patterns are not generally complete solutions, but rather characteristics of solutions, only some patterns can be automated. The best approach is to identify excessive repetition in your designs or your implementations and use automated patterns as a tool to simplify your work.

*Use automated patterns as a tool to simplify your work.*

## Other Methods

Traditional waterfall development details all the design before implementing and testing. Patterns can be incorporated in this approach, but waterfall development does not provide the opportunity to validate these patterns on a small amount of code before they are used broadly.

Patterns are a key part of the Unified Process's focus on architecture. Patterns are validated by implementing and testing examples before they are widely implemented, allowing the patterns to be improved without impacting a lot of the design and code.

*Patterns are a key part of the Unified Process's focus on architecture.*

Early implementation of patterns is consistent with XP's principle of "incremental design," which states that "design done close to when it is used is more efficient."[9] However, the Unified Process explicitly recommends looking for key patterns and implementing them. XP doesn't have this same architecture focus; rather, patterns and consistency emerge through continuous refactoring.

RUP encourages automated application of patterns and reuse of patterns to increase productivity, although this is an advanced application of RUP. XP doesn't discuss this topic explicitly, but XP's value of simplicity and principle of "baby steps" remind teams to be cautious about doing too much too soon.

---

9. Beck 2004.

## Levels of Adoption

This practice can be adopted at different levels:

- **Basic.** Learn patterns. It is important for developers to be familiar with key patterns relevant to their field and to use them as basic tools for solving problems and communicating solutions.

  Create and follow good examples of cross-cutting patterns.

  Understanding and applying patterns can speed development and enhance communication. Less design documentation is needed if standard patterns are followed.

- **Intermediate.** Use reference architectures; these partial solutions can add a lot of value relative to the effort required to use them.

  Understanding and applying reference architectures can speed development of projects that can leverage a reference architecture.

  Use UML to document design patterns; the visual representation provides a compact and precise means of documenting patterns.

  Documenting patterns using UML takes time, but it is an investment that can pay off in more accurate communication and, more important, be the basis of reusable pattern assets.

- **Advanced.** Use pattern automation to speed repetitive work and improve consistency.

  Apply patterns across the enterprise as part of an enterprise architecture. Create repositories of reusable patterns as part of a reuse program.

  Advanced applications of pattern automation, enterprise reuse, and aspect orientation are investments that suggest more discipline, at least initially.

## Related Practices

- *Practice 2: Execute Your Project in Iterations* describes iterative development as offering the opportunity to discover and test patterns in early iterations, make any necessary corrections, and then use those patterns consistently through the rest of the development effort.

- *Practice 10: Prioritize Requirements for Implementation* illustrates that examples of cross-cutting patterns should be developed early. Prioritize requirements that will create such examples and allow you to get them right.
- *Practice 16: Architect with Components and Services* describes many useful patterns for identifying components and for using components.
- *Practice 17: Actively Promote Reuse* shows that patterns are reusable assets and should be a part of any systematic reuse effort.
- *Practice 18: Model Key Perspectives* demonstrates that UML collaborations are a good way to document design patterns.

## Additional Information

### Information in the Unified Process

OpenUP/Basic covers the basics of applying patterns and reference architectures. RUP and RUP plug-ins elaborate on these basics. For example, the J2EE plug-in to RUP describes important J2EE design patterns, while the Service-Oriented plug-in describes patterns that apply to service-oriented architectures.

### Additional Reading

The following classic work popularized design patterns:

Erich Gamma et al. *Design Patterns: Elements of Reusable Object-Oriented Software*. Addison-Wesley, 1995.

There are many books on patterns. The following address patterns of architectural scope:

F. Buschmann et al. *Pattern-Oriented Software Architecture: A System of Patterns*. John Wiley & Sons, 1996.

Douglas Schmidt, Michael Stal, et al. *Pattern-Oriented Software Architecture, Volume 2: Patterns for Concurrent and Networked Objects*. John Wiley & Sons, 2000.

Michael Kircher and Prashant Jain. *Pattern-Oriented Software Architecture, Patterns for Resource Management (Wiley Software Patterns Series)*. John Wiley & Sons, 2004.

Martin Fowler. *Patterns of Enterprise Application Architecture*. Addison-Wesley, 2003.

Gregor Hohpe and Bobby Woolf. *Enterprise Integration Patterns*. Addison-Wesley, 2004.

For guidance on improving existing code with patterns, see the following:

Joshua Kerievsky. *Refactoring to Patterns*. Addison-Wesley, 2005.

For guidance on applying patterns and UML in the context of an overall software development process, see the following:

Craig Larman. *Applying UML and Patterns: An Introduction to Object-Oriented Analysis and Design and Iterative Development*. Prentice Hall, 2005.

# Architect with Components and Services

by Bruce MacIsaac

*Component and service-oriented architectures help you to build software that is more easily understood, changed, and reused.*

## Problem

Components are relatively independent units that can be assembled to build larger systems. The benefits of components include the following:

- An architecture that is more easily understood, as each component defines a cohesive capability and hides internal complexity.
- A system that can be more easily changed, as individual components can be modified without affecting other components.
- Greater potential for reuse, as components can be assembled for different uses.

Service-oriented architectures are similar to component architectures, in that systems can be composed using services. Services are published capabilities that can be discovered and used dynamically. Identifying services and designing service providers act as an extension to the basic approach for identifying interfaces and designing components that implement them.

This practice describes how to identify and document components and services.

## Background

Let's discuss why components are needed and review the different kinds of components.

## The Need for Components and Services

Early on in my career as a software developer, I was asked to review some code. Sadly this was not because of my great expertise, but because a quality requirement box needed to be checked, and nobody else was available.

This code was part of a highly successful commercial product, critical to the company. I looked forward to learning how professionals designed software. My first disillusionment was that there was little design documentation, and it was out of date. "Look at the code" was the recommendation. After studying the code for several hours, I went to a senior developer and expressed my confusion. "I don't understand how this software is organized. There are lots of modules, but I don't understand the grouping." His response was that the low-level modules had become numerous over time and so were grouped alphabetically. Any module could invoke any other. Large data structures were passed around or shared by different modules, and it was difficult to determine what data each module used. The result was a system that was very difficult to understand. Fixing bugs in one module often introduced new bugs as side-effects, because the dependencies between modules were not clear.[10]

*Components that hide complexity make systems understandable.* Eventually, that system was completely reengineered, at great expense. Instead of having lots of small modules organized alphabetically, components with specific responsibilities were organized into subsystems and layers. Instead of large shared data structures, interfaces explicitly defined inputs and outputs. Instead of minor changes and bug fixes having broad impact across the system, most changes could be isolated to a single component, while other code, which depended only on the interfaces to the component, was unaffected. From this and other experiences with both good and bad architectures, I have learned an important lesson: components that hide complexity behind interfaces are the key to creating understandable systems.

---

10. I wish I could say that I learned the code, recommended key improvements, and saved the day. Unfortunately, I was unable to figure out the big picture, and my review added little value.

## Definition of Component, Service, and Subsystem[11]

The term "component" has been overused. It is often used generally to mean "any constituent part." RUP defines it much more narrowly as *"a non-trivial, nearly independent, and replaceable part of a system that fulfills a clear function in the context of a well-defined architecture."*

The key term is "replaceability." Anyone who has upgraded a computer or repaired a car understands the basic principles of component parts: there are connection points that have to fit, and the part has to meet certain specifications. These specifications allow you to replace an old part with a new one, even one built by a different manufacturer.

*A component's specification allows it to be replaced.*

The most basic form of replaceability is design and implementation replaceability. The component is a "black box," exposing a set of interfaces. Since clients depend only on these interfaces, the underlying component can be modified or replaced, provided it continues to support the specified interfaces.

A "service," in simplified terms, is a capability that is published to a directory so that clients can dynamically discover its interface. This allows flexible composition of new capabilities from loosely coupled services. A "service component" implements one or more services much as a regular component implements interfaces. The difference is that services are dynamically discoverable.

*Services are published capabilities that can be dynamically discovered and composed.*

In this practice the term "component" applies equally to service components.

Note the term "design subsystem" is used interchangeably with "design component," reflecting the evolution of these terms; once different, they have evolved in the latest UML 2.0 specification to be essentially equivalent, with "subsystem" generally used to refer to larger granularity components.

---

11. These "kinds of components" are abstracted from RUP 7.0.

## Applying the Practice

This practice provides an overview of how to identify and specify components.

### Identify Components and Services from the Problem Space

*Components encapsulate concepts in the problem space.*

Components can often be discovered from the problem that the software is intended to solve. The largest components (often called subsystems) or services can often be identified by modeling the overall business and encapsulating business rules or parts of the business process.[12]

To identify components within an application, start by identifying the "things in the system which have responsibilities and behavior." Nouns used in the requirements are a good starting point, as are domain objects (see *Practice 8: Understand the Domain*). A more structured approach[13] is to identify "analysis classes," including the following:

- Boundary classes that encapsulate interactions with an external system, device, or human actor.
- Entity classes encapsulating information that must be stored, and the business rules associated with that stored information.
- Control classes to coordinate behavior.

These analysis classes provide a key starting point for components. Start by grouping highly interdependent or closely related classes into components, and separate classes that are relatively independent.

### Identify Components and Services from Existing Assets

*Components encapsulate resources.*

Often, there are existing company resources, such as databases or existing systems. Encapsulating resources with a standard interface allows the resource to be accessed in a consistent manner and enables it to be replaced or modified as needed.

---

12. Modeling of business processes and business rules is covered by the Business Modeling discipline in RUP.

13. This is the approach of "analysis modeling" found in RUP.

## Use a Layered Architecture

Components should encapsulate functionality, but they should also be able to take advantage of common services. A layered architecture classifies functionality into layers in such a way that upper layers use services from lower layers. This classification clarifies the dependencies and responsibilities of components. It also helps identify reusable components, as functionality that logically belongs to a lower layer can be refactored into a component at that lower layer.

*Separating concerns with a layered architecture makes it easier to identify components.*

Figure 6.6 shows a typical layering approach.

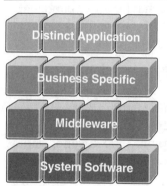

**Distinct Application** subsystems that make up an application—contain the value adding software developed by the organization.

**Business Specific**—contains a number of reusable subsystems specific to the type of business.

**Middleware**—offers subsystems for utility classes and platform-independent services such as distribution, security, database access, messaging, and so on.

**System Software**—contains the software for the actual infrastructure such as operating systems, interfaces to specific hardware, device drivers, and so on.

**FIGURE 6.6  A Typical Layering Approach.** *The separation of concerns in each layer makes it easier to identify components and make changes. (From RUP v7.0.)*

Notice how this layered approach isolates hardware and operating system dependencies to the lowest layer, making it easier for the upper layers to migrate to other platforms.

Layering is equally applicable to service-oriented architectures. Although services discussions often focus on the peer-to-peer interactions within the top layers of the architecture, services can still benefit from layering to increase reuse and reduce dependencies.[14] And even when the services themselves are not layered, the components that implement services can usually benefit from a layered architecture.

---

14. See Stojanovic 2005 and Greenfield 2004 for examples of layering applied to service-oriented architectures.

## Factor Out Common Behavior

Several classes may have similar requirements that can be factored out and moved into another component. In particular, mechanisms such as persistent storage, interprocess communication, security, transactions, error reporting, format conversion, and so on are natural components.

Look at design patterns with similar challenges (see *Practice 15: Leverage Patterns*). Patterns often suggest how class responsibilities can be refactored to reduce coupling in ways that create better component boundaries.

*Isolate reusable behavior into components.* Looking more broadly, consider behavior that may be reusable for other systems in the future and try to isolate such behavior into components.

## Consider Likely Changes

*Isolating potential areas of change enables future changes.* Stakeholders often have ideas about what they would like the system to do in the future. For example, they may wish a product to be configurable to support other languages, other platforms, or different working environments. You should not expend a lot of effort designing for requirements that may never materialize. However, isolating potential areas of change can be an inexpensive means of enabling easier changes in the future. For example, the simple layering approach described earlier shows how to isolate platform dependencies to ease future migration.

## Separate Specification and Realization

UML provides for the separation of a component's design into specification and realization. The specification serves as a contract that defines everything a client needs to know to use the component. The realization is the detailed internal design intended to guide the implementer. You can even create two or more "realization" components for one specification component if you wish to have different implementations.[15] A similar approach is used to specify services separately from services components.

---

15. A component specification can have a different implementation when, for example, different companies provide competing implementations for the same specification, or when components are implemented and optimized for specific platforms.

Figure 6.7 shows how an engine can be specified. The provided interface (shown as a circle) is a powertrain. The required interface (a half circle) is a power source or fuel. An engine can be reused in a car or boat, provided the right connections are present. The realizations of the engine specification are not shown in this diagram, but would be actual engines provided by various engine manufacturers.

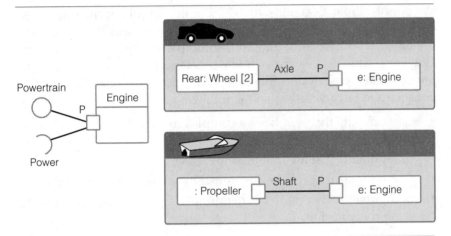

**FIGURE 6.7 Example of Connected Components.** *An engine can be used in a car or a boat, provided it has the right connections. (From the OMG UML 2.0 specification.)*

Figure 6.8 gives a software example based on Java Database Connectivity (JDBC). JDBC is a component that has two connections. The first provides a standard interface for client applications to access a database. The second is a driver interface that the database vendor must realize.

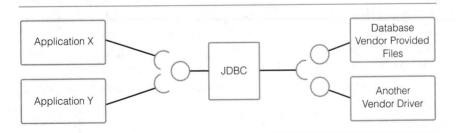

**FIGURE 6.8 Example of Connected Software Components.**

*Provided and required interfaces allow components to be replaced.*

These examples show that components both provide and require interfaces, and that the interfaces allow one component to be replaced by another compatible component.

Specifications often hide the internal complexity of a component. So while the design of a component realization can include a detailed description of interactions between internal elements—using structure, state, activity, and interaction diagrams—specifications are usually simpler. Specifications usually focus on describing the interfaces, dependencies on other interfaces, and required quality of service. Usually a UML structure diagram, accompanied by text, is sufficient. However, you can use the rich UML notation to provide a rich and precise visual description for the specification. Such precise descriptions tend to be most useful in the following cases:

- Components that will have a complex externally visible state and behavior.
- Components that are intended for reuse.
- Components that will be developed by a separate organization.
- Components that will have multiple implementations for the same specification.

Services and service components frequently have one or more of the above characteristics, and so benefit from a precise UML specification.

UML can be used to precisely specify components and services.

## Provide the Right Level of Interconnection

Some components encapsulate resources or capabilities that need to be accessed by multiple distributed applications. These are natural candidates for wrapping as a service, because service frameworks generally provide a standard and flexible means of managing distributed capabilities. Because accessing a distributed capability involves sending and receiving data over the network, performance and scalability are significant concerns. Message-based asynchronous protocols are often the best choice, as these allow the requestor and provider of a service to work in parallel, rather than await a response from the other.

Not all components should be exposed as services, as the flexibility provided by services comes with a cost. Distribution needs to be administered, interfaces are complicated by the need to minimize the number of message interactions, and asynchronous messaging and parallel processing can be tricky. Most smaller components do not need this complexity.

*Not all components should be exposed as services.*

## Develop Components Iteratively

It can be difficult and costly to refactor components after they have been fully implemented. To validate the design of components and their interfaces, implement basic scenarios that prove the integration of the components and interfaces. Add functionality in each iteration to refine and expand upon the interfaces. Developing components iteratively enables you to find problems, such as coupling or performance issues. You can then correct these problems through refactoring, without impacting a lot of code. This issue is discussed in more detail in *Practice 2: Execute Your Project in Iterations* and in *Practice 10: Prioritize Requirements for Implementation*.

*Develop components iteratively to enable inexpensive refactoring.*

## Other Methods

Traditional waterfall development can be used to design and implement components. However, this method can lead to late discovery of problems, and it is difficult and costly to refactor components after they have been fully implemented. The iterative approach validates that components integrate and perform well using partial implementations, and even stubs. The component can then be refactored as necessary without impacting a lot of code.

In an XP approach, components are not a focus. Some can be expected to emerge through refactoring and general good design. The Unified Process explicitly focuses on architecture, and it recommends identifying key components and interfaces and initially implementing just enough to validate architectural decisions. Whereas the Unified Process considers components useful for organizing teams, especially on larger projects, XP recommends a flat organization in which all code is shared.

*The Unified Process recommends implementing just enough to validate architectural decisions.*

Unlike XP, RUP also extends to cover the needs of larger projects, enterprise reuse, and enterprise architecture by describing how and when to use detailed component specifications. RUP also provides technology-specific information, such as how to design and implement services using J2EE and IBM Rational Software Architect.

## Levels of Adoption

This practice can be adopted at different levels:

- **Basic.** Understanding components and services. It is important for developers to know how components and services can be applied to the systems they develop, and to understand the heuristics for good design, including principles of cohesion, coupling, and information hiding. Understanding and applying good design principles can speed development and enhance communication.

- **Intermediate.** Use analysis models and collaborations to discover components.

  Modeling can be applied as needed, in an agile fashion, or as a concerted effort of up-front modeling suited to more formal projects. In both cases, early identification of components, services, and their interfaces helps to stabilize the software early and allows developers to work more independently, thus increasing the team's ability to deliver iteratively.

- **Advanced.** Create detailed component and service behavior specifications to enable completely independent and even multiple implementations.

  Detailed specification requires investment, training, and discipline. Such investments are usually associated with large projects, or enterprise-level reuse and architecture efforts.

## Related Practices

- *Practice 2: Execute Your Project in Iterations* explains that component interactions should be identified and validated in early iterations using partial implementations, allowing you to make corrections inexpensively.

- *Practice 11: Leverage Legacy Systems* describes how to maximize the benefits of existing legacy systems, including how to incorporate them as components and services in larger enterprise systems.
- *Practice 13: Organize Around the Architecture* describes how teams are organized around the components in the architecture.
- *Practice 15: Leverage Patterns* describes how to use patterns as tried and true solutions. Patterns can help you to identify and refactor components. You can create your own patterns to show how your components should be used.
- *Practice 17: Actively Promote Reuse* includes components as key reusable assets that should be a part of any systematic reuse effort.
- *Practice 18: Model Key Perspectives* describes how visualizing software aids understanding. Visualizing dependencies and interactions can help you identify, understand, and evaluate components.

In general, good practices lead to more effective component development, which in turn leads to more effective overall system development.

---

## Additional Information

## Information in the Unified Process

OpenUP/Basic describes how to design and develop component-based systems. RUP includes more advanced techniques, such as how to apply business modeling and systems engineering techniques to identify large-scale components and how to build systems of systems using techniques such as use-case flow down. RUP and RUP plug-ins also provide technology and tool-specific guidance. For example, the service-oriented architecture plug-in to RUP includes a UML profile for service-oriented architectures and guidelines for designing and developing services using IBM Rational Software Architect.

## Additional Reading

For guidance on component identification and design, see the Additional Reading section in *Practice 15: Leverage Patterns* (component identification and design are key concerns of many architectural patterns).

For a good overall reference for object-oriented analysis and design and component-based development, see the following:

> Jim Arlow and Ila Neustadt. *UML and the Unified Process: Practical Object-Oriented Analysis and Design.* Addison-Wesley, 2002.

For discussion of components from the large to the small, and for guidance on adopting component-based development at an enterprise scale, see the following:

> Peter Herzum and Oliver Sims. *Business Component Factory: A Comprehensive Overview of Component-Based Development for the Enterprise.* John Wiley & Sons, 1999.

For guidance on creating detailed component specifications[16] see the following:

> John Cheesman and John Daniels. *UML Components: A Simple Process for Specifying Component-Based Software.* Addison-Wesley, 2000.

For some up-to-date examples for modeling components using UML 2.0:

> Scott W. Ambler. *The Object Primer: Agile Model-Driven Development with UML 2.0.* Cambridge University Press, 2004.

The following is an excellent article on how to move beyond abstract theory and practically implement replaceability:

> Fredrik Ferm. "The What, Why, and How of a Subsystem." *The Rational Edge,* 2003. Found online at http://www.ibm.com/developerworks.

---

16. The authors do not use standard UML, and the work predates UML 2.0, nevertheless, the guidelines and examples are worth reading.

For a description of service-oriented architectures and their relationship to components, see the following:

Dirk Krafzig, Karl Banke, and Dirk Slama. *Enterprise SOA: Service-Oriented Architecture Best Practices*. Prentice Hall, 2005.

Zoran Stojanovic and Ajantha Dahanayake, eds. *Service-Oriented Software System Engineering: Challenges and Practices*. Idea Group Publishing, 2005.

# Actively Promote Reuse

by Bruce MacIsaac

*Reusing assets can save you time and money,*
*while increasing overall quality.*

## Problem

Many organizations repeatedly build similar software and other assets that could have been reused. The problem is not only the cost of developing these assets but also the complexity and costs of maintaining the volume of unnecessary artifacts. Reuse promises a number of benefits:

- Reduced cost by building assets only once.
- Quicker delivery of new capabilities by assembling and configuring reusable components in new ways.
- Better quality through use of proven components.
- Reduced complexity through architected, standardized components.

Unfortunately, reuse at many organizations is ad hoc at best. This practice describes how to overcome barriers to reuse and how to foster a reuse culture in your organization.

## Background

We start by defining an "asset" and discussing barriers to reuse and trends enabling greater reuse.

### What Is an Asset?

When most people talk about reuse, they are usually thinking of reusing code. Reuse, however, is not limited to code. Patterns, requirements, guidelines, processes, and so forth are all candidates for reuse. For example, a reusable asset could be a collection of Java coding patterns or a set of requirements.

An asset has several desirable characteristics:

- It serves a clear purpose.
- It solves a recurring problem.
- It is relatively independent, portable, flexible, and extensible and can be reused in different contexts.
- It includes documentation of how and when it should be used, including instructions and guidance for customization.

Here are some examples of successful code assets:

- Large customizable, componentized commercial offerings like PeopleSoft and SAP.
- Middleware for integrating business systems, such as MQSeries.
- Smaller commercial components, available from retailers like ComponentSource.
- Component frameworks, such as J2EE and Microsoft .NET.
- Open source tools, frameworks, and components included in Linux, Eclipse, and Apache projects.
- Smaller open source components in repositories like SourceForge.

Here are some examples of reusable assets:

- Reusable patterns, such as IBM's e-business patterns and Microsoft's blueprints.
- Reusable requirements, such as standard requirements for globalization and supportability across an organization.[17]
- Reusable development processes, such as plug-ins to EPF or RUP.

## Barriers to Reuse

Several years ago I needed a library of geometric services for lines and surfaces on the earth. My problem was that I was dealing with large distances, and two-dimensional geometry was inadequate given the

---

17. IBM has many products with many different technologies, but despite this, many requirements, such as globalization and supportability requirements, have been standardized for the organization.

earth's spheroid shape. Knowing little about spheroids, I was strongly motivated to find code that I could reuse or adapt. I spent a lot of time asking around the company, searching the Web, and consulting various literature sources. It was difficult to know if such a library existed at all, and even more frustrating to think that the perfect library might exist, but I lacked the tools to find it.

I did find something, but it was a poor fit, as it had few of the needed services and was written in another programming language. In the end we built our own library and designed it to be reusable by any application. However, it was built for our project, and if a future project ever needed such a library, I wonder how anyone would know that our library exists. There were no mechanisms in place to encourage cross-project reuse.

Reuse has such compelling benefits that you may wonder why it tends to be the exception rather than the rule. The answer is that there are significant barriers to reuse, including the following:[18]

- Lack of incentives to identify and produce suitable reusable assets.
- Difficulty finding, assessing, and using assets.
- Architectures do not enable new items to be added.

The rest of this chapter discusses how to overcome these barriers.

## Trends Enabling Greater Reuse

Reuse is becoming easier with new technologies and approaches, including the following:

- The growth of Web-based communities sharing knowledge and assets, including both "interest groups" and open source communities. One of the newest such communities is one that inspired this book, the EPF community. This new community enables common representation and shared evolution of methodologies and methodology-related assets.
- Object Management Group (OMG) Reusable Asset Specification (RAS) effort, which standardizes the format of reusable asset libraries.

---

18. Summarized from Jacobson 1997.

Tools supporting this standard will make it easier to manage and access reusable assets.

- Rich platforms and component frameworks like Eclipse, Microsoft .NET, and J2EE make it easier to create components that integrate well with other components.
- Web services and middleware are making it easier to integrate components and existing systems in flexible ways.
- Model-driven development approaches, including platform-independent models and domain-specific languages, raise the level of abstraction, allowing for more flexible implementations, including targeting different platforms and automated application of patterns.

## Applying the Practice

The following are some strategies that can be used to foster reuse in your organization:

- Establish standards for representation.
- Capture examples.
- Promote sharing of good examples and reusable assets through communities.
- Create asset repositories.
- Foster consumption of reusable assets.
- Fund creation of reusable assets.
- Develop reusable assets incrementally.

These strategies are discussed in turn below.

## Establish Standards for Representation

Whatever the asset, reuse is easier if the representation follows some standard. The following are some different kinds of standards:

*Assets that use a standard representation are easier to reuse.*

- **External standards.** For example, standardize on UML as a modeling representation.

- **Common tools.** For example, choosing a standard tool to manage requirements allows sharing of examples and best practices for the use of the tool to manage requirements.
- **Templates.** For example, if you want to reuse requirements, a standard format for representing use cases will make them easier to reuse.
- **Technologies.** Choosing standard technologies such as .NET, and then building components that work in the resulting framework, will make it easier to mix and match components. Consider standards-based platforms such as J2EE and open platforms like Eclipse if you wish to avoid locking into a single vendor's solution.
- **Guidelines.** For example, standard coding guidelines result in code that is easier to use and understand across a broad community.

A standard methodology like RUP is a great facilitator for standardizing representation. Many companies have created plug-ins to RUP to deliver standard templates, notations, guidelines, and tool usage guidelines (tool mentors).

## Capture Examples

Copying and modifying from examples are generally the most common forms of reuse. They don't have the visibility of large-scale systematic reuse, because you can't easily tell that the reuse happens; material reused this way is rarely cited. However, improving efficiency on lots of small tasks adds up, so this kind of reuse should be encouraged.[19] How does it happen?

Let's say you need to produce a certain kind of document, code, or data, and you don't know what to do. You could thumb through some books, read through guidance in RUP or EPF, or work through guidance in a template, but after a while you become frustrated with trying to interpret the guidance. You cry out, "Don't tell me—show me!"

---

19. Note that this is about adapting examples to learn how to apply a pattern, not about duplication. Duplication of code is discouraged, because duplicated code is hard to maintain.

Many practitioners turn to the example grapevine; they ask their colleagues, post requests on forums, and if they are lucky they unearth an example. If they are very lucky, it is a good example.

A lot of time could be saved if good examples were made available. Sometimes there are confidentiality concerns, sometimes there is resistance just because the examples aren't "showcase quality." One way to start is to make a repository available for completed project artifacts and require these artifacts to be stored in the shared repository upon project completion.

*Sharing good examples adds up to major savings.*

Some companies have confidentiality concerns that prevent cross-company sharing of all artifacts, which limits the effectiveness of this simple approach. "Sanitizing"—removing sensitive information—is a solution that can still allow many artifacts to be shared.

Sharing artifacts has many limitations: it doesn't scale, there is no way to assess quality, and each "reuser" has to make changes to take advantage of the assets. Defects in the original artifact multiply with each copy, and improvements in one copy don't easily flow to others. More systematic approaches to reuse are described in later sections.

## Promote Sharing of Good Examples and Reusable Assets Through Communities

One way to promote good examples is to establish communities with a focus on excellence in a particular part of the software development process. For example, IBM has communities for visual modeling, testing, requirements, and so on. If you need to find a good example, you can post requests on the community forum, contact community experts directly, or search through a community's shared file area. This approach is one step up from the informal grapevine.

Communities can also provide feedback and encouragement to practitioners who create good examples or reusable assets. Additional incentives, either as recognition in annual appraisals or some financial incentive program, can also promote the creation of assets. Incentives should be based on actual reuse, to avoid collecting a lot of supposedly reusable assets that are never reused.

*Communities provide a forum and incentives to share assets.*

Some organizations go beyond simple communities by creating "community source" projects. The idea of "community source" is to mimic the successful practices of open source projects, but within the scope of an organization. As with open source projects, community source projects are successful only if there is a critical mass of individuals willing to participate.

Communities are easy to set up. Free services are offered by Yahoo!, MSN, and several other online services.[20]

## Create Asset Repositories

*Asset repositories need categorization, search, and feedback mechanisms.*

As the number and diversity of reusable assets grow, some method of managing these assets becomes necessary. The keys to managing large reusable asset repositories are an effective categorization scheme, search mechanism, and feedback mechanism. Consider the Amazon online bookstore as a model for reuse, except that "asset" replaces "book." You can browse or search by categories such as subject or author. More important, it is easy for individuals to post comments and provide a rating so that a potential buyer can benefit from the experience of others.

Note that the OMG has recently adopted a reusable asset specification (RAS). This specification provides a set of guidelines and recommendations about the structure, content, and descriptions of reusable software assets. There are some advantages to standardizing asset repositories on such a standard:

- You can migrate easily to other tools and environments that support the standard.
- It becomes possible to search across repositories, even repositories produced by third parties (a virtual super-repository).
- It fosters good documentation of assets, including categorization, examples, feedback, and so on.

---

20. For Yahoo! groups, see http://groups.yahoo.com. For MSN groups, see http://groups.msn.com.

## Foster Consumption of Reusable Assets

If you have taken the time to produce reusable assets, you should take the following steps to foster their use:

- Advertise the existence of assets to end users.
- Train end users in how to find and assess assets.
- Use a development process that encourages reuse.

## Fund Creation of Reusable Assets

The biggest benefits of reuse accrue when substantial assets are reused many times. Creating such assets can be a valuable investment, but they need to be identified, produced, managed, and made available for consumption (see Figure 6.9).

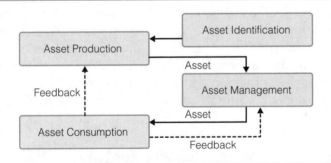

**FIGURE 6.9 Reuse Program Management.** *Reuse of significant assets across the enterprise requires a dedicated reuse program that enables assets to be identified, produced, managed, and consumed.*

Reuse of significant assets across an enterprise requires a dedicated reuse program.

*Reuse of significant assets across an enterprise requires a dedicated reuse program.*

As with every project, an enterprise-level reuse program should have the following:

- A vision that defines objectives and sets the direction.
- A business case that justifies the required expenditures.
- Adequate funding to realize the objectives.

- An architecture that enables reuse.
- A software development process that covers the following:
  - Management of requirements and change requests from clients
  - Management of different versions of assets and dependencies between assets
  - Measurement of success/return on investment

In addition, an enterprise-level reuse program benefits from the following:

- An enterprise business model that defines the goals and processes that drive the business.
- An enterprise architecture that allows for improved integration between systems, coordinated adoption of new technologies, and ensured effectiveness of overall business processes.[21]

You also need a governance process to manage dependencies and priorities as you evolve assets. Users of an asset may have competing needs that drive the asset in different directions. Which changes should be included? Should everybody update to the latest version? If not, how will you maintain multiple versions? The references listed in the Additional Information section can help you address these and other management, cultural, and technical challenges facing enterprise reuse efforts.

## Develop Reusable Assets Incrementally

Building a successful reuse program is a challenging endeavor, and failures are common. Many programs result in repositories full of "reuseless"[22] assets, that is, assets that are potentially reusable but are nevertheless not reused. Why does this happen?

If you build an asset to meet the needs of future projects, you are assuming that you can predict the needs of those projects. Unfortunately, it is very difficult to predict future needs, because needs

---

21. See the Additional Information section for references on these topics.
22. The term "reuseless" comes from Ambler 2005.

change and technologies evolve. Assets built for the "future" clutter repositories waiting for a future that never comes.

Instead of focusing on reuse for an unknown future, consider the reuse needs of existing projects. Identify two projects that have a common need, and evaluate the likelihood that additional projects will have a similar need. If you have a family of related systems, the benefits of reuse can be obvious.[23] But sometimes there is simply not enough commonality to justify a reuse effort.

A rule of thumb is that unless you expect to reuse an asset more than three times,[24] it is not worth trying to make it reusable.

Once you have a business case for creating an asset, focus on the needs of the immediate projects that plan to use it, and evolve the asset over time to support additional projects. Generalizing a few assets of proven value to meet the needs of specific projects builds early success, and avoids building assets that don't get reused.

*Generalize assets for specific projects to ensure good return on investment.*

## Other Methods

While XP doesn't directly say much about reuse, its principles and practices affect how reuse is applied on XP projects. Let's discuss some examples.

The high level of communication on XP teams, along with shared development, enables the team to share knowledge of potential assets and reuse opportunities. The XP search for "the simplest thing that could possibly work" encourages reuse when this is the simplest solution. The incremental design approach discourages big up-front design of reusable components, but continuous testing and continuous improvement through refactoring can result in quality components with potential for reuse.

---

23. Glass 2003 points out that most reuse success stories come from families of related systems.

24. Glass 2003 and Ambler 2005 make reference to this rule of 3.

*Integrate reused components in early iterations to ensure that they work as expected.*

These principles and practices are compatible with the Unified Process. However, the Unified Process explicitly addresses reuse as one of many architectural decisions, including guidance for making build versus buy versus reuse decisions, as well as advice on the benefits and pitfalls inherent in reusing existing assets. In particular, the Unified Process recommends integrating reused components in early iterations to ensure that they work as expected.

Creation of reusable assets is not part of OpenUP/Basic, but is included in RUP. Partner extensions to RUP provide additional depth (see the Additional Information section on page 299).

Scrum doesn't directly address reuse.

## Levels of Adoption

This practice can be adopted at three different levels:

- **Basic.** Establish a common representation for each kind of artifact that you want to reuse.

    Promote sharing of examples and reusable assets through communities that have a shared file area and forum.

    All reuse efforts involve some investment, and they pay off in increased ability to deliver more and deliver more quickly. This basic approach requires a minimum of investment, yet generates good results.

- **Intermediate.** Promote education and use of open standards, reference architectures, patterns, common and shared processes, component frameworks, component architectures, and service-oriented architectures.

    Investing in your organizations' technical knowledge in these areas increases their ability to create better-quality assets that are potentially reusable.

- **Advanced.** Fund the creation of reusable assets through a dedicated reuse program.

    Dedicated reuse programs involve substantial investment and risk. However, in cases where the organization has substantially overlapping development work, there can be significant payoffs.

## Related Practices

- *Practice 16: Architect with Components and Services* and *Practice 15: Leverage Patterns* describes components, services, and patterns. These practices encourage reuse and aid in the creation of reusable assets, because they define systems in terms of reused and potentially reusable parts.
- *Practice 18: Model Key Perspectives* describes how modeling aids understanding and communication. Modeling is an effective way to document reusable software assets. Model-driven development approaches can also raise the level of abstraction, resulting in more flexible components. For example, a component can be expressed using a platform-independent model that is transformed into different platform-specific models.
- *Other practices*: Reusable assets are created following the same principles as nonreusable assets. In this sense all the practices in this book are applicable.

## Additional Information

### Information in the Unified Process

OpenUP/Basic recommends that projects reuse existing assets, but it doesn't go into the details of organizational reuse efforts. OpenUP/Basic, however, can be applied to projects that produce or improve reusable assets.

RUP provides specific guidance for asset production, consumption, and management in the *Asset-Based Development* plug-in. In addition, the *Systems Engineering* plug-in to RUP covers how systems of systems can be constructed, and the *Business Modeling* plug-in to RUP describes how to model business processes to identify opportunities for automation and reuse.

Flashline is a company that specializes in software reuse consulting and has produced a RUP plug-in for managing software asset portfolios. This plug-in is available from the company's Web site at http://www.flashline.com.

## Additional Reading

For guidance on setting up and running a dedicated reuse program:

> Jacobson, Griss, and Jonsson. *Software Reuse: Architecture, Process, and Organization for Business Success*. Addison-Wesley, 1997.

> Hafedh Mili. *Reuse-Based Software Engineering: Techniques, Organizations, and Controls*. John Wiley & Sons, 2002.

For guidance on enterprise-level reuse as an extension to RUP, including enterprise business models and enterprise architecture:

> Scott Ambler et al. *The Enterprise Unified Process: Extending the Rational Unified Process*. Prentice Hall, 2005.

For guidance on reuse as part of product line development:

> Paul Clements. *Software Product Lines: Practices and Patterns*. Addison-Wesley, 2002.

> Jack Greenfield et al. *Software Factories: Assembling Applications with Patterns, Models, Frameworks, and Tools*. John Wiley & Sons, 2004.

# Model Key Perspectives

by Bruce MacIsaac

*Modeling raises the level of abstraction and allows the system to be more easily understood from different perspectives.*

## Problem

As software systems become more and more complex, and as distributed teams strive to communicate more effectively, there is an increasing need to use abstraction to deal with complexity, to simplify understanding, and to become more productive.

Models raise the level of abstraction, and their powerful ability to provide information in a simple, intuitive form improves the understanding of everyone involved. Models can focus on a particular perspective

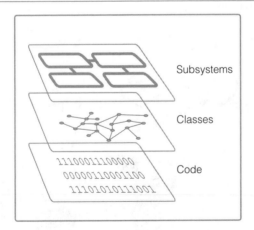

**FIGURE 6.10 Levels of Abstraction.** *Models raise the level of abstraction, allowing you to focus on important aspects such as relationships and patterns rather than getting bogged down in details. (From RUP v7.0.)*

that addresses particular concerns of particular stakeholders, which aids communication. This in turn helps teams to do the following:

- Detect errors and omissions.
- Explore and compare alternatives at a low cost.
- Understand the impact of changes.

These general benefits apply to all forms of modeling, including requirements modeling, business process modeling, software design, and even your house's wiring diagrams. This practice focuses on modeling key perspectives for software development.

## Background

*Models filter out unwanted details so that you can focus.*

Imagine you wanted to meet someone through a dating service, and your date was described solely in terms of his or her chemical makeup and relative positions of molecules in space. While completely accurate, such a description would be useless; you really want a higher abstraction, such as height, intelligence, and personality. Models are simplifications of systems that filter out unwanted details so that you can focus on particular aspects.

**FIGURE 6.11 Models Are Simplifications of Systems.**

As software systems get larger, models that capture the "big picture," the major structural elements and patterns of behavior, become especially important. Visual representations are particularly useful, as human beings are very efficient at processing visual information. Graphics that show relationships and interactions of software elements can be read at a glance. Many errors have patterns that are easily spotted in a visual representation (see Figure 6.12).

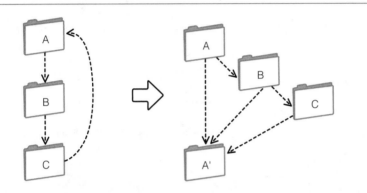

**FIGURE 6.12 Structure Diagrams.** *Structure diagrams are one way to visualize a system. In this example the first diagram shows a cyclic dependency between packages. The second diagram shows this corrected through refactoring.*

For example, Figure 6.12 shows dependencies between packages A, B, and C. You can easily see the circular dependency relationship between A and C. Structure diagrams like these enable developers to reason about a system, exploring alternatives such as splitting A to remove the cyclic dependency, as shown in the right half of the figure.

Behavior can also be represented visually, for example using a UML activity diagram, as shown in Figure 6.13.

The arrows show how the processing flows, while decision nodes such as "baggage/no baggage" show alternative flows. Because it doesn't take long to learn the meaning of the various symbols, subject matter experts can evaluate the system behavior for missing steps or incorrect sequences even if they cannot read code.

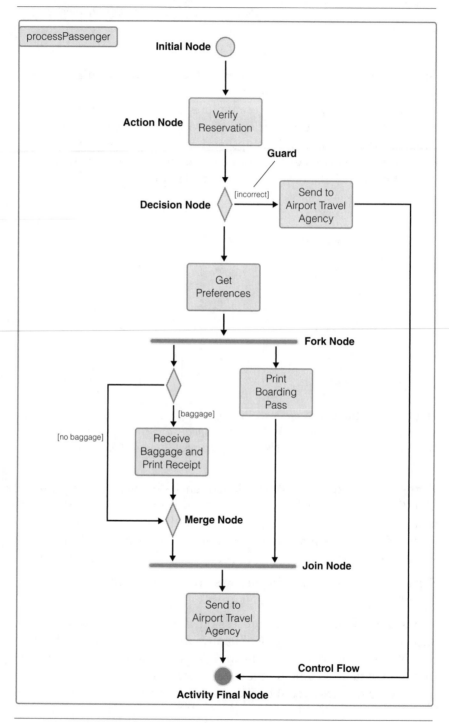

**FIGURE 6.13 Example of a UML Activity Diagram.** *UML diagrams visually model behaviors. (From RUP v7.0.)*

Visual modeling is just one way to model. This practice describes some useful modeling practices and explains when they are best applied.

## Applying the Practice

This section describes how to focus your modeling efforts on key perspectives, starting with basic design sketches. It also provides an overview of model-driven development approaches in which a visual model becomes the implementation.

## Identify the Key Perspectives

The most important perspectives are not the same for every system. For systems with a large and complex database, the data perspective is important to model. For others, concurrency may be important. When deciding what to model, you should start with the most complex aspects of the system, which is where modeling can help the most.

*Focus on the most complex aspects of the system first.*

Before modeling anything, you should understand the purpose of the model. What information should be conveyed? What information should be hidden? Who will benefit from the model? Is the model worth the effort to maintain?

Usually, it is best to start with informal models—such as rough sketches, tables in a spreadsheet, or notes in an e-mail—that focus on a single purpose.

## Sketch the Design

Design sketches are an effective way to capture ideas, so that you can see the "big picture." Sketches are particularly useful for design brainstorming sessions, because you can use them to focus on aspects that your group is interested in.

For example, sketches of a large system should include major subsystems, their interfaces, and their interactions. Such sketches are key to understanding how a large system is composed. Sketches of structure and behavior within subsystems in turn help to provide an understanding of the internals of subsystems.

Initial sketches should be created quickly and revised dynamically as new ideas and trade-offs are considered. Because whiteboards are quick and easy to use, they are good for design sketches. However, results are hard to capture and share with geographically dispersed colleagues. Software modeling tools can be great as a "virtual whiteboard" for design sketching, as they allow standard shapes to be selected and connected quickly and easily. However, once a sketch conveys the right information, it is more important to validate the design than make the sketch pretty. The best software designers refactor their designs, so don't waste time cleaning up a graphic in the early stages of design.

*Intersperse sketching, implementation, and refactoring.* Sketches should be considered as a way to capture or communicate ideas, not as a step that has to precede implementation. It is often useful to write some code to try out a design idea or to learn how to use an unfamiliar component, while a sketch may work better as a way to understand relationships and communicate with others. Each activity benefits and complements the other.

In particular, you should avoid creating volumes of detailed design before creating an implementation. Implementing should be done early, to ensure that design ideas actually work in practice—not just on paper.

## Agree on a Standard Notation

For a small group of people, informal notations can work reasonably well; you can draw some shapes and invent a notation as you go along. However, for larger audiences, a formal notation helps avoid confusion.

Many notations have been proposed for various languages and environments. For object-oriented software design, the UML is dominant. UML has also been extended to other domains, such as business modeling and data modeling, but competes with other notations in these domains.

*The common notation of UML makes cross-domain communication easier.* All other things being equal (tool support, richness of notation, and so on), we recommend UML-based notations. Once you know the basics of UML, it's easier to learn additional UML-based notations. If business modelers, data modelers, and object modelers are using similar notations, it will be easier to evolve business objects into classes in object models and transform classes in object models to tables in data models. The common notation of UML makes cross-domain communication easier.

## Visualize the Code

The latest software development platforms are providing more and more ways to view code. For example, you can capture the results of running tests as sequence diagrams. As another example, you can automatically generate diagrams to show dependencies between code elements. These visualizations help developers to understand their code better and relate it to the intended design.

*Code visualization helps developers to relate code to design.*

## Document Key Architectural Perspectives

There are many arguments for and against documenting design. Up-to-date design documentation can help testers, developers, and maintainers understand the system, enabling them to work more effectively. However, design documentation can easily become obsolete and cause harm by communicating wrong information.

Managers responsible for large legacy systems often suffer from the following problem: the original developers have left and nobody understands the implementation, so it is very difficult to make changes. How could this problem have been avoided? One way would have been to maintain the design documentation. Another would have been to ensure that the code remained well structured and self-documenting as it evolved.

Well-written, understandable code is better than poor code that is well documented. But documentation still has value if you can maintain it efficiently.

One approach to ensure efficiency is to focus on the highest-value documentation. It is this part of the design that many people need to understand and that will be referenced frequently as the system evolves.

You'll want to start by documenting the architecture. Architecture encompasses the key design decisions, including the most important components, patterns, and interactions. A concise description of the architecture is usually worth maintaining, as it helps your team understand how the parts fit into the whole and reminds them of the

*An architectural description enables understanding of key parts and patterns.*

patterns to be followed. Diagrams can be particularly useful to hide unnecessary detail and focus on a particular architectural concern.

Architecture is best described from multiple perspectives or "views." RUP suggests the following views:[25]

- *Logical view*—describes the structure and interactions of design classes and components.
- *Implementation view*—describes how the code is organized into elements for version control and deployment.
- *Process view*—describes concurrency.
- *Deployment view*—describes how software is distributed across processing nodes.
- *Requirements (or use case) view*—describes the requirements that drive the other views.

Most projects start with the logical and requirements views and then add other views as needed.

## Use a Model-Driven Development Approach

Software development started with binary language, moved to assembly languages, shifted to higher-level languages such as FORTRAN and C, and later moved to languages such as Java and C#. Each step on the way enabled great gains in expressiveness; developers could solve problems with less effort.

*Model-driven development is the next step in the evolution of software implementation.*

Model-driven development (MDD) is the next step in that evolution. In an MDD approach, the model is essentially a high-level language. Developers create and evolve models that can be transformed into code or executed directly. By modeling instead of coding, developers can express solutions in terms closer to the problem being solved, and by using a visual notation, developers can better understand and communicate how a system works.

The Object Management Group (OMG) is defining a standard approach to MDD, called model-driven architecture (MDA). MDA describes

---

25. First proposed in Kruchten 1995 as the "4+1 Views."

development in terms of successive model transformations. For example, a model is created that describes the structure and behavior of the system in conceptual terms, without specifying a particular platform. This is called a platform-independent model (PIM). Transformations can then be applied to create a model that targets a specific platform, such as J2EE or Microsoft .NET. The result is a platform-specific model (PSM). The PSM can, in turn, be transformed into executable code.

This approach promises a number of benefits:

- **More efficient development.** Descriptions of the problem to be solved are more quickly converted into implementations.
- **Higher quality.** Each model can be evaluated from a quality perspective.
- **Greater reuse.** More abstract models have more general applicability.
- **Long-term maintainability.** A platform-independent design is less affected by technology churn as platforms evolve.

MDA is still in an early stage of evolution. However, early adopters are reporting some successes,[26] and there are many tools[27] that support MDA in terms of generating code from models, and transforming models to models.

One notable example is the Eclipse modeling framework (EMF), an open source MDA implementation with broad applicability. With EMF you can specify a model using UML, XML, or annotated Java and use that model to generate a nearly complete Java application with a default user interface and data persistency. The generated Java classes provide basic create, update, and delete code, as well as notification, persistency to XMI, and lots of other code that can be used as is or extended as needed. Models or code can be updated and synchronized with each other. [28]

---

26. See http://www.omg.org/mda/products_success.htm.

27. See http://www.omg.org/mda/committed-products.htm.

28. EMF was used to develop both EPF (see Appendix A), and RMC (see Appendix B).

## Other Methods

Traditional waterfall development is based on an up-front design approach, usually using some kind of model. However, waterfall development does not validate the model with running code until late in the project, which is a risky time to discover design flaws. Traditional development methods also tend to create a lot of design documentation that is difficult to maintain, rather than focusing on key architectural perspectives.

XP takes an incremental design approach, focusing on constantly improving the code through refactoring. XP is compatible with an MDD approach; you just recognize that the model represents a higher-level programming language[29] and develop incrementally using that language. XP doesn't encourage or discourage sketching the design using UML diagrams. You can diagram if you want, but diagram only what you need, create tests and code, and then discard the diagrams.

*The Unified Process encourages diagramming to evolve designs and to document key architectural perspectives.*

Like XP, the Unified Process encourages an evolving design, but unlike XP, the Unified Process encourages diagramming as a means of evolving the design and documenting the architecture from key perspectives. The most important diagrams are maintained. Others are maintained only if there is tool support that makes it easy.

In terms of visual modeling, the Unified Process and XP differ on the topic of architecture. The Unified Process encourages defining an architecture, whereas XP does not. RUP then goes beyond the needs of most small projects by including optional specialized techniques, such as business modeling, simulation, round-trip engineering, and code-and-test visualization.

Agile modeling is a development approach that recognizes the value of using models (both visual and nonvisual) and includes guidance on how to model efficiently and effectively. Most of the core principles and practices, such as "software is your primary goal" and "model in small increments," are consistent with the Unified Process. Agile

---

29. Beck 2000 discusses this in "role of pictures in design."

modeling focuses on design sketching, because it offers high value and is relatively easy for developers to adopt. The Unified Process recognizes the value of design sketching but also encourages MDD.

## Levels of Adoption

This practice can be adopted at different levels:

- **Basic.** Use informal models to understand and communicate ideas.

  Creating informal models, such as design sketches, can speed development by enhancing understanding and communication. This moves you down and to the left on the process map.

- **Intermediate.** Document the architecture using UML.

  Maintaining the architecture is a moderate investment that pays off in many ways: the entire team understands the system better; software is stabilized early; and developers can work more independently, thus increasing the team's ability to deliver iteratively. This moves you down on the process map.

- **Advanced.** Use an MDD approach.

  MDD requires investment and training. However, both small and large teams may benefit significantly from the increased productivity. This moves you down and to the right on the process map.

## Related Practices

- *Practice 15: Leverage Patterns* describes how to use patterns as tried and true solutions and how they can be applied in modeling environments.
- *Practice 16: Architect with Components and Services* describes how components and services lead to better architectures. Visual modeling is an effective way to document components and services.

More generally, visual modeling helps you to define a clear architecture, which supports practices related to managing change, organizing teams, and so on.

## Additional Information

### Information in the Unified Process

Visual modeling plays a role throughout RUP and OpenUP/Basic. However, OpenUP/Basic takes a very light approach—models are informal and optional and are used to communicate and understand. RUP expands on informal modeling to cover additional model-driven approaches, including round-trip engineering and MDA approaches. RUP also provides technology-specific guidance, such as J2EE and .NET, as well as tool-specific guidance, such as guidance for a variety of visual modeling environments.

### Additional Reading

To learn more about UML, see the following:

> Michael Chonoles. *UML 2 for Dummies*. John Wiley & Sons, 2003.
>
> James Rumbaugh, Ivar Jacobson, and Grady Booch. *The Unified Modeling Language Reference Manual, Second Edition*. Addison-Wesley, 2004.

For guidance on how to practice modeling in an agile fashion, see the following:

> Scott Ambler. *The Object Primer, Third Edition, Agile Model-Driven Development with UML 2.0*. Cambridge University Press, 2004.
>
> Martin Fowler. *Is Design Dead?* (Keynote XP 2000 conference). Found online at http://www.martinfowler.com/.

For the latest on the evolution of MDA and MDD, see the following:

> http://www.omg.org/mda and http://www.ibm.com/software/rational/mda/

To learn more about EMF, see the following:

> Bill Moore et al. *Eclipse Development Using the Graphical Editing Framework and the Eclipse Modeling Framework*, IBM 2004, available at http://ibm.com/redbook.

# CHAPTER 7

# Adapt the Process

| | |
|---|---|
| *Benefits* | • Lifecycle efficiency. |
| | • Open and honest communication of risks. |
| *Patterns* | 1. Rightsize the process to the project needs, including the size and distribution of the project team, to the complexity of the application, and to the need for compliance. |
| | 2. Adapt process ceremony to lifecycle phase. |
| | 3. Improve the process continuously. |
| | 4. Balance project plans and associated estimates with the uncertainty of a project. |
| *Anti-Patterns* | • Always see more process, more documentation, and more detailed up-front planning as better, including insistence on early estimates and adherence to those estimates. |
| | • Use the same amount of process throughout the project. |

This principle states that it is critical to rightsize the development process to the needs of the project. It is not a question of more being better, or of less being better. Rather, the amount of ceremony, precision, and control present in a project must be tailored according to a variety of factors—including the size and distribution of teams, the amount of externally imposed constraints, and the phase the project is in.

More process—whether usage of more artifacts, production of more detailed documentation, development and maintenance of more models that need to be synchronized, or more formal reviews—is not necessarily better. Rather, you need to *rightsize the process to project needs*. As a project grows in size, becomes more distributed, uses more complex technology, has more stakeholders, and needs to adhere to more stringent compliance standards, the process needs to become more disciplined. But for smaller projects with collocated teams and known technology, the process should be more streamlined.

Second, a project should *adapt process ceremony to lifecycle phase*. The beginning of a project is typically accompanied by considerable uncertainty, and you want to encourage a lot of creativity to develop an application that addresses the business needs. More process typically leads to less creativity, not more, so you should use less process at the beginning of a project, when uncertainty is an everyday factor. On the other hand, late in the project you often want to introduce more control, such as feature freeze or change control boards, to remove undesired creativity and risks associated with late introduction of defects. This situation translates to more process late in the project.

Third, an organization should strive to *continuously improve the process*. Do an assessment at the end of each iteration and at the project's end to capture lessons learned, and leverage that knowledge to improve the process. Encourage all team members to look continuously for opportunities to improve.

Fourth, you need to *balance project plans and associated estimates with the uncertainty of a project*. This means that early on in a project, when uncertainty typically runs fairly high, plans and associated estimates need to focus on big-picture planning and outlines rather than aim to provide five-digit levels of precision where clearly none exist. Early development activities should aim to drive out uncertainty and enable gradual increases in planning precision.

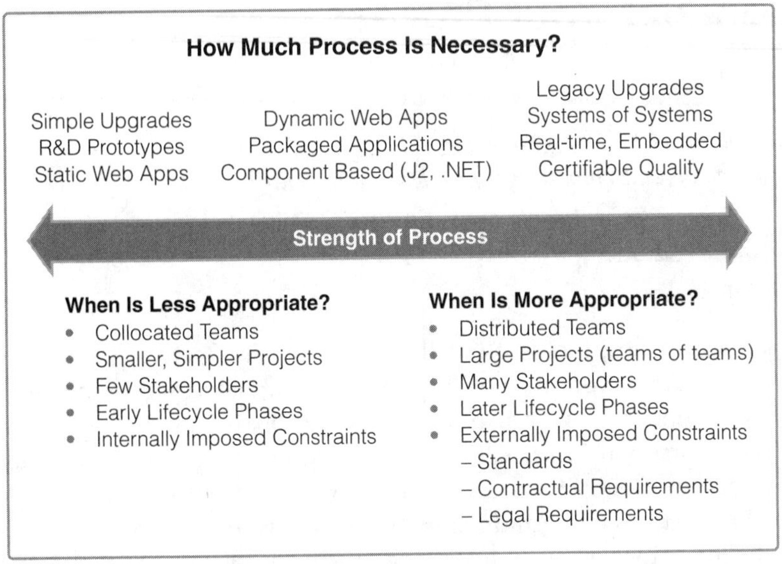

**How Much Process Is Necessary?**

|  |  |  |
|---|---|---|
| Simple Upgrades<br>R&D Prototypes<br>Static Web Apps | Dynamic Web Apps<br>Packaged Applications<br>Component Based (J2, .NET) | Legacy Upgrades<br>Systems of Systems<br>Real-time, Embedded<br>Certifiable Quality |

**Strength of Process**

**When Is Less Appropriate?**
- Collocated Teams
- Smaller, Simpler Projects
- Few Stakeholders
- Early Lifecycle Phases
- Internally Imposed Constraints

**When Is More Appropriate?**
- Distributed Teams
- Large Projects (teams of teams)
- Many Stakeholders
- Later Lifecycle Phases
- Externally Imposed Constraints
  - Standards
  - Contractual Requirements
  - Legal Requirements

**FIGURE 7.1 Factors Driving the Amount of Process Discipline.** *Many factors— project size, team distributions, complexity of technology, the number of stakeholders, compliance requirements, the particular stage of the project—determine how disciplined a process you need.*

An anti-pattern to following this principle would be to see more process and more detailed up-front planning as always better, including insistence on early estimates and adherence to those estimates. Another anti-pattern would be to use the same amount of process throughout the project.

This chapter describes a series of practices that will help you to adapt the process to the context of your project or organization:

- *Practice 19: Rightsize Your Process* explains how you can work more effectively by focusing only on the activities in your process for which the benefit of the activity is greater than the cost.

- *Practice 20: Continuously Reevaluate What You Do* offers guidelines for how you can improve your working procedures by always challenging what you do.

Let's have a look at these practices!

# Rightsize Your Process

by Per Kroll

*Choosing the right amount of process allows your
project to maximize productivity while gaining agility.*

## Problem

Projects with no process typically do not work effectively, since they
are forced to reinvent proven approaches to attack common problems
and also tend to run into more collaboration issues due to unclear
division of responsibilities. Projects with too much process may suffer
from lack of creativity and productivity due to enforcement of artifacts and activities that add limited or no value to the challenges at
hand. This practice provides guidelines on how to choose the right
amount of process based on your needs.

## Background

We have come a long way in the United States since the days of the
Wild West, when an alleged criminal got a quick, though not always
fair, trial. But given the large number of crimes, the rapid population
growth, and the lack of trained professionals, most people in Wild
West society were probably happy with the process and saw little reason to change it. Speed and simplicity were more important than
quality.

However, we believe that today most people prefer the more rigorous
trial process currently used in the United States. It may not be perfect,
but it provides much stricter guidelines for the police, prosecutor, and
defense lawyers regarding what is and is not acceptable behavior. In
the end, hopefully, it leads to fewer unfair trials, which most people in
today's society find more reprehensible than delayed trials. From this
example we see that the amount of process needs to be adapted to fit

the needs of the various stakeholders. What is right for one situation may not be right for another.

My wife and I are currently building a new balcony, and to do so we need a construction permit. One of our neighbors is probably very happy that one of the prerequisites for this permit is permission from all our neighbors, because that enabled him to insist that we plant some trees to provide him with a reasonable amount of privacy. However, the process of obtaining a permit involved many other steps that I did not care too much for. We needed to prove that the other houses in the neighborhood have a similar look and feel, we needed to provide three revisions of the plans, we needed to get approval from several different departments, we had to meet with some departments many times, we had to have several inspections, and so on. Overall, the permit process probably increased our cost by 50 percent and more than doubled the duration of this pretty simple project, as well as forcing us to reduce the size of the balcony to avoid an even more rigorous permit process. All in all, even though certain steps were very valuable, I found the permit process overly cumbersome and unhelpful. If you do not continuously take active steps to simplify a process, it often ends up being overly bureaucratic and inefficient.

Philippe Kruchten expressed it well[1]: "The purpose of a software engineering process is not to make developers' lives miserable, or to squash creativity under massive amounts of paperwork. Its only real purpose is to ensure that a software development organization can predictably engineer and deliver high-quality software that meets all of the needs and requirements of its users—on schedule and within budget."

But how do you choose the right amount of process for your project to ensure productivity, predictability, and quality without losing too much in creativity and flexibility? The answer will vary based on your situation. Let's have a look at some guidelines that will help you to "rightsize" your process.

---

1. Kroll 2003.

## Applying the Practice

A project will be more effective if you rightsize your process, that is, focus on executable software rather than supporting artifacts and produce only artifacts that add value. You need to choose both the right level of ceremony for your project and the extent to which you should do iterative development—what we refer to as understanding where you should be on the process map (see Figure 7.2), and you need to scale your process accordingly. You need to automate mundane tasks and continuously improve your process through assessment and refinement. Let's have a look at each of these activities.

## Focus on Executable Software, Not Supporting Artifacts

*Producing executable software is often the fastest way of mitigating risk.*

A clear focus on executable software promotes the right thinking among your team; you run less risk of overanalyzing and theorizing and can instead get down to work to prove whether solution A or B is better. Forcing closure by producing executable software is often the fastest way of mitigating risk.

*Artifacts other than the actual software are supporting artifacts.*

A focus on executable software means that *artifacts other than the actual software are supporting artifacts.* They are there to allow you to produce better software. By staying focused on executable software, you are better prepared to assess whether producing other artifacts—such as requirement management plans, configuration management plans, use cases, test plans, and so on—will really lead to software that works better and is easier to maintain. In many cases the answer is yes, but not always.

You need to weigh the cost of producing and maintaining an artifact against the benefit of producing it. The benefit of producing many artifacts typically increases as your project grows larger; you have more complicated stakeholder relations, your team becomes distributed, the cost of quality issues increases, and the software becomes more critical to the business. All these factors are an incentive to produce more artifacts and treat them more formally. But for every project you should strive to minimize the number of artifacts produced, to reduce overhead, and to focus on executable software.

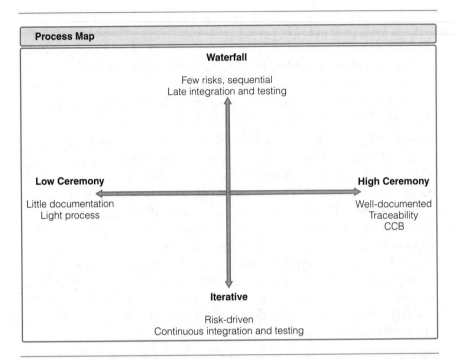

**FIGURE 7.2 Process Map for Process Comparison.** *By organizing processes and process assessment frameworks along two dimensions—Low Ceremony/High Ceremony and Waterfall/Iterative—you can compare them and analyze which are the most suitable for your project or organization. (Adapted from Kroll 2003.)*

## Produce Only Artifacts That Add Value

In most projects you will ask yourself, "Should we produce this artifact or not?" On the one hand, "cowboy projects" pay no attention to process and, as can be expected, leverage too few artifacts. On the other hand, some projects pay too much attention to process and tend to use too many artifacts rather than too few. As an example, one of the most common mistakes RUP users make is to produce artifacts just because RUP describes how to produce them. RUP is a rich, customizable knowledge base, with, among others, artifacts suitable for large-scale, safety-critical systems. But that doesn't mean that those artifacts should be used. Small, nonsafety-critical projects simply should not use artifacts not aimed at them. To reduce the number of artifacts you produce, cut down on the number of *types* of artifacts you have in your process. Also, do not assume that just because your process describes an artifact of a certain type, such as a use-case realization, you need to produce a use-case realization for *every* use case. It may be sufficient to produce use-case realizations only for the use cases for which you have complex collaborations.

*Reduce the amount of artifacts by changing the way team members collaborate.*

You should also look for opportunities to reduce the amount of artifacts, and the level of details used when producing an artifact, by changing the way team members collaborate. In the past you may, for example, have produced very comprehensive requirements specifications to ensure that developers understood what they should implement. By improving the collaboration between analysts and developers, you may be able to reduce the time spent on formal documentation of requirements. When requirements are unclear, developers ask for clarifications, and by having developers show prototypes as they evolve, analysts can clarify the requirements as needed. The closer collaboration may not only reduce the documentation cost but also improve the quality of both the requirements and the code.

*If you are in doubt as to whether or not to produce an artifact, don't.*[2] But do not use this guideline as an excuse to skip essential activities such as setting a vision, clarifying a business case, documenting requirements, developing a design, and planning the testing effort. Each of these activities produces artifacts of obvious value. If the cost of producing an artifact is going to be higher than the value of having it, however, you should skip it.

*Some artifacts are not there to assist the project team, but to assist the organization.*

It is worth noting that some artifacts are not there to assist the project team per se, but to assist the organization to achieve certain objectives, such as ISO-9001 certification, enterprise reuse, financial reporting, management oversight, tracking of metrics to improve predictability of future projects, and so on. For such artifacts, it is essential for the project team to involve appropriate stakeholders in decisions regarding whether or not the artifacts should be produced.

---

2. Ambler 2004 refers to this as "Model with a Purpose."

If you choose to produce an artifact, you also need to determine the right strategy for maintaining the artifact. Some artifacts may be treated as throwaways, others may always need to be kept current, and some may be updated only when it hurts.[3]

## Understand Where Your Project Should Be on the Process Map

To guide you in how much process to use, and what type, it helps to think of where your projects should be on the process map described in Chapter 1 and shown in Figure 7.2. By figuring out where the "sweet spot" for your project is on the process map, you can better understand how to customize or augment the process you are using now. Should you go for more or less discipline? Table 7.1 lists some of the factors that determine how much discipline is appropriate for your project. If your project requires more discipline, use the practice adoption levels cited in this book to determine what steps you need to take to move your project to the right on the process map. For information on what factors drive iteration length, and hence where you should be on the $y$ axis of the process map, see Table 2.3 in *Practice 2: Execute Your Project in Iterations*.

As listed in Table 7.1, one of the factors that determines the appropriate amount of discipline is where you are in the project, or whether you are in early or late lifecycle phases. This factor is often poorly understood. Early in the project you are working with a great many unknowns, so you want to follow a process that enables you to change and augment your solution rapidly, without being bogged down by a lot of rigor and discipline. Late in the project, you want to stabilize your code and make only changes that are well motivated. You thus need to introduce more rigor toward later lifecycle phases (see *Practice 3: Embrace and Manage Change*). A common anti-pattern is to have high degrees of ceremony throughout the project, but more process has never helped foster the creativity you often need in early phases to build the right solution.

*One factor that determines the appropriate amount of discipline is where you are in the project.*

---

3. The latter is a practice from agile modeling; see Ambler 2004.

**TABLE 7.1 Factors Impacting the Appropriate Amount of Discipline.** *Examples of factors driving the need for more discipline within a project include large project size, distributed development, regulatory and contractual requirements, complex stakeholder relations, long application life span, late lifecycle phases, or complex projects.*

| Factors Driving Less Discipline | Factors Driving More Discipline |
|---|---|
| Small team | Large team |
| Collocated team | Distributed team |
| Few stakeholders | Many stakeholders |
| No regulatory requirements | Regulatory requirements (Sarbanes-Oxley, Food and Drug Administration, etc.) |
| No contractual relationships | Contractual relationships |
| Short projects | Long projects |
| Early lifecycle phases | Late lifecycle phases |
| Simple projects | Complex projects |

## Scaling Your Process with the Eclipse Process Framework and Rational Method Composer

A capability pattern is a recurring process pattern that accomplishes a well-defined objective. Capability patterns are a key construct in the architecture of the Eclipse Process Framework (EPF) and Rational Method Composer (RMC) (see Appendices A and B), allowing you to scale your process incrementally from very light to very disciplined.

*Capability patterns provide a simple mechanism for scaling your process.*

Let's look at an example. In EPF, OpenUP/Basic contains a capability pattern that provides a lightweight and agile approach to defining, designing, implementing, and testing a scenario. A larger project may need a capability pattern providing a little more discipline, if, for example, the design is more formally documented. In this case the project team can choose a different capability pattern that better addresses the desire for discipline. A third project that builds safety-critical systems may need yet more discipline and may use even more rigorous capability patterns, available in RUP within the RMC product, for defining, designing, implementing, and testing a scenario. All three capability patterns are different, but they achieve the same objective: to define, design, implement, and test a scenario. So capability patterns provide a simple mechanism for scaling your process by exchanging one set of capability patterns for another, matching set, thus providing a more or less disciplined process. Our expectation is that the concept of capability patterns, combined with the creativity of the open source community, will over time provide us with access to a broad set of exchangeable capability patterns suitable for different styles of development.

## Automate Mundane Tasks

Each product has a series of mundane or administrative tasks that need to be performed. To the extent possible, such tasks should be automated. Rather than having each team member report weekly status, can we automate status reporting by having a reporting tool extract relevant information from repositories and tools? Can we automate the production, and at least basic testing, of builds?

## Continuously Improve Your Process Through Assessments

Rightsizing the process is a continuous activity throughout the project. Daily scrum meetings are a great opportunity to bring up issues preventing progress, and some of them may require a process change. Iteration assessments and retrospectives[4] at the end of iterations provide you with an opportunity not only to assess what you accomplished in the iteration but also to improve your way of working. Each project should also end with an overall project assessment, allowing you to understand what improvements can be done for future projects (see *Practice 20: Continuously Reevaluate What You Do*).

*Retrospectives provide you with an opportunity to improve your way of working.*

---

4. Kerth 2001

## Other Methods

All agile methods focus on the need to streamline process by avoiding unnecessary bureaucracy.

*XP minimizes documentation by relying primarily on verbal communication.*

XP goes to the extreme, minimizing documentation and modeling, and capturing secondary artifacts by relying primarily on verbal communication. When items are written down, they are typically noted on index cards or whiteboards. Some guidance is given on how to scale the process for the needs of larger or distributed teams—the use of Wikis, for example, or ideas from Scrum, such as the use of "scrums of scrums" as a communication vehicle allowing daily management meetings to occur across larger organizations. Even though XP has reportedly also been used successfully for larger projects, and XP has been extended to scale it up,[5] the target audience for XP is still primarily teams that want to be in very lower left corner on the process map (see Figure 7.3).

In his book *Agile Software Development*,[6] Alistair Cockburn captured a map similar to the process map in Figure 7.2. The $x$ axis represents project size, and the $y$ axis is the potential damage a system could produce, with a safety-critical system being on the high end. Cockburn has also built a series of processes that scale from less disciplined to more disciplined: Crystal Clear, Crystal Yellow, Crystal Orange, Crystal Red, and so on. He leverages his map to guide people when to use which process.

Scrum has already been used in smaller as well as larger projects and organizations. One of the scalable techniques is to use "scrum of scrums," meetings in which representatives from each team involved in the larger effort meet daily or as often as needed to sort out cross-team issues. New teams are also introduced to dealing with cross-project issues such as reuse, testing, and production support.

Agile Modeling articulates a number of different principles with the objective of streamlining process, including the principles of Traveling

---

5. See, for example, Industrial XP, www.industrialXP.org.
6. Cockburn 2002.

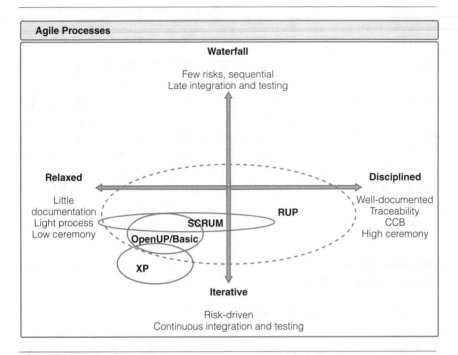

**FIGURE 7.3 Process Map for XP, Scrum, OpenUP/Basic, and RUP.** *XP targets projects with iterations of one to two weeks, OpenUP/Basic two to four weeks, and Scrum four weeks; RUP provides the broadest range based on how it is customized or what configuration of RUP you use. In a similar fashion, each process provides a different amount of ceremony, with XP being the process with the strongest focus on lightweight documentation.*

Light and Model with a Purpose. The former guides us in carefully choosing which artifacts to maintain, since some artifacts may be too costly to maintain and may have fulfilled their purpose once created. The latter guides us in being clear on what the objective is in creating a model or parts of a model, and modeling as little as possible while still addressing the objective.

OpenUP/Basic is focused on iterative and agile development for small teams. It focuses on the most essential tasks and artifacts, to make the process easy to learn and adopt. It provides guidance on when to capture artifacts more formally in tools or documents and when a whiteboard may suffice. It also borrows from many concepts found in Scrum, such as Product Backlog, Sprint Backlog, and Daily Scrum, even though the terminology is different.

*RUP is a customizable framework containing several out-of-the-box processes.*

RUP differs from the other processes mentioned above by being a customizable framework that contains several out-of-the-box processes, rather than a single process. RUP also scales OpenUP/Basic to cover enterprise needs, by allowing you to add guidelines for larger or distributed teams around technologies such as J2EE and .NET, or for products such as the IBM software development platform. It also provides guidance on various project types, such as packaged application development, legacy evolution, custom application development, systems engineering, business engineering, portfolio management, program management, or service-oriented architecture.

## Levels of Adoption

This practice can be adopted at three levels:

- **Basic.** The project team determines which artifacts and process steps to use as they progress through the project. The decisions are not formally documented.

   The basic practice of deciding as you go minimizes the amount of discipline and brings you down and to the left on the process map.

- **Intermediate.** The project team documents which artifacts and process it will use, allowing clear communication regarding what process is to be used. As an example, training material can now be customized to train the team on (only) the relevant aspects of the process being used.

   The intermediate practice of documenting the process facilitates reuse across projects and capturing lessons learned, and it should provide team members with a clearer understanding of how to do the work. Capturing these lessons learned should allow you to streamline the work and thus shorten the iteration length. It will, however, force you to spend some time documenting and continuously updating the process.

- **Advanced.** The project team assesses what worked and did not work for each iteration and project and leverages this assessment to fine-tune the process.

  The advanced practice of continuously improving the process is crucial to a team's optimal performance and should allow you to move down and to the left on the process map. The key is to time-box this activity and to communicate the process in the most effective way. Lengthy process descriptions are not always the optimal communication vehicle, especially for small audiences.

## Related Practices

- *Practice 4: Measure Progress Objectively* describes how to avoid getting a false perception of status by focusing more on primary than secondary artifacts. That same focus is essential as you rightsize your process.
- *Practice 12: Build High-Performance Teams* discusses the characteristics of a high-performance team and how to build a culture that breeds them. Having the right amount of process for your needs is essential for a high-performance environment.
- *Practice 20: Continuously Reevaluate What You Do* provides guidelines for how you can improve your process by always challenging what you do.

## Additional Information

## Information in the Unified Process

OpenUP/Basic is base process meant either to be used as is or extended with additional guidance in required domains. Its focus is on simplicity, with minimum documentation. RUP extends OpenUP/Basic by providing many specialized out-of-the-box processes, covering a variety of project types. RUP focuses on more specialized content, as well as content appropriate for larger projects. RUP also discusses topics such as how to customize a process and effectively implement it in an organization.

## Additional Reading

For information on process configuration, see the following:

Peter M. Senge. *The Fifth Discipline*. Doubleday, 1990.

Alistair Cockburn. *Agile Software Development*. Addison-Wesley, 2002.

Barry Boehm and Richard Turner. *Balancing Agility and Discipline*. Addison-Wesley, 2003.

Robert McFeeley. *IDEAL: A User's Guide for Software Process Improvement*. Software Engineering Institute, 1996.

For information on how to customize RUP, see the following:

Stefan Bergström and Lotta Råberg. *Adopting the Rational Unified Process: Success with RUP*. Addison-Wesley, 2004.

Per Kroll and Philippe Kruchten. *The Rational Unified Process Made Easy: A Practitioner's Guide to the RUP*. Addison-Wesley, 2003.

# Continuously Reevaluate What You Do

by Heath Newburn

*If we always challenge what we do and seek innovative ways to develop software, we can improve how we work and achieve better project results.*

## Problem

In life it's often the actions we don't take rather than the deeds we do that cause us the greatest problems. A real danger any software project faces is the inertia and mediocrity of the mundane. We're usually so pressed for time in our rush to get our applications out the door while checking all of our process boxes that we don't have time to look for ways to improve how we work. Unless there's an edict from the top or a fire to put out, we rarely look at how we can or should improve our methods. This inertia leads to more of the same, which can be costly to our projects.

## Background

We often make unjustified assumptions. Take this story, for example. A grandfather sat down to lunch at his grandson's house to celebrate the grandson's promotion to vice president at his company. The younger man knew that porterhouse steak was his grandfather's favorite, so he brought his grandfather a four-ounce steak just like those he had always seen his father make. The older man looked up in surprise and grinned: "Cheap, just like your dad." The grandson turned a little red and asked, "What do you mean, Grandpa? I thought you liked your steaks small; that's how Dad always makes them, and you taught him." The grandfather laughed and shook his head: "It's not that we liked small steaks, it was just all we could afford!"

Sometimes we make assumptions about the "best" or "right" way to do something because that's the way we've usually seen it done.

Often, in fact, it's the only way we've seen it done. But as the example above illustrates, that doesn't mean our assumptions are right.

When I moved back to Austin after a four-year absence, I started taking what I knew to be the shortest route to my new workplace. A few months later, I had to run an errand on the way home and encountered a new road that hadn't existed when I left town, though I later found out that it had been there for more than a year! That accidental discovery saved me 20 minutes a day, and cutting more than an hour a week off my commuting time made a real difference to my life. The way I had thought was best was no longer best, since my assumptions were now wrong!

Within our development process we often do the same thing. The way we've done things in the past has obviously worked to some degree, so what's the need for change? If it ain't broke, don't fix it, right? And while development processes often become a religious discussion—whether it's spiral, RUP, XP, or some other form of agile development—everybody's got a reason to use or not use a particular approach.

What's important for you to understand is the best way to leverage your process. What changes do you need to make to your process to make your project successful? For the activities and artifacts that you can influence the most, what should you look at changing now, and how should you drive those changes?

## Applying the Practice

Continuously refining your process is critical to the long-term success of your team and project. You can start looking at all the parts of your process by asking "Why do we do it that way?" Once you understand why, you can quickly eliminate problems by verifying that the assumptions that have been made are still valid.

### Start by Asking Questions

One of the most effective ways to begin reexamining what you're doing is to start asking questions. "Why" questions can be particularly effective. If you've ever been around a small child, you know that at some point the constant questions can become infuriating, but they often turn out to be gems worth pondering. "Why do you work so late, Daddy?", "Why do I have to wear clothes?" (my son's current favorite), "Why do we sleep?", "Why do I have to go to bed early?" . . .

Such questions help us evaluate our habits and actions. Why do we do the things we do? Are they the best choices for us? We may take a route to school that saves us five minutes, but if the more leisurely route boasts better scenery, has no stop-and-go traffic, and is free of aggressive drivers, are we making the right decision?

Once we understand the "why," we can address the "how" and the "what." If our goal is to get to school in the shortest amount of time, then we are indeed making the right choice. If our goal is to use the trip to talk to the kids in the car and enjoy a relaxing start to the day, maybe we should take a different approach. Almost all of us take the same route to work every day. Is it always the best way, even on those days when there's an accident? Are some routes slower than others depending on what time of day it is? Or do we just end up taking the same route every day because that's what we did the day before? How many things do we do because that's the way we did them the day before?

*Once we understand the "why," we can address the "how" and the "what."*

## Continuously Verify Assumptions

Throughout the project, we should continuously challenge what we do by verifying assumptions. As we progress through a project, we have to ensure that our assumptions, that is, what we believe to be valid and true, still are. Or, as Allen Carter[7] asked in thousands of English classes at Clayton High School:

What are we doing?

Why are we doing it?

What is it good for?

How do we know?

---

7. High school humanities teacher in Clayton, New Mexico.

These questions could constitute the core of a checkpoint for every iteration in your process.

Verifying the integrity of your project at regular checkpoints can be extremely useful. If nothing else, it's worth asking whether or not the project should be continued. A classic example is the Iridium satellite project. This $6 billion project was undertaken for one simple reason: to allow you to carry a single phone with which to make or receive a phone call anywhere in the world. In the early 1990s, phone coverage was a concern for global travelers. Executives, salespeople, oilfield workers, and others had to either rent phones at outrageous rates, own multiple phones, or (horror of horrors!) be out of touch. With a huge number of competing cell standards, large areas with no cell coverage, and no clear leader who could drive adoption of a worldwide standard, the idea of a satellite system seemed like a winner. For Iridium, launching more than eighty satellites to cover the world would be an expensive proposition but would fill a gap for all of these potential customers with big pocket books. However, while the company was setting up the system, the world quickly changed. As GSM became the European standard and no-cost roaming covered the United States, other areas of the globe fell into line; pretty soon the reason for Iridium's existence became moot. By focusing only on the end goal, the project headed for rapid doom, and the system was eventually sold for pennies on the dollar. If someone had challenged, "What are we trying to accomplish here?" as the business environment was evolving, they would have changed the business plan before spending billions of dollars.

## Always Be Challenging

A good way to challenge your processes, your assumptions, and your habits is to build a paradigm for asking the right questions. Simply asking why isn't enough. If nothing else, you'll end up seriously annoying the people around you and making yourself nuts. As you look at your process and work flows, if you hear or see something that doesn't seem quite right, use a questioning approach to engage discussions and ensure that you're on your current path for a real reason, rather than just for lack of a reason to do something else. Whatever choices you've made, you must be able to articulate a reason for them.

While Carter's four questions above are great, you need to be able to answer not only if it's the right thing but also if it's the best thing. Edward de Bono describes several approaches to evaluating any situation in his ABC (Always Be Challenging)[8] approach (see Figure 7.4). Whenever we look at a particular situation, we have to determine three things. Being a lateral thinker, he starts backwards.

- **C**—Cut: Is there still a need to do what we're doing? Is the goal still relevant? Do we now have other priorities? Are our assumptions still valid?

- **B**—Because: What are the reasons that we've adopted this approach? Are we doing the same thing because that's the way we've always done it?

- **A**—Alternatives: if there is no other approach, how can we refine and improve the one we have to make it more effective or efficient?

*Cut what is not worth doing, validate the why, and improve what you need to do.*

**FIGURE 7.4 The ABCs of Improvement: Always Be Challenging.** *To improve the way you are working, you should always challenge current practices. Using Edward de Bono's ABCs, cut out what is not worth doing, validate the reason you're using your current methods, and improve the way you are doing what you need to do if there are no alternatives.*

This approach works well when we look at our test methodology at the beginning of a project. We'll look at what we've done in past projects and determine whether it will work for this project. If the reasons that we took the particular approach in the past are still valid—

---

8. de Bono 1970.

that is, we have to do testing—and we have the same skills, same personnel, and same sets of problems, we might still take this approach. However, there may be new tools available that will allow us to enhance our capabilities. So we'll add some additional training cycles and make sure we can show our reasoning behind the decision to move forward on this new path, rather than just blindly doing the same things we did last time.

## "Sunset" Processes

*If you can't articulate the value, eliminate the item.*

Another way to force rethinking is by "sunsetting" processes. Governments often "sunset" laws or committees, which means that those laws or entities expire after some period of time and can be renewed only by an overt act. This strategy forces the owners of sunsetted items to continue to justify their existence and provide evidence that they are actually adding value. If you can't articulate the value, then you can probably safely eliminate the item. Finding the right way to establish the value proposition in this method, or any other described here, can be a big challenge. Knowing how to measure success is the key to knowing what to keep, what to change, and what to lose.

## Measure Success

The issue of measuring success brings up a crucial point. It's important to understand just how to determine what parts of your process are working. This is a conundrum for process owners. Although you don't want to drown people in metrics and measurement, you have to have some method to determine the effectiveness of the process. While the method can be subjective, it's much better to determine and focus on what can be objectively measured. Examine the work products from the process; how can they be quantified and qualified? It is also important to set up measures to drive improvements of your weakest area(s) within the overall system, rather than improvement of an area that is already strong.[9]

---

9. Goldratt 2004.

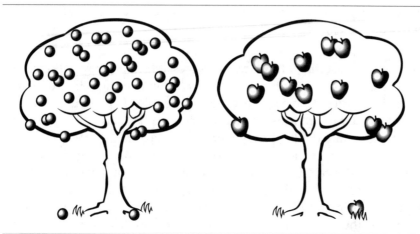

**FIGURE 7.5 Measure Success.** *To know which process to keep and which to throw away, you need to know what characterizes success. Measuring success crystallizes which processes are worth keeping and which are not. Is it better with many small fruits, or a few large fruits?*

One common measurement of success during a project is the quality of code, as defined by the number of defects discovered. This measurement is often taken by comparing a defect projection rate against the actual number of defects. If the number of defects in your project exceeds the target by 300 percent, is the project successful? Before you say no, what if you had a test team whose skill far exceeded that of previous testers? What if the defect projections themselves were flawed?

In other words, it's not enough to have a single measure of success. You might also rate code quality by the number of blocked test cases, customer satisfaction surveys from early release programs, depth and breadth of execution of automated test buckets, or many other factors. Most measurements will be defined in terms of the constraints of quality, cost, and speed, all three of which need to be measurable at any time. This may mean cost and budget analysis, alignment with milestone delivery dates, the amount of overtime being burned on a project, or usability test scores. While any number of methods may be relevant to your project, make sure you're not evaluating in a single dimension. Overlapping measurements will ensure that you have a better understanding of your project.

*Make sure that measurements are readily accessible and easily gathered.*

Whatever metrics you choose to measure your product, make sure that those measurements are readily accessible and easily gathered by your teams. One of the things that can become a huge drag on team leads is metrics reporting to different people. I've been on teams where we had to produce six different sets of charts to satisfy the measurement required by all the layers of management. One team lead finally got fed up, created a two-page chart that could be generated by tools, and advocated it all the way to the executive level until he got buy-in across the board. By focusing on what was really needed in his status reporting and being able to gather it automatically, he greatly improved the quality of his work life and that of his team. With these measurements in hand, he could easily show what was and wasn't working and enabled the leadership team to make the right decisions.

## Do Iteration Reviews and Retrospectives

*In iterative development you assess your team and process at the end of each iteration.*

One of the benefits of iterative development is that you have an opportunity to assess the effectiveness of your team and the process you use at the end of each iteration. You can then use what you have learned in the review to improve the way you work in the next iteration.

The term *retrospective*[10] is frequently used to describe a review focused on learning how to work more effectively. As an example, the Agile Manifesto states[11]: "At regular intervals, the team reflects on how to become more effective, then tunes and adjusts its behavior accordingly." We have found that a retrospective is best done at the end of each iteration together with an assessment of the results of the iteration. This review often creates a sobering awareness of potential problems the project may face. For example, if you realize that you implemented the capabilities you had planned to implement within the iteration, but the quality of the code is so low that it is close to unusable, you gain a lot of insights into where you can look for

---

10. Kerth 2001.
11. www.agilemanifesto.org/.

improvements in the way you are working. You can probably understand what improvements are required by analyzing your test approach, the amount of time spent on using the application within each iteration, and the prioritization you put on developing new capabilities versus improving the quality of the application.

When conducting a retrospective, make sure you focus on how to improve, not on blaming people for not doing a good job, as discussed in the section Build Trust in *Practice 12: Build High-Performance Teams*. To address this issue, Norman Kerth defines what he calls the Prime Directive for retrospectives[12]: "Regardless of what we discover, we understand and truly believe that everyone did the best job they could, given what they knew at the time, their skills and abilities, the resources available, and the situation at hand." He also defines four key questions to focus on during the retrospective:

- What did we do well, that if we don't discuss we might forget?
- What did we learn?
- What should we do differently next time?
- What still puzzles us?

To ensure that the retrospective is a good learning experience, Ellen Gottesdiener[13] defines three required parameters:

- **Immediacy.** Make sure that you can apply lessons learned within days of the retrospective. This fits well with doing the retrospective in conjunction with the iteration assessment.
- **Relevance.** Make sure that the learning deals with topics that team members care about, such as how to improve test efforts, collaboration across various functions within the teams, or how to be more effective in the build process.
- **Self-direction.** Make sure that all team members take ownership and control of their learning and actions to make improvements. Make sure that a plan is produced during the retrospective outlining who should change what.

---

12. See Kerth 2001.
13. Gottesdiener 2003.

Note that it is important to conduct retrospectives at the end of each iteration rather than, as many projects unfortunately do, only at the end of the project. Waiting until the end of the project creates several problems:

- It is at this point too late to improve upon your current project.
- Teams often disperse at the end of the project, and lessons learned from one project may not apply to the next project, where you may have very different team dynamics and issues.
- If teams disperse at the end of the project, team members are less likely to put the required energy into the brainstorming session, since they may not benefit from the lessons learned.
- Technology issues addressed in one project may not be relevant for the next project, which may use other technology.
- There is no incentive to apply lessons learned when the project is over, and in most cases, nobody sees it as his or her responsibility to make effective use of the lessons learned.

**FIGURE 7.6 Iteration Assessment.** *By assessing the processes and results achieved at the end of each iteration, team members can understand how to improve the way they work for the remainder of the project.*

## Don't Go to Abilene Just Because Everyone Else Is Going

There are lots of methods that assist in decision making: risk avoidance mechanisms, Monte Carlo analysis, idea generation techniques, causal analysis, and many others. Find a method that is repeatable and useful for your team and use it. Again, making a decision based solely on lack of failure with a past experience isn't optimizing your talent pool. By the same consideration, "going along to get along" is a road to hell paved with good intentions.

*"Going along to get along" is a road to hell paved with good intentions.*

A death spiral for any group is to get caught up in group-think or appeasement. You have to challenge assumptions when they don't look very smart. Professor Jerry Harvey described what he called the "Abilene paradox," based on a real-life event that might sound familiar to some of us.[14]

**FIGURE 7.7  Challenge Assumptions to Avoid the Abilene Paradox.** *In many everyday situations we do things a certain way just because we assume that everybody thinks this approach is a good one. As we can learn from the Abilene paradox, we may find that nobody thinks what we are doing is a good idea, but that nobody ever raised the issue of whether the process should be followed.*

---

14. Harvey 1996.

A woman takes her East-Coast-raised husband home to West Texas in the middle of a blistering summer. The family spends most of the days on a nice screened-in porch with ceiling fans and ice-cold lemonade to keep the heat away, and much to the son-in-law's surprise the atmosphere is actually very pleasant and conversational. One day the father-in-law, noticing a lull in the conversation, asks, "Y'all want to go to Abilene for dinner?" No one seems in disagreement, so they all pack into the car and head down the dusty road.

After a three-hour round trip with no air conditioning in a broiling sun, choking dust, carnivorous horse flies, and a greasy meal that some prisons wouldn't serve, they all clamber back onto the porch at the homestead. They're grumpy, sweaty, and generally miserable. The daughter notes that the meal wasn't much and maybe Mom could get out some of her fried chicken from lunch. The father and son-in-law begin to argue over whose meal was worse. After a little bit of lemonade, they cool down some, and the father-in-law remarks "Yep, I can't even believe y'all wanted to go." The others look on in shock. No one remembers pressing the idea, and it was clearly the father who proposed it. The father shakes his head defensively. "I thought you were bored, and I was just trying to be polite! If you didn't want to go, why didn't you say so?" Everyone descends into silence and private fuming. Because everyone had wanted to be polite, no one had voiced any disagreement, each thinking that only he or she didn't want to go.

The moral here is that in your product directions, development process, and day-to-day decisions, make sure you're not headed to Abilene. Ensure that you're going somewhere for a reason, rather than just going along for the ride because that's what you think everyone else wants.

## Closing Thoughts

Allowing your decision-making process to be governed by the laziness of "that's the way it's always been done" is a bad road to take. Create positive change rather than just being carried by the inertia of your organization. Ensure that you've examined the rationale behind your actions and that you can clearly articulate what you are doing, why you are doing it, and how you know it's valuable. Avoid the pit-falls of the Abilene paradox and don't blindly do what you did before. By making sure that you're actually adding value to your project and not just following the well-worn path, you'll avoid the "good enough" syndrome and make your project more successful.

## Other Methods

If you follow a waterfall process, you will at least theoretically do requirements, design, implementation, integration, and testing only once and in a sequential order. This process therefore provides you with limited ability to learn from your mistakes, because if you determine after the requirements phase that you can improve the way you work with requirements, you cannot apply that knowledge until the next project.

Unlike waterfall development, iterative development gives you the excellent ability to improve what you are doing in each iteration through iteration review and retrospectives.

Agile development approaches, such as XP and Scrum, clearly emphasize the value of continuously improving. Both of these methods recommend retrospectives at the end of each iteration. Scrum calls these Sprint Reviews. Scrum also prescribes daily Scrum meetings, where three questions are answered by each team member:

*   What have you done since last meeting?
*   What will you do between now and next meeting?
*   What obstacles stood in the way of doing work?

The last questions provide the Scrum Master with information about what stands in the way of progress, so that obstacles can be removed and related improvements to the working procedure can be implemented as appropriate.

XP also prescribes pair programming, where two developers work side by side to develop parts of the application, enabling both to learn from each other.

RUP and OpenUP/Basic articulate the importance of doing reviews at the end of each iteration, milestone reviews at the end of each phase, and a review at the end of the project to learn how you can work more effectively. RUP and OpenUP/Basic include daily status meetings and pair programming as optional techniques you may consider using. RUP and OpenUP/Basic also have a built-in review step for most tasks and checklists for most artifacts, allowing the team to continuously improve both the quality of artifacts and how to do things. It should be noted that the value of reviews diminishes as collaboration increases, and that collaboration may therefore have a better pay-off than more reviews.

## Levels of Adoption

This practice can be adopted at three different levels:

- **Basic.** Work product owners reevaluate parts of the process on an ad hoc basis. This should lead to more effective processes with less overhead, and hence also the opportunity for shorter iterations.

- **Intermediate.** The team carries out end-of-iteration reviews and retrospectives and uses the results to continuously improve the process. This should lead to more effective processes with less overhead, and hence also the opportunity for shorter iterations.

- **Advanced.** A governing body ensures that the entire process has had active reviews to verify that each part of the process is the most useful for the team. All team members continually strive to find better ways of building their part of the solution.

  The governance introduces more overhead, and hence more discipline and longer iterations, but this system should in the end lead to a process that better addresses the specific needs of the organization.

## Related Practices

- *Practice 2: Execute Your Project in Iterations* shows that using iterative development allows you to continuously reexamine what you're creating.
- *Practice 12: Build High-Performance Teams* discusses building trust, which is crucial to enabling all team members to discuss openly and constructively how to improve the way they work.
- *Practice 19: Rightsize Your Process* explains how to work more effectively by focusing only on the activities in your process for which the benefit is greater than the cost. Continuously improving your process is core to reevaluating what you do.

## Additional Information

## Information in the Unified Process

OpenUP/Basic provides guidance on iteration reviews, retrospectives, pair programming, and other basic and intermediate practices. RUP adds guidelines on how team members can assess the artifacts they produce and provides guidance on process improvement.

## Additional Reading

Books on improving software development processes:

> Alistair Cockburn. *Agile Software Development*. Addison-Wesley, 2002.

> Norman L. Kerth. *Project Retrospectives: A Handbook for Team Reviews*. Dorset House, 2001.

Relevant books outside the field of software development:

> Edward de Bono. *Serious Creativity: Using the Power of Lateral Thinking to Create New Ideas*. HarperBusiness, 1993.

> Edward de Bono. *Lateral Thinking: Creativity Step by Step*. Perennial, 1970.

Jerry Harvey. *The Abilene Paradox and Other Meditations on Management*. Jossey-Bass, 1996.

Eliyahu M. Goldratt and Jeff Cox. *The Goal, Third Edition*. North River Press, 2004.

# CHAPTER 8

# Making Practical Use of the Best Practices

You have hopefully been inspired by a number of the best practices in this book. You may have picked up new ideas on how to develop software more effectively and had a chance to reflect on opportunities for improvements within your team. But how do you actually use these practices? Which practice should you adopt first? Should you adopt the practices one at a time, or should you adopt many at once? On what type of project should you adopt your first practices?

This chapter aims to answer these and other questions related to adopting the practices described in this book.

## Which Practices Should I Adopt First?

The reason for introducing a best practice into your organization is to obtain business benefits measured in improved project results. Introducing a practice is an investment. As with all investments, you need to make a business case with a return, such as, higher-quality, lower cost, and/or shorter time to market.

*Introducing a practice is an investment.*

*To determine which practice(s) to adopt first, create a shortlist of problems to fix.*

You can choose many different starting points for adopting best practices, and most of them will provide you with value (see Figure 8.1). But are some better than others? To determine which practice(s) to adopt first, you need to create a shortlist of problems that you need to fix. This can be done using either of the following two approaches. The first approach is to walk through the problem statement for each practice and see which problems resonate with you. Do you experience the problem described? If you do, put the problem and the related practice on the shortlist.

The other approach is to consider the issues your team has faced in the past and assess their impact on your business. If the impact is big, write the problem down. This book contains many practices, so to help you to find the practices that fix problems in a certain area, we have organized them around key principles. If you are trying to find a cure for a specific problem you are experiencing, review the principles to see which one(s) are the most relevant. Then go through the practices for the relevant principle(s) and put them on your shortlist.

**FIGURE 8.1 There Are Many Roads Leading to Good Results.** *Most practices will provide you with benefits, but some will have higher pay-offs than others. You need to decide what your end goal is and then determine the best way to get there.*

Once you have a shortlist of relevant problems and related practices for your project or organization, the next step is to identify the value of fixing them. If it is hard to attach real numbers to the value of fixing individual problems, articulate their relative value. After a while, you should have a prioritized list of practices to adopt.

But what if you are doing fine, but there is a drive to "do better"? You can use the same approach as described above to identify the practices to adopt first, but with a more positive spin. Rather than looking for problems, you are looking for opportunities for improvements.

Will you ever be "done" adopting practices? We will answer that question in the next section.

## Start with the Basics

For each of the practices, the "levels of adoption" describe basic, intermediate, and advanced adoption (see Table 8.1). When adopting a practice, start with the basic level, gain some familiarity and success with the basic practice, and then consider whether a more advanced adoption makes sense.

The goal should not be to adopt the advanced practices on every topic. Basic adoption suggests that the practice can be adopted with a smaller effort, or by people with less advanced skills. Because they require low investment but offer high potential for results, these basic levels are usually worth adopting. Advanced adoption means more investment and complexity in applying the practice, usually involving a higher cost; therefore, there is a greater burden to make sure that a particular project needs to take on this cost. Figure 8.2 shows the relative cost (investment) of sample practices and their relative value by adoption level. The gradient indicates the return on investment (ROI), with a steeper gradient indicating a higher return. In this example, practice A and B have a higher ROI for adoption of basic levels than for adoption of intermediate and advanced levels, whereas practice C has a lower ROI for adopting basic than for adopting intermediate and advanced levels.

*The goal should not be to adopt the advanced practices on every topic.*

**TABLE 8.1 Summary of Practices by Adoption Levels.** *Each practice can be adopted at the basic, intermediate, and advanced level. Choose what practices to adopt at what level based on the needs of your project.*

| # | Practice Name | Basic | Intermediate | Advanced |
|---|---|---|---|---|
| 1 | Manage risk. | Decide what risk to address in each iteration. | Update risk list and make visible. | Use risk management tool and traceability. |
| 2 | Execute your project in iterations. | Deliver incrementally. Replan based on feedback. | Plan iterations based on risk. | Use mini- and super-iterations. |
| 3 | Embrace and manage change. | Do partial implementation. Keep documentation simple. | Use Unified Process lifecycle. Refactor. Manage change. | Automate change management and use CCB. |
| 4 | Measure progress objectively. | Measure and re-estimate each iteration. | Chart progress. | Automate measurements and record in a database. |
| 5 | Test your own code. | Use coding guidelines and standards. | Developers actively test their own code. | Formally inspect code. Use static, structural, runtime analysis, and performance test tools. |
| 6 | Leverage test automation appropriately. | Provision each test machine. | Create automated test suites. | Automate stress and performance testing. |
| 7 | Everyone owns the product! | Openly share info. Evaluate 10% complete work. | Cross-functional collaboration. Assess progress through working code. | Use scalable collaboration platform and enterprise architecture. |
| 8 | Understand the domain. | Include customer in project, and use a glossary. | Visualize a domain object model. | Leverage business rules and business process modeling. |
| 9 | Describe requirements from the user perspective. | Identify scenarios. | Capture use cases, and link scenarios to use cases. | Chunk use cases into separately managed requirements. |

**TABLE 8.1 Continued**

| # | Practice Name | Basic | Intermediate | Advanced |
|---|---|---|---|---|
| 10 | Prioritize requirements for implementation. | Prioritize most essential requirements for each iteration. | Balance priorities of architecture, business, and customer. | Systematically manage requirements categories and attributes. |
| 11 | Leverage legacy systems. | Ensure continuous improvement of systems in maintenance. | Plan incremental improvement. | Establish long-term enterprise vision and plans. |
| 12 | Build high-performance teams. | Clearly communicate project vision and responsibilities. | Establish trust, encourage constructive feedback, and communicate openly. | Couple performance evaluations to established values. |
| 13 | Organize around the architecture. | Organize around features. Architect oversees architecture. | Organize vertically and horizontally. Approve architectural changes. | Formalize changes through an Architecture Control Board. |
| 14 | Manage versions. | Manage version-controlled files. Manually manage change sets. | Set up isolated workspaces, with activity-based delivery. | Share version-controlled components across products. |
| 15 | Leverage patterns. | Learn patterns and provide examples. | Use reference architectures and document patterns with UML. | Use pattern automation and enterprise-wide patterns. |
| 16 | Architect with components and services. | Apply component and service design principles. | Model components, services, and interfaces. | Create detailed component and service specifications. |
| 17 | Actively promote reuse. | Common templates/representations, form communities. | Educate on available assets. | Fund creation of assets. |
| 18 | Model key perspectives. | Use informal sketching. | Document UML architectures. | Use model-driven development. |
| 19 | Rightsize your process. | Decide on process to use as you go. | Document the process you use. | Improve the process after each iteration. |
| 20 | Continuously reevaluate what you do. | Each person assesses his or her own working procedure. | Do iteration reviews and retrospectives. | Centrally coordinate process improvement. |

A smaller project that wants to follow a low-ceremony process would apply the most basic or intermediate level for most practices. However, the advanced level does not always mean more ceremony or overhead. It may instead indicate that you need a higher degree of skills, or more advanced tooling. As an example, adopting advanced change management practices may allow you to work with a minimum of ceremony, because the tools handle all the bookkeeping. Use the symbol associated with each practice level to understand how the practice relates to the process map.

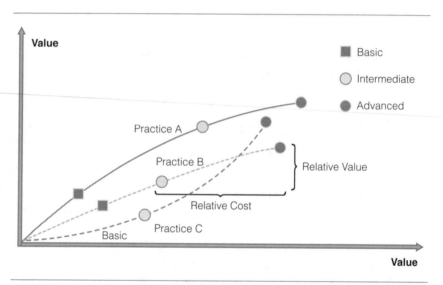

**FIGURE 8.2 Relative Cost and Value by Practice Level.** *For each organization, each practice creates a unique cost-value profile. Some practices make more sense to adopt than others. In most cases, as you move to higher levels, the relative cost increases, while the relative value decreases. Thus, each organization needs to assess whether the optimal level for each practice is basic, intermediate, advanced, or none.*

As your team adopts a practice, commit to using the practice for a certain number of iterations and then review the results to see whether you want to continue. Some practices may take some time to get right, and giving up after one iteration typically does not allow you to learn the practice well enough to assess its usefulness properly.

One approach we have found very useful when doing process improvement is first to assess how well we are doing today. This assessment should involve all team members, so that they (1) get a sense of ownership of the assessment results and (2) buy into them. Second, have the team agree on where they would like to be in the future. Choose a time line that is beyond any immediate deadlines, but not so far away that it becomes irrelevant to what you are doing today. It is often good to have a roughly one-year horizon. Lastly, do a short-term plan for how to improve over the next iteration or the next few months. Do not have a horizon longer than three to six months, or you will not take any immediate actions. Table 8.2 provides an example using the practices in this book as a driver for your process improvement effort.

*Create a short-term plan for how to improve over the next iteration or the next few months.*

**TABLE 8.2 Example of a Process Improvement Plan.** *This plan has been produced in three steps. Step 1 is to assess how well the team is doing relative to a practice. Step 2 is to have the team agree on what is a desirable end goal. Note that the team may choose never to adopt some practices, or to adopt them only at a basic or intermediate level. In Step 4, the team produces a short-term plan for what to improve in the next three months.*

| # | Practice Name | Where Are We? | Where We Would Like to Be | Short-Term Plan |
|---|---|---|---|---|
| 1 | Manage risk. | Basic | Intermediate | Key focus. Couple with Practice 10. |
| 2 | Execute your project in iterations. | Intermediate | Intermediate | N/A |
| 3 | Embrace and manage change. | Basic | Advanced | Key focus. Manage change request more effectively. |
| 4 | Measure progress objectively. | None | Intermediate | Not a focus now. |
| 5 | Test your own code. | Basic | Advanced | Key focus. Apply test-first design. |

*continues*

**TABLE 8.2  Continued**

| # | Practice Name | Where Are We? | Where We Would Like to Be | Short-Term Plan |
|---|---|---|---|---|
| 6 | Leverage test automation appropriately. | Intermediate | Advanced | Good if we can improve. Send Karen on training course. |
| 7 | Everyone owns the product! | Intermediate | Advanced | Not a focus now. |
| 8 | Understand the domain. | Basic | Intermediate | Start by using a basic domain object model. |
| 9 | Describe requirements from the user perspective. | Intermediate | Intermediate | N/A |
| 10 | Prioritize requirements for implementation. | None | Intermediate | We need to involve our customers and architect in prioritization work. |
| 11 | Leverage legacy systems. | None | None | N/A |
| 12 | Build high-performance teams. | Basic | Advanced | Not a focus now. |
| 13 | Organize around the architecture. | None | None | N/A |
| 14 | Manage versions. | Intermediate | Advanced | Focus. We must do a better job on parallel development! |
| 15 | Leverage patterns. | Basic | Intermediate | Deploy tool with patterns and get mentor to assist. |
| 16 | Architect with components and services. | None | Advanced | Not a focus now. |
| 17 | Actively promote reuse. | Basic | Intermediate | Not a focus now. |
| 18 | Model key perspectives. | None | Intermediate | Not a focus now. |
| 19 | Rightsize your process. | Basic | Advanced | Download EPF and check it out. Jane |
| 20 | Continuously reevaluate what you do. | Basic | Intermediate | Have Ken run retrospectives for each iteration. |

## Adopt Related Practices

In most cases you would not adopt one practice at a time, but rather a few or more practices at once. There is no obvious grouping of practices. In some cases three or four practices seem to address a problem you are facing, and you choose to adopt all of them. In other cases you may decide that you want to adopt all or most of the practices related to a certain principle. You may want to consider adopting a few other common combinations or themes of practices together.

## Practices Supporting Iterative Development

Most practices in this book support iterative development, directly or indirectly. The following list includes some of the more critical practices:

*Most practices in this book support iterative development.*

- *Practice 1: Manage Risk* explains how to identify and prioritize key risks. Key risks are used to determine what to focus on in the next iteration.
- *Practice 2: Execute Your Project in Iterations* describes how to plan iterative development and think about dividing up your project into a series of iterations.
- *Practice 3: Embrace and Manage Change* describes what changes to encourage and discourage at what time within a project. Discouraging certain types of changes late in the project is essential to manage risk effectively.
- *Practice 4: Measure Progress Objectively* explains how to assess progress better through iterative development.
- *Practice 5: Test Your Own Code* details how developers can approach testing their own code holistically and includes techniques that will potentially participate in a broader test automation strategy.
- *Practice 6: Leverage Test Automation Appropriately* describes how automating appropriate amounts of the test effort can also realize improved product quality and shorter product development schedules.
- *Practice 7: Everyone Owns the Product!* addresses how all team members need to orient their mindset to enable effective iterative development.

- *Practice 10: Prioritize Requirements for Implementation* shows how to determine which requirements to address first to deliver customer value and to mitigate key risks.
- *Practice 14: Manage Versions* discusses how to manage the complexity of evolving hundreds of artifacts as you iterate.

If you want to move toward iterative development, these practices should be on your shortlist to adopt.

## Practices Improving Your Ability to Manage Requirements

Problems with requirements management are often quoted as a primary source for project failures. As an example, the 1995 Chaos Report by the Standish Group listed requirements management issues as five of the top ten reasons for project failure. A number of practices in this book will help you improve the management of requirements:

- *Practice 2: Execute Your Project in Iterations* describes how to plan iterative development and think about dividing up your project into a series of iterations, so that you can get feedback on the requirements.
- *Practice 7: Everyone Owns the Product!* addresses how all team members need to orient their mindset to enable effective iterative development.
- *Practice 8: Understand the Domain* describes how to document key aspects of the problem domain to minimize communication issues and to increase every team member's understanding of the problem domain.
- *Practice 9: Describe Requirements from the User Perspective* outlines how to document requirements in the form of use cases, scenarios, and user stories and how to support your requirements with storyboards and user-interface prototypes.

*No matter how good you are, you will make many incorrect assumptions regarding requirements.*

- *Practice 10: Prioritize Requirements for Implementation* shows how to determine which requirements to address first to deliver customer value and to mitigate key risks.

No matter how good you are at managing requirements, you will make many incorrect assumptions regarding them, and the best medicine for flawed requirements is often iterative development, because it allows you to showcase a partial solution to make sure that you are on track. Therefore, also take a close look at all the practices for iterative development.

## Practices Improving Your Ability to Do Architecture, Design, and Implementation

A majority of people in most projects are involved in architecture, design, and implementation activities. Making these people more effective is hence of great value. The following practices will help you improve in this area:

- *Practice 5: Test Your Own Code* details how developers can approach testing their own code holistically and includes techniques that will potentially participate in a broader test automation strategy.

- *Practice 6: Leverage Test Automation Appropriately* describes how automating appropriate amounts of the test effort can also realize improved product quality and shorter product development schedules.

- *Practice 7: Everyone Owns the Product!* addresses how all team members need to orient their mindset to enable effective iterative development.

- *Practice 10: Prioritize Requirements for Implementation* shows how to determine which requirements to address first to deliver customer value and to mitigate key risks.

- *Practice 11: Leverage Legacy Systems* provides information about reuse of another type of asset, that is, how to leverage the many valuable assets you have in your organization.

- *Practice 15: Leverage Patterns* explains how patterns allow you to produce an architecture more effectively and how patterns can be used to help enforce the architecture.

- *Practice 16: Architect with Components and Services* describes the benefits of developing with components and services and explains how to go about developing a component- and services-based architecture.

- *Practice 17: Actively Promote Reuse* offers guidelines for how to enable and promote reuse of assets.

- *Practice 18: Model Key Perspectives* explains how models can help you understand, communicate, and accelerate development.

*Practices around architecture, design, and implementation are rapidly evolving.*

This is an area where practices are rapidly evolving. New technologies help us architect, design, and implement our applications more effectively, while innovative approaches to design and implementation, such as agile approaches, make us look at how we work from new perspectives.

## Practices Improving Your Ability to Do Testing

*Testing needs to be initiated early in the project.*

Testers may be some of the most undervalued resources in a project, often thrown in at the bitter end in an attempt to raise quality. Throughout the book we have provided guidance on how testing needs to be initiated early in the project and to continue throughout the project. A number of practices in this book focus on testing and quality assurance:

- *Practice 1: Manage Risk* explains how to identify and prioritize key risks. Key risks are used to determine what to focus on in the next iteration.

- *Practice 2: Execute Your Project in Iterations* describes how to plan iterative development and think about dividing up your project into a series of iterations, so that you can start testing early in the project.

- *Practice 4: Measure Progress Objectively* explains how to assess progress better through iterative development.

- *Practice 5: Test Your Own Code* details how developers can approach testing their own code holistically and includes techniques that will potentially participate in a broader test automation strategy.

- *Practice 6: Leverage Test Automation Appropriately* describes how automating appropriate amounts of the test effort can also realize improved product quality and shorter product development schedules.

- *Practice 7: Everyone Owns the Product!* addresses how all team members need to change their mindset to take more responsibility for the ultimate quality of the application you are developing.

- *Practice 20: Continuously Reevaluate What You Do* offers guidelines for how you can improve your working procedures by always challenging what you do.

Testing is where the rubber hits the road. It provides invaluable feedback on how well you are doing and allows your teams to improve the way they work.

## How Can RUP and EPF Help Me?

EPF is an open source process framework for authoring, configuring, publishing, and viewing software practices and processes. One of the processes in EPF is OpenUP/Basic, which is a stripped-down, simplified version of the Unified Process, suitable for smaller teams looking for an agile development approach consistent with Unified Process principles. Even though the practices in this book are process agnostic, they are well aligned with RUP and OpenUP/Basic. You find that many of the basic and sometimes intermediate levels of practices in this book are consistent with OpenUP/Basic.

*OpenUP/Basic is a simplified version of the Unified Process.*

EPF also enables scalable processes and process frameworks to be built on top of it. One such scalable process framework is RUP.[1] RUP can be daunting at first glance, providing guidance on hundreds of best practices. These best practices are integrated into a coherent, full lifecycle process, allowing you to scale from the needs of smaller projects to those of large and complex projects. Through a clear articulation of roles, artifacts, and activities, team members understand what they need to produce and how to produce it. Tool mentors provide guidance on how best to leverage the tools at hand to carry out the work. The coherent story ensures that team members understand how to execute a project from start to finish.

*EPF enables scalable processes and process frameworks to be built on top of it.*

It is, however, not obvious from OpenUP/Basic and RUP how to take out a small slice and adopt only that thin slice. That is really what we are trying to achieve with this book. Each practice in this book represents a slice of OpenUP/Basic and RUP, articulates what problem that slice is solving, and provides pragmatic guidance on how to solve the problems. The practices help you improve your software effort by attacking one problem at a time. Each practice describes how OpenUP/Basic and RUP can help you adopt the practice and also references other processes such as XP[2] and Scrum[3] so that you can understand differences and similarities between what the practice and other processes suggest. Work is going on to incorporate these and

---

1. Kroll 2003.
2. See Beck 2004.
3. See Schwaber 2002.

other processes into the EPF, which will provide you with a broader set of practices and processes to choose from—some consistent with this book, some not. This development will help drive innovation and will provide users of EPF with a broader set of tools to choose from.

*OpenUP/Basic and RUP provide details of how to execute the practice.*

OpenUP/Basic and RUP provide the details on how to execute the practice—the roles responsible, the step-by-step tasks to be performed, templates for the artifacts to be produced. Throughout the book you can incrementally adopt more and more practices. As you do so, you will discover that you are adopting a larger percentage of first OpenUP/Basic and then RUP. At some stage you will find that you are ready to adopt large chunks of RUP,[4] such as a whole discipline. The book is a springboard, allowing you to jump more effectively into the land of RUP without getting overwhelmed.

As you are following OpenUP/Basic and RUP, you can use the practices in this book to understand which aspects of OpenUP/Basic and RUP to focus on.

## Choosing the Right Pilot Project[5]

Introducing change always brings with it the risk of undesired negative effects. A key benefit of adopting a few practices at a time is the ability to improve incrementally, hence minimizing the risks of negative effects. However, if you choose to adopt many practices in a project, you should choose your initial project, or pilot project, carefully. Here are the things to consider:

- **Staffing profile.** Choose for your pilot people those who (1) have an interest in learning something new and (2) have the ability and the opportunity to act as mentors on future projects. Having pilot team members act as internal mentors on other projects is the fastest way of transferring knowledge. Also make sure that the project manager and the architect are qualified and work together as a team, because these are the two most important roles.

---

4. See Bergstrom 2004 for more information on adopting RUP.

5. This section adapted from Kroll 2003, Chapter 11.

- **Importance and complexity.** A pilot project should build real software that has a reasonably important business purpose. If the application isn't important enough, it may not garner sufficient resources to be successful. If not complex enough, people will say, "Well, building that application doesn't prove anything. Over here, we're building *real* software, and we still don't think you can do that with your process." In most cases you don't want your project to be so critical and complex that there are heavy pressures to take shortcuts on the process. That won't prove anything, except that the first time you used your process under suboptimal conditions, it did not save a doomed project. In certain cases, however, you actually want to choose a very high-profile, critical project—for example, when you have nothing to lose, or when you must force a rapid improvement of the process and tool environment to ensure business success. The advantage of choosing a critical project is that it will be likely to employ the most talented people, the strongest management support, and the deepest pockets to pay for necessary training, mentoring, and tool support.

- **Team size.** Most pilot projects work best if you have six to eight people on the project team, that is, enough people to introduce some elements of complexity, but not so many that people are overwhelmed. The ideal number of people may vary, however, based on the nature of the practice you are trying to adopt. Certain practices require larger teams to experience their value, such as those deemed more appropriate for medium or large projects.

- **Length and time constraints.** You want fast feedback on whether the practice works for you or not. Often, you do not have to run a complete pilot project to obtain the feedback you are looking for. The ideal length of a pilot project is typically two to six months, which is long enough to allow for some complexity and short enough to allow you to move on and put your experience to work on other projects. Furthermore, you don't want the time constraints to be too tight. You need to be able to take enough time for the project to learn to apply the practices and associated tools appropriately.

> *A pilot project should build real software that has a reasonably important business purpose.*

## Conclusions

The authors of this book hope that you find some practices in this book that you can easily adopt to improve your or your team's software development capabilities. We encourage you to check out EPF and RUP for more detailed guidance on these and other practices, and to keep up to speed with the latest practices on software development.

*Best practices allow you to avoid repeating mistakes for which others have already found solutions.*

Remember, best practices codify recipes for success, allowing you to avoid repeating mistakes many others have already made and found solutions for. As the philosopher George Santayana said, "Those who cannot remember the past are doomed to repeat it."[6]

---

6. Santayana 1905.

# APPENDIX A

# The Eclipse Process Framework (EPF)

## Why EPF?

The software industry abounds with expert knowledge of how to develop software effectively. That knowledge may be centered on (1) technologies, such as J2EE, .NET, or various tool environments; (2) various specialty domains, such as how to build secure software, how to best leverage service-oriented architectures, or how to do distributed development; and (3) various industry-specific bodies of knowledge, such as how to deal with straight-through processing in the financial world, or how to build embedded systems for the auto industry.

The sources for all of these great ideas and knowledge include companies doing software development; the agile community; Software Process Improvement Networks (SPIN groups); product and technology companies; academia and software research groups, such as SEI Carnegie Mellon and USC Center for Software Engineering; and a variety of thought leaders, practice leaders, and companies capturing industry best practices into various knowledge bases, books, and processes.

Presently, most of these process assets have a number of limitations:

- **Inadequate integration.** Different media, notations, language, and terminology are used to express process assets, making integration of the process assets difficult to achieve.

- **Redundancy or overlapping.** Process assets are developed with limited collaboration among different groups, leading some groups to reinvent the wheel rather than add value to preexisting work. This results in redundant or partially overlapping assets.

*Best practices are currently inadequately integrated, redundant, and poorly communicated.*

- **Poor communication.** Process assets are developed without an infrastructure that allows for integration and customization to the specific needs of an organization or project and are delivered in a form that often is hard for the end user to understand and use. As a result, the knowledge captured in the asset is not effectively communicated.

The purpose of EPF is to address the above issues by facilitating cohesion and usefulness of process assets and best practices. EPF also aims to foster an environment for effective collaboration and innovation in software development by bringing together communities and having them express process assets using a standard format. EPF also supports the ability to express a diversity of views in how to develop software, since this diversity drives innovation. The goals of EPF are further discussed in the following section.

## What Is EPF?

EPF, a project carried out under the auspices of the Eclipse Foundation, is aimed at building an open source process framework. IBM originally suggested the initiative, and many other companies and organizations jointly proposed and supported it. At the project's inception, the following companies were joint proposers: 2-Pro Mentor, Adaptive, AmbySoft, Armstrong Process Group, BearingPoint, Bedarra Research Lab, Capgemini, Catalysts, Covansys, European Software Institute, Ivar Jacobson International, Kruchten Engineering Services, Number Six Software, Object Mentor, Softeam, and the University of British Columbia. Project supporters included Jaczone, Object Management Group (OMG), NTTComware, Sogeti, Unisys, and Wind River. Additional companies and individuals with an interest in furthering the state of software development are continually joining this growing team.

EPF has two goals. The first is to provide an extensible process engineering framework and tools. The extensible process framework provides an executable language for processes (see the section Software Process Engineering Metamodel on page 368). It also provides tools to support method authoring, process authoring, library management, configuring, and publishing of a process, as well as a core set of process engineering capabilities on which additional process engineering tools can be built (see the section Extensible Process Engineering Tools on page 374).

*EPF provides an executable language for processes.*

The second goal of EPF is to provide the software development community with extensible process content that promotes iterative and agile development practices such as continuous integration and testing throughout the project lifecycle, while minimizing overhead and high degrees of formality. These practices should serve as sample content as well as a foundation for a variety of processes that may reuse this content. The section Extensible Process Content on page 367 provides more information.

*EPF promotes iterative and agile development practices.*

To jumpstart the project, IBM contributed an initial set of tools and content, as well as an evolving metamodel foundation.

## Potential Users of EPF

We expect to see a variety of usage models for EPF. Let's look at a few potential users of EPF and some usage scenarios they might encounter.

## Individual Project Teams

Teams working on individual projects within various software development organizations can easily download and deploy the out-of-the-box processes captured in EPF. The out-of-the box processes can be customized by mixing and matching content from various processes, removing content, or adding or customizing content by applying content plug-ins provided by the larger ecosystem around EPF. The teams can also capture their own practices with the content-authoring tools included in EPF. The resulting processes can be deployed and continually evolved to accommodate lessons learned as the project progresses.

## Enterprises or Line-of-Businesses

*Research shows 66 percent of projects fail or are challenged.*

Many organizations have problems implementing software projects successfully, and according to the Standish Group's research,[1] 66 percent of projects fail or are challenged. The main problem, however, is not that we do not *know* how to develop software in a predictable manner, but that most project teams do not use this knowledge. As a result, organizations that leverage practices with a proven track record have a much higher success rate than those that reinvent the wheel. As an example, the Standish Group's research shows that in 2000, projects using a formal methodology were 64 percent more likely to succeed than was the average project. This percentage is amazingly high, especially considering that many formal methodologies preach out-of-date practices such as waterfall development. It is also important for organizations to incorporate their own lessons learned to allow continuous process improvement, as well as being able to include unique in-house knowledge for their domain to make the process applicable.

*Projects using a formal methodology are 64 percent more likely to succeed.*

Let's consider how EPF can be used to address these needs.

Through the EPF ecosystem, that is, the organizations and community members that support EPF by delivering services or products or being involved in discussion and collaboration with EPF, development organizations can access a large volume of content. Examples include the open source content, content provided free of charge, and content that can be purchased from vendors. These organizations can thus obtain diverse software development knowledge that is integrated

---

1. Chaos 2003.

within the same framework. Companies can also capture their own best practices using the content-authoring capabilities in EPF.

All of this content can be packaged into a set of delivery processes that capture the relevant aspects of the process content for different project types (see the section Delivery Processes on page 371). Delivery processes can also specify project plan templates that may be appropriate starting points for different projects and link those templates to relevant process guidance, describing milestones and how to accomplish various objectives specified in the project plan template.

As project teams within an organization learn how to improve their approach to software development, they can then capture these learned practices and deploy them effectively. As the EPF ecosystem evolves content, this content can be continually rolled out to the organization, enabling continuous process improvements.

*Project teams can capture learned practices and deploy them effectively.*

Some select enterprises and line-of-businesses will see the value of evolving key process building blocks in EPF and will be willing to make investments to help improve the framework.

## Academic Institutions

Colleges and universities will play two important roles in the EPF ecosystem. First, as consumers, universities can leverage EPF to teach current best practices in their curricula. We expect that supporting material, such as textbooks and ready-made curricula, will be made available, making it easy for universities to develop courses. We also expect that discussion forums about EPF will allow students to exchange ideas about software development best practices with people in the industry.

*Universities can leverage EPF to teach current best practices in their curricula.*

The second role for academic institutions is to bring state-of-the-art software best practices into the mainstream software industry. Researchers can capture and share their experiences and research data within EPF, for example, research regarding which best practices increase productivity or quality the most. They can then discuss this research in associated discussion forums.

*Researchers can capture and share their research within EPF.*

## Vendors, Technology Companies, and Companies Interested in a Specific Domain

*Vendors can wrap their solutions within the context of a process.*

Vendors and technology companies, as well as the companies they collaborate with, typically have unique knowledge of a specific solution or technology. These companies can use EPF to capture this specialized knowledge. They, or consumers of their solutions and technology, can then wrap these solutions within the context of a process. For example, a vendor producing a software requirements tool can now capture guidance on how best to use this technology. The vendor can choose to ship a variant of EPF, including the requirements content, with the product. Companies using their requirements tool can then combine the requirements content with any other set of content available through the EPF ecosystem.

Companies that share an interest in a particular technology or domain may also use EPF to collaborate and develop content for that domain. For example, a handful of companies could jointly develop FDA-compliant guidelines inside or outside the Eclipse organization. They can keep this content as private, sell it, or make it freely available.

## System Integrators

System integrators will typically use EPF in the same way as enterprises or line-of-businesses (see above). Some system integrators, however, will add an additional usage scenario. They may be thought leaders or practice specialists within a certain domain and want to use EPF to improve the framework within that area, thus making at least some of their knowledge available through EPF. This approach enables domain specialists to showcase their expertise, which will in turn create more business for them, while providing the larger Eclipse community with an enhanced framework.

## Extensible Process Content

A key objective of EPF is to provide best practices that team members can easily adopt and assemble into a series of alternative, modifiable, and extensible processes that can be applied to different projects. The focus is on core development activities: requirements, analysis and design, implementation, testing, change management, and project management. Content includes role descriptions, work products/ artifacts for capturing information, activities and tasks, and various guidelines.

A second key objective of EPF is to provide software development teams with essential practices for iterative and agile software development, including the following: continuous integration; test-driven development; customer involvement throughout the project; iterative development; pair programming; use-case, scenario, or user-story-driven development; and the practices presented in this book. The goal is to be inclusive in the choice of best practices and to incorporate practices that may be accepted by some, but not necessarily all, constituencies.

While EPF strives for inclusivity, another key objective is simplicity. If EPF is too large and unmanageable, content will be difficult to find, maintain, and refresh. Consequently, overhead could creep into the process. Simplification can be achieved through continuous refactoring, which unifies two or more process elements that cover similar concepts and allows them to be expressed once and reused several times.

*EPF strives for simplicity, which can be achieved through continuous refactoring.*

This continuous refactoring has the advantage of driving convergence within the industry, encouraging agreement regarding proven practices and allowing the industry to derive further innovation from a common baseline. It is important, however, to ensure that EPF, while remaining simple, also provides a fertile environment for innovation by being open to, and in no way preventing, the expression of diverse views.

To meet these three key objectives, EPF currently works on two process frameworks:

- **Open Unified Process (OpenUP)** is an open-source version of the Unified Process. One of the contained processes is OpenUP/Basic, which is a very lightweight adaptation of the Unified Process with influences from Scrum.
- **Agile Process Framework** is a process framework reflecting XP, Agile Modeling, and other leading agile development approaches.

More processes can be created if deemed necessary, especially if we have people to contribute time and assets. It is easy to assemble new processes or create derivatives from existing processes on the fly, which reduces the number of processes that need to be provided out-of-the-box.

Reusable process fragments or process patterns can also be captured in capability patterns, as shown in the section Capability Patterns on page 372. Capability patterns can be used to construct a delivery process rapidly and offer the flexibility to supply the right process for the right situation while still providing commonalities between the processes.

## Software Process Engineering Metamodel[2]

*EPF provides flexibility while maximizing reuse of common best practices.*

EPF and the processes built on top of it share a common structure aimed at providing flexibility in supplying processes to users while maximizing reuse of common best practices. IBM has developed this metamodel, currently called the Unified Method Architecture (UMA), as an evolution of current OMG industry standard *Software Process Engineering Metamodel (SPEM) v1.0*.[3] With OMG, IBM and other OMG partners are working on improving UMA to become SPEM 2.0. As SPEM 2.0 stabilizes, EPF is expected to adopt this and other relevant industry standards around software process and software project management.

The metamodel provides a rich process engineering language. Below we will provide a brief overview of five core concepts: method content, delivery processes, capability patterns, categories, and plug-ins. Note that these and other concepts are optional. For example, you can author a process that does not define any tasks (part of the method content), or you can skip organizing method content into categories.

---

2. This section borrows from material contributed by Peter Haumer.
3. See http://www.omg.org/docs/formal/05-01-06.pdf.

## Method Content

The method content defines key reusable process building blocks (see Figure A.1):

*The method content defines key reusable process building blocks.*

- **Work products.** What is produced, or desired outcomes.
- **Roles.** Who performs the work.
- **Tasks.** How to perform the work.
- **Guidance.** Additional information linked to the other method elements.

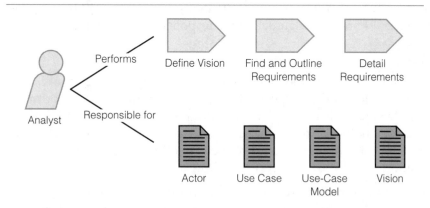

**FIGURE A.1  Work Products, Roles, and Tasks.** *Method guidance defines reusable process building blocks. The figure shows that the analyst role is responsible for a number of work products: actor, use case, use-case model, and vision. The analyst also performs a set of tasks: define vision, find and outline requirements, and detail requirements.*

### Work Products

**Work products** can take various shapes or forms, such as the following:

- An *artifact* is a physical piece of information that is used or produced by a software development process. Examples of artifacts include documents such as a vision document or software development plan; models, such as a use-case model or design model; source files; scripts; and a binary executable.

- A *deliverable* is one or more work products that are of value to a stakeholder and are packaged for delivery to a stakeholder.
- An *outcome* is an intangible work product that is a result or state, such as an installed server, optimized network, or approved funding.

## Roles

A role describes a set of skills and responsibilities that must be supplied and assumed by a team member. Examples of roles include *analyst, developer,* and *tester.* An individual will typically take on several roles at one time and frequently change roles over the duration of a project. For instance, in a specific project you may take on some of the responsibilities of an analyst and all of the responsibilities of a developer.

## Tasks

Tasks define how to move the project forward by creating or updating one or more work products. The work is performed by one or more people in specific roles, relates to work products as input and output, and is usually defined as a series of steps that involve creating or updating one or more work products. The following are examples of tasks:

- **Find and outline requirements.** This task is performed by a person taking on the analyst role to identify use cases and key supporting requirements, and define a basic outline for them. The main input is the vision for the project, and the major outputs are outlined requirements.
- **Analyze architecture.** This task is performed by a person taking on the software architecture role to come up with a candidate architecture for the system. The major inputs are requirements, including the vision. The major output is a description of the architecture.

## Guidance

Guidance provides additional information related to key elements such as roles, tasks, work products, and processes (see following sections). Guidance includes guidelines, templates, checklists, tool mentors, supporting material, reports, and concepts.

## Delivery Processes

A delivery process describes a complete project lifecycle end to end and will be used as a reference or template for running projects with similar characteristics as defined for the process (see Figure A.2). A delivery process can, for example, provide guidance for a small J2EE project developing a new application, a large package implementation project, or a medium-sized project enhancing an existing application. The delivery process template provides users with a lifecycle, including a suggested iteration pattern.

*A delivery process describes a complete project lifecycle end to end.*

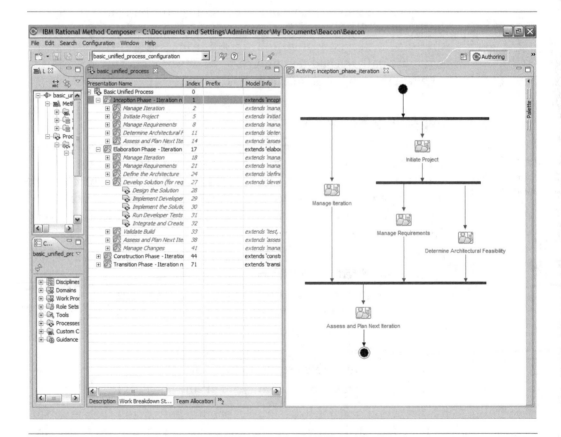

**FIGURE A.2 The Inception Iteration Template in the OpenUP/Basic Delivery Process.** *On the left the OpenUP/Basic delivery process is represented as a work breakdown structure (WBS). On the right is a graphical depiction of the same information for the Inception iteration template. The WBS editor and graphical editor operate on the same data, ensuring that the two representations remain consistent.*

The delivery process suggests which capability patterns (see below) to use in each phase. The delivery process also suggests which activities should be assigned and tracked, because managing every task is typically too much overhead. This can be modified to fit the management style and size of the project.

It is critical to understand that a delivery process is a template. One cannot know in advance exactly how many iterations a project should use. The number will be determined based on the specific problems and issues the project faces through its lifecycle. Likewise, one cannot know in advance which capability patterns to apply at what time. This question will be answered as current status, mitigated risks, and the goals of the current iteration are assessed. A delivery process, however, is very valuable to a project team, since it conveys what capability patterns and iteration patterns other teams have found useful when working on similar projects.

## Capability Patterns

*A capability pattern is a recurring process pattern.*

A capability pattern is a recurring process pattern that describes a reusable cluster of activities in a common process area. Capability patterns are used as building blocks to assemble delivery processes or larger capability patterns to enable reuse of the key practices they express. Capability patterns aim to accomplish a well-defined objective, for example:

- Produce a high-level understanding of requirements that have been validated with customers.
- Detail requirements and in parallel design, implement, integrate, test, and validate a related scenario or use case with the end user.
- Detail requirements and in parallel design, implement, integrate, and test a related component or capability.
- Produce a candidate architecture.
- Create a contract for a commercial off-the-shelf (COTS) solution.

It is also good practice to design a capability pattern to produce one or more generic deliverables, so that the process engineer can select patterns for assembly by deciding which deliverables are required. You can also use capability patterns as a learning tool by describing knowledge for a key area such as a discipline (e.g., requirements management) or a specific technical area (e.g., relational database design).

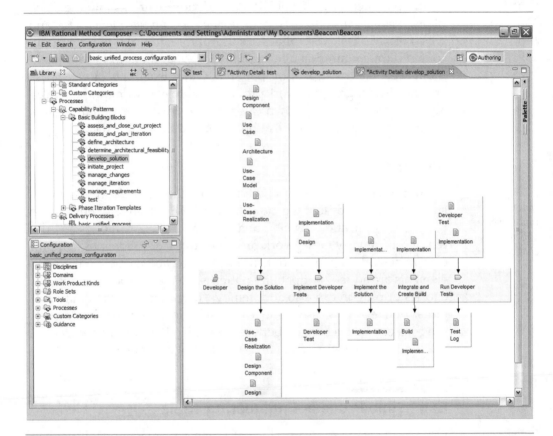

**FIGURE A.3 Capability Pattern in OpenUP/Basic.** *OpenUP/Basic is constructed from a number of capability patterns. The figure shows a capability pattern for designing, implementing, and testing a scenario or other type of requirement. It comprises five tasks (shown in the central horizontal box on the right side: Design the Solution . . . Run Developer Tests) all performed by a developer. Each task has a set of defined input work products (shown above each task) and produces or updates a set of work products (shown below each task).*

## Categories

*A category is a logical grouping of process elements.*

A category is a logical grouping of process elements. There are many different types of categories, for example, a discipline, which is used to group related tasks. OpenUP/Basic divides its tasks into the disciplines *requirements, architecture, development, implementation, test,* and *project management.* Disciplines are useful for end users to learn about content in a certain domain and for process authors to ensure maximum reuse across capability patterns. Other examples of categories are domains for grouping work products and role sets for grouping roles. You can also define your own categories to create, for example, navigation structures or categorization of content into SEI CMMI levels.[4]

## Plug-Ins

*A plug-in is a container of any type of method and process content.*

A **plug-in** is a container of any type of method and process content, such as content describing how to use J2EE effectively, how to do packaged application development, or how to use JUnit. It can add, remove, or modify tasks, work products, roles, or guidelines in a process framework. A plug-in contains information about how these process elements are added to capability patterns, delivery processes, and categories. A plug-in can also add, remove, or modify the capability patterns, delivery processes, and disciplines in a process framework. Plug-ins can be exchanged between organizations and project teams, enabling the development of an ecosystem of best practices.

## Extensible Process Engineering Tools

*EPF provides tools for authoring, library management, configuring, and publishing.*

EPF leverages the software process engineering metamodel described above to provide tools and a basic framework for method authoring, process authoring, library management, and configuring and publishing. The framework is extensible, allowing alternative or additional process engineering tools to be built by extending the core functionality.

---

4. See www.sei.cmu.edu/cmmi/.

Let's have a look at some of the tool capabilities:

- **Method authoring.** Best practices can be captured as a set of reusable method building blocks as defined in the metamodel: roles, work products, tasks, and guidance—such as templates, guidelines, examples, and checklists. Relationships between method elements can be defined through forms. A rich-text editor allows you to document method elements, and graphical views present diagrams showing relevant relationships. Reuse is facilitated by the ability to create a method element as a derivative of another method element through various inheritance-type relationships. As a result, you can, for example, specify that a systems architect has similar responsibilities to a software architect by expressing the differences and reusing everything that is common.

- **Process authoring.** Reusable process building blocks can be organized into processes along a lifecycle dimension by defining, for example, work breakdown structures and specifying when in the lifecycle what work products are produced in which state. The tool allows you to construct reusable chunks of processes through capability patterns. A capability pattern that specifies, for example, how to define, design, implement, and test a scenario can now be reused in a variety of processes. The tool also allows you to define delivery processes, which are end-to-end processes. Structural information can often be edited with graphical as well as nongraphical editors.

- **Library management and content extensibility.** An XMI-based library enables persistency and configuration management as well as content interchange for distributed client-server implementations. Method and process content can be packaged into content plug-ins and content packages, allowing simple distribution, management, and extensibility of content. As content plug-ins are added to your content library, the tool will resolve dependencies between process elements. Plug-ins can also be exported to XML to allow interchange with other tools.

- **Configuring and publishing.** You can create a process configuration by selecting a set of content plug-ins and content packages. Optionally, you can use an existing process configuration as a starting point and add or remove content plug-ins and content packages to or from the configuration. For example, you may start with a generic configuration suitable for small collocated teams and add content plug-ins containing specific guidance for each of Eclipse, JUnit, J2EE, and IBM Rational RequisitePro. The delivery processes associated with a configuration can be further customized. As the configuration is published, the tool resolves the many relationships that may exist among process elements in the selected plug-ins and packages, and generates a set of html pages with links representing relationships among process elements. The resulting Web site that project members use to view the process they have decided to use is thus easy to navigate, and viewable via a Web browser without a Web server. This process will allow users on all platforms to view the published process (see Figure A.4).

## Participating in the Development of EPF

*Anyone can help enhance EPF.*

Because EPF is developed applying the same open source principles and rules as any other Eclipse project, anyone can view the open source code and content as it evolves, and anyone can help enhance it. For this approach to work, there need to be some rules of engagement.

Eclipse is run as a meritocracy: you earn your entitlement to collaborate by demonstrating an ability to add value. Anybody can submit suggestions for enhancements, and anybody can submit content or code to be included in future versions of EPF. People who submit content or code are called "contributors."

Those who have the right actually to make changes to the product are called "committers." This group determines which of the changes proposed by contributors should be included in the next release. Typically, committers are also contributors. Contributors who have proved themselves over an extended period of time can become committers.

You can find more information about how Eclipse works, and about EPF, at www.eclipse.org.

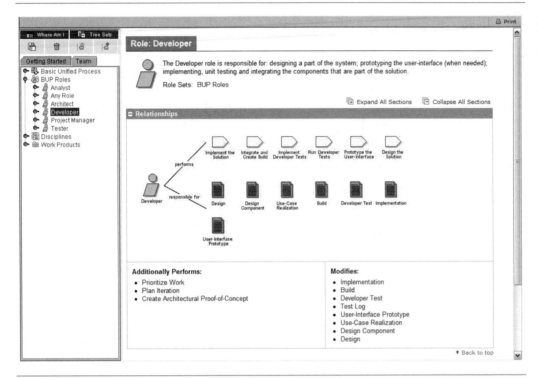

**FIGURE A.4 A Published Web Site Representing a Process Configuration.** *A published Web site consists of a set of html pages, which can be viewed with a standard Web browser. This example gives a brief description of the developer's role and graphically depicts the tasks a developer performs and the work product for which the developer is responsible. Hyperlinks make it easy to find additional information, such as guidelines or templates, for tasks and work products.*

# APPENDIX B

# IBM Rational Method Composer (RMC)

The IBM Rational Method Composer (RMC) is a commercial product built on top of EPF (see Appendix A). It is the next major evolution of the product previously called RUP and, among other things, integrates the methods from RUP[1] and IBM Rational SUMMIT Ascendant.[2]

The objective of RMC is to provide a comprehensive process solution for the enterprise. RMC consists of three major components:

1. The RUP process framework for guiding people in the development of a variety of software-intensive systems, including *legacy evolution, commercial-off-the-shelf (COTS) development, service-oriented architecture, systems engineering, and maintenance.*

2. Enterprise process guidance derived from IBM Rational SUMMIT Ascendant, RUP, and newly created content.

3. Eclipse-based tooling for authoring, configuring, viewing, and publishing processes, including integration with IBM Rational Portfolio Manager to provide an execution environment of an enterprise process framework.

*RMC provides a comprehensive process solution for the enterprise.*

---

1. RUP came to IBM through the acquisition of Rational Software.

2. IBM SUMMIT Ascendant came to IBM through the acquisition of PriceWaterhouseCoopers.

For organizations focused on software, systems, or enterprise IT capability, RMC provides processes for defining existing or improved business processes and describes the organization and IT requirements for implementing desired improvements. It can guide projects ranging from small collocated development to distributed or large-scale development, from packaged application and legacy evolution to maintenance and custom application development projects. It provides a framework for executing projects within the context of a project, program, or a portfolio, and it links IT investments to high-priority business improvements while leveraging various development and deployment environments, such as service-oriented architectures.

RMC also provides tools that allow you to capture your own best practices, assemble what is suitable for a project or set of projects, and communicate those best practices to the project team. RMC integrates the process with tools for analysis, development, and testing as well as for management of projects and portfolios.

Let's look at the content RMC provides for projects of different types, as well as its cross-project and enterprise-level guidance. We will also look at how RMC can deliver value to practitioners and team members, project managers, and process managers or process engineers.

## Process for a Variety of Projects

*The RMC product comes with a set of out-of-the-box processes.*

The RMC product comes with a set of *out-of-the-box processes*, or *delivery processes*. These describe an end-to-end process, including a suggested order of activities, such as what phases to plan for and typical iteration patterns. These can be used out of the box, or as a starting point for further customizations. New delivery processes are added and made available via the DeveloperWorks Web site.[3] At the time of publishing, the following processes are available:

- **RUP for small projects.** This process guides small and collocated teams in how to develop new software or make major improvements to existing software.

---

3. See www.ibm.com/developerworks.

- **RUP for medium-sized projects.** This process guides distributed and medium-sized teams in how to develop new software or make major improvements to existing software.

- **RUP for large projects (classic RUP).** This process guides distributed and large-scale teams in how to develop or refine business models, how to develop new software, and how to make major improvements to existing software to support an evolving business. This process is most appropriate for organizations working to meet industry or regulatory compliance guidelines, such as Sarbanes-Oxley, SEI CMMI, Basel, and ISO 9001.

- **RUP for COTS or packaged application development.** This process describes how to choose the right components for reuse and how to make the right trade-offs among reuse, addressing requirements, programmatic risk, and marketplace concerns. The process addresses how to incorporate one or several smaller components, as well as how to customize large packages to your needs (see Figure B.1).

- **RUP for systems engineering.** This process describes how to develop systems that consist of a combination of software, hardware, and people, addressing the common problems these resources present through effective, unified collaboration. This process is used in a variety of projects, from large-scale defense and communications projects to embedded software projects in the automobile industry.

- **RUP for service-oriented architecture.** This process describes how to define business processes and couple them with services (see Figure B.2). It provides a variety of approaches for identifying the appropriate business elements to expose as service components by analyzing current assets and data structures. The approach includes specific guidance on how to leverage J2EE and other technologies to implement Web services effectively.

- **RUP for maintenance.** This process describes how to take a set of defects and change requests and drive an incremental release of an existing product.

- **SUMMIT systems delivery.** This process describes how to develop an application using traditional structured systems development techniques.

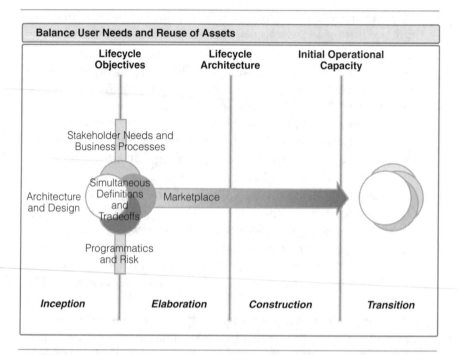

**FIGURE B.1 RUP for COTS/Packaged Application Development.** *RUP for COTS or packaged application development describes how to balance trade-offs among stakeholders, availability of commercial components, architectural concerns, and program risks as you develop applications using COTS or implement packaged applications.*

*RMC provides specialized content to support a variety of domains and technologies.*

RMC also provides specialized content to support a variety of domains and technologies that can be used to augment or alter the delivery processes listed above, or to build completely new delivery processes. This content is packaged as downloadable "plug-ins," which can be added to your processes library at any time. IBM and partners continuously develop new plug-ins.

Following are some key content areas covered by these plug-ins:

- **J2EE development.** This includes guidance on architectural patterns, designs targeting various deployment environments, and effective use of tools to develop J2EE applications.

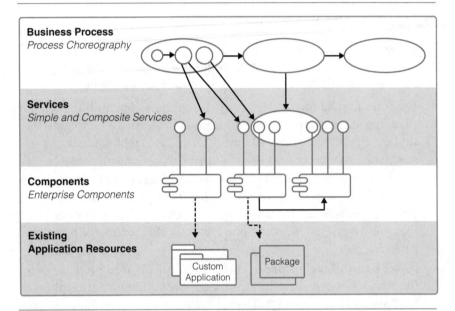

**FIGURE B.2 RUP for Service-Oriented Architecture.** *RUP for service-oriented architecture describes how to define and simulate business processes; how to identify services from business processes, use cases, existing data, and legacy components; how to couple services to business processes to allow close coupling between business needs and IT assets; and how to implement services and service components.*

- **.NET development.** This includes guidance on distribution patterns, application design, .NET platform elements, architectural layering, and effective use of tools to develop .NET applications.
- **User-centered engineering.** This includes user experience modeling, navigation maps, storyboards, wire frames, usability testing, and user-centered design.
- **Tool-specific guidance.** This includes how to leverage IBM Rational software development tools, as well as partner tools, effectively.

## Process for the Enterprise

*RMC addresses cross-project concerns at the program, portfolio, and enterprise level.*

RMC also addresses cross-project concerns at the program, portfolio, and enterprise level. We expect to expand upon this content rapidly. At the time of publishing, the content includes the following:

- **Program management.** This provides guidance on mobilizing and planning large or very large program efforts, such as implementation of a program office, planning, and the establishment of program governance, controls, and supporting infrastructure.

- **Portfolio management.** This provides guidance on planning and executing a portfolio assessment, managing business cases, conducting periodic and strategic reviews of ongoing initiatives, and making decisions about whether to continue or discontinue the project.

- **Asset-based development.** This provides guidance on asset production, asset consumption, and asset portfolio management.

- **Business engineering.** This provides guidance on modeling business goals, existing and future business processes, and organizational structure, as well as simulation of business process. It also describes how to link business processes to existing or future software assets.

- **Process engineering.** This provides guidance on effective leveraging of IBM RMC for your process initiative, as well as on carrying out process improvement efforts.

- **Systems engineering.** As described in the section Process for a Variety of Projects on page 380, this process is used both at a project level and for large programs, where an overall system is defined and a large number of integrated projects are developing individual components—all leveraging the same system architecture.

IBM has also released the IBM Tivoli Unified Process, which addresses the needs of operations and systems management organizations. This process is based on a UK-based standard, IT Information Library (ITIL). IBM Tivoli Unified Process is not included in the RMC product but is hosted on the same tooling platform. Content from RMC and IBM Tivoli Unified Process can therefore be customized and used together.

## How the Practitioner Uses RMC

RMC provides structure for the practitioner in three areas: productivity, guidance, and personalization. Let's walk through what RMC provides in each of these areas.

*RMC provides practitioners with productivity tools, guidance, and personalization technology.*

- **Productivity.** A key reason for following a process is to be more productive. RMC provides a number of productivity tools:
  - *Templates* to provide a starting point for producing key artifacts.
  - *Roles, tasks,* and *artifacts* to understand how to collaborate effectively with the rest of the team.
  - *Tool mentors* that provide detailed guidance on how to use a specific tool to carry out tasks described in the process.
  - *Process advisor* to understand how best to leverage tools by providing context-sensitive process guidance directly within your development environment.
- **Guidance.** RMC provides a number of different types of guidance:
  - *Guidelines, techniques,* and *concepts* to help teams learn about new approaches in software development and how to leverage key technologies and techniques effectively.
  - *Examples* so that teams can learn from the success of others.
  - *Checklists* for rapid assessment of work in progress and for seeing how it can be improved.
- **Personalization.** Based on your experience level, role, and interest, you can personalize your interface toward the process to focus on what matters to you, either through MyView for Web browser access or through Process Advisor using an Eclipse-based interface.

## How a Project Manager Uses RMC

RMC focuses on addressing three critical areas for the project managers: rapid project initiation, flexibility, and reality-based management.

1. **Rapid project initiation.** Once a decision has been made to initiate a project, time is usually a precious commodity. The purpose of the out-of-the-box *delivery processes* (see Figure B.3) is to provide the project manager with a quick starting point for planning and

*Delivery processes provide the project manager with a quick starting point.*

initiating a project. The delivery process will provide an initial project template, identify what type of project milestones to include, specify what work products to deliver at each milestone, and state what resources are needed for each phase. The integration between RMC and IBM Rational Portfolio Manager allows the manager to instantiate a project plan rapidly based on a starting template and project specifics. Microsoft Project plan templates can also be generated from RMC.

2. **Flexibility.** No two projects are alike; a project manager needs to modify the process rapidly to address specific project needs. He or she can do this through *plug-ins* and *selectable method packages*, allowing content around various domains—such as database modeling or advanced requirements management—to be added or removed. *Capability patterns* allow project managers to add or remove quickly process patterns that pertain to specific problems. RMC also allows a project manager to modify rapidly any aspect of a delivery process.

*RPM provides a complete environment for managing RUP projects.*

3. **Reality-based management.** Experience has shown that most *detailed* project plans produced at project inception are worthless halfway to completion. For this reason a delivery process is assembled from capability patterns. You can apply these process patterns as needed as you go through a project, rather than creating a detailed plan for the entire project up front. You can transfer delivery processes and capability patterns to RPM and instantiate your project plan in increments, one or a few capability patterns at a time. RPM provides a complete environment for managing RUP projects and makes it possible for (1) team members to understand what tasks are the most important, estimate time to complete tasks, and manage documents and reviews; and (2) project managers to distribute assignments, manage schedules and resources, and collaborate with the team to understand project issues. RPM also provides portfolio management capabilities, as well as enabling the entire team to view a variety of metrics related to project health and status, such as requirement and code churn, defect trends, and progress relative to the project/iteration plan.

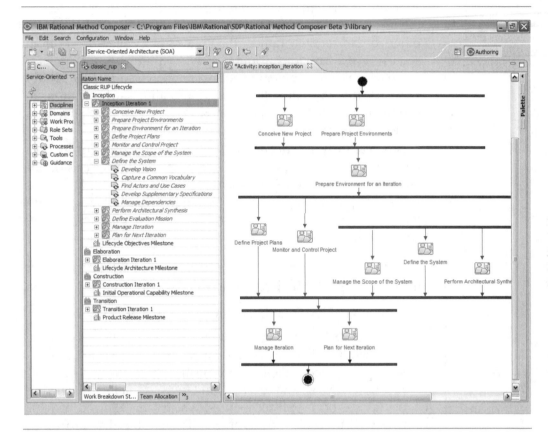

**FIGURE B.3 Delivery Process Depicted Graphically and as a Work Breakdown Structure.** *A delivery process provides, among other things, a work breakdown structure that can be exported to IBM Rational Portfolio Manager and Microsoft Project. The delivery process also depicts graphically what activities and tasks should be done in what order, what work products and artifacts will be produced at what time, and what roles you need to staff at different stages of a project.*

## How Process Managers Use RMC

Process managers, process engineers, or content owners must determine the appropriate process for various teams within the organization. To accomplish this, the process manager requires *breadth of content* and the ability to *customize* the process to the needs of different project types, as follows:

*RMC allows organizations to capture their own best practices.*

- **Breadth of content.** To address the breadth of process needs of organizations, teams need to reuse best practices that work for other organizations rather than inventing everything from scratch. RMC provides a foundation of enterprise-level process content, which is supplemented by commercial and open source plug-ins from IBM and others. RMC also allows organizations to capture their own best practices by seamlessly extending the RMC content libraries.

- **Customizability.** It is not enough to have a lot of content; you also need to be able to leverage that content to execute projects of different types effectively. This goal is achieved by enabling process managers, process engineers, and content owners to package content into reusable *capability patterns* and to construct *delivery processes* for various project types out of capability patterns.

---

## History of the RMC Product

The evolution of RMC has gone through a number of phases:

- **Phase 1: 1987–1996.** In 1987, the company Objectory AB launched the Objectory process[4] (principal author Ivar Jacobson). The process focused on business modeling, requirements, analysis, and design, and was formally modeled using object-oriented techniques, which later allowed us to make the process customizable and extensible. The process was use-case-driven, to ensure that the requirements were not only captured but also designed, implemented, and tested.

- **Phase 2: 1996–1999.** In 1995 Rational Software Corporation acquired Objectory and started to integrate the Objectory process with the Rational Approach.[5] The Rational Approach (principal authors Grady Booch, Walker Royce, and Philippe Kruchten) was an iterative and architecture-driven process that used the four phases currently in RUP. The result was

---

4. Jacobson 1994.
5. Devlin 1995.

launched in 1996 under the name Rational Objectory Process (with Philippe Kruchten as developer manager and Per Kroll as product manager). Over the next four years Rational acquired a large number of companies, and integrated its processes into RUP, including requirements management content[6] (principal author Dean Leffingwell) from Requisite Inc., test content from SQA, and configuration and change management content from Pure-Atria. In 1998, the name was changed to Rational Unified Process as the process was made to support UML, and in 1999 RUP covered the full project lifecycle.

- **Phase 3: 2000–2005.** In 2000 we started to rely increasingly on partners for specialized content. We worked with Microsoft and Applied Information Sciences to create a WinDNA version of RUP and with IBM, BEA, and Sun Microsystems to create a J2EE version of RUP. As we worked with more and more partners, and as the customer base expanded, we needed a more sophisticated process environment. In 2001 we launched authoring and configuring tools, allowing content producers to develop content plug-ins and consumers to configure a process from plug-ins. A large number of plug-ins were made available, and many companies did extensive customizations of RUP.

- **Phase 4: 2005– .** In 2005 we completely rebuilt the process tooling, with the capabilities described above. The process content expanded beyond RUP, to include, among other things, portfolio management content and content from SUMMIT Ascendant. The name of the product was changed to IBM Rational Method Composer to reflect these changes. In 2006 the RMC product was localized to nine languages: French, German, Italian, Spanish, Brazilian Portuguese, Simplified Chinese, Traditional Chinese, Korean, and Japanese. In 2005, the EPF open source project was created with +20 organizations supporting the effort within the first few months.

---

6. Leffingwell 2000.

## Guiding Principles for Evolving IBM Rational Method Composer

Since we are playing a key role in the evolution of RMC, as well as the foundation of EPF, we have some final words.

During the last decade, RUP has continuously evolved by leveraging best practices from a variety of sources. This evolution occurred through integration with other proven processes, such as the Objectory Process, the Rational Process, and SUMMIT Ascendant; through collaboration with leading edge companies and institutions, such as SEI Carnegie Mellon, USC Center for Computer Engineering, and a large number of companies that have pushed the state of the art in software development; and through efforts from the broader software development community, which has contributed innovations such as agile development techniques. Every year we receive more than 1,000 enhancement requests for our process framework from our customers. As we move forward with broader support for the expanding software development process arena, we rely on you to "keep us honest" and to continue to help us evolve the RMC product.

RMC and its predecessors have always provided a stand-alone process, independent of tools. At the same time, these process frameworks have ensured tight integration with software tools for teams seeking automated tool environments, especially IBM Rational Software Development Platform and the Eclipse platform. We strongly believe that the greatest productivity gains are reached by integrating process with tools.

*A process works only when it helps team members to collaborate more effectively.*

Since RUP made its debut in 1996, the Rational team has firmly believed that a superior process framework must empower individual team members. Only then will a process be successfully adopted within an organization. Far too many process improvement initiatives are driven by management's desire to standardize a process simply because it will drive "rigor" or "predictability," but these efforts fail when practitioners cannot see how the process makes their lives easier. For this reason we have always focused on what the individual team members need. In the end, software is built by teams, and a process works only when it helps team members to collaborate more effectively.

# GLOSSARY

This glossary captures key terms that may be especially important for those who read the book in nonsequential order. Terms in italics are defined elsewhere in the glossary.

**Actor** (from *RUP*)   Someone or something, outside the system (or business), that interacts with the system (or business).

**Agile Modeling**   An agile process, created by Scott Ambler, for modeling and documentation of software-based systems.

**Architecture** (from *RUP*)   The highest-level concept of a system in its environment, according to IEEE. The architecture of a software system (at a given point in time) is its organization or structure of significant components interacting through interfaces; these components comprise successively smaller components and interfaces.

**Component** (from *RUP*)   A nontrivial, nearly independent, and replaceable part of a system that fulfills a clear function in the context of a well-defined architecture. A component conforms to and provides the physical realization of a set of interfaces.

**Construction**   The third phase of the *Unified Process lifecycle*, where most of the software is developed, leading to the development of an operational system or a beta release.

**Crystal**   A family of agile processes developed by Alistair Cockburn. They scale from less disciplined to more disciplined: Crystal Clear, Crystal Yellow, Crystal Orange, Crystal Red, and so on.

**Eclipse Process Framework (EPF)**   An open source process framework developed within the Eclipse open source organization.

**Elaboration**    The second phase of the *Unified Process lifecycle*, in which the product vision, its requirements, and its *architecture* are fully defined. Major risks are mitigated to update cost and schedule estimates.

**EPF**    See Eclipse Process Framework.

**eXtreme Programming (XP)**    An agile process created by Kent Beck. XP articulates five values to guide you in your project: Communication, Simplicity, Feedback, Courage, and Respect.

**IBM Rational Method Composer (RMC)**    A commercial process product built on top of *EPF*. It includes *RUP*, other method content, and method tooling.

**Inception**    The first phase of the *Unified Process lifecycle*, in which the scope of the project and its motivations are defined, and all stakeholders either buy into the project or decide not to proceed with it.

**Iteration**    A time-box within a project with a plan and evaluation criteria, allowing for incremental delivery of code and supporting documentation that can be assessed by stakeholders at the end of each iteration.

**Legacy System**    A mature system that serves ongoing needs. Legacy systems are often old, monolithic systems, built using older design approaches and older technologies.

**Open Unified Process (OpenUP)**    An open-source process framework based on the *Unified Process lifecycle*. *OpenUP/Basic* is a subset of OpenUP.

**OpenUP/Basic**    A simplified version of the *Unified Process*, targeting smaller and collocated teams interested in agile and iterative development. OpenUP/Basic is a subset of OpenUP, and is a part of the *Eclipse Process Framework*.

**OpenUP**    See Open Unified Process.

**Pattern**    A named strategy for solving a recurring problem.

**Phase** (from Kroll 2003)    The time between two major project milestones, during which a well-defined set of objectives is met, *work* *products* are completed, and decisions are made to move or not move into the next phase.

**Plug-In**  A container of any type of method and process content. It can add, remove, or modify content in a method framework.

**Product Backlog**  A list of all to-do items for an application used in *Scrum*, corresponding to the *OpenUP/Basic* concept of a *work item list*.

**Rational Unified Process (RUP)**  A customizable method framework providing guidance for a variety of project types and enterprise needs. RUP is an extension of *OpenUP/Basic* and is delivered through the *IBM Rational Method Composer*.

**Risk** (from Kroll 2003)  An ongoing or upcoming concern that has a significant probability of adversely affecting the success of major milestones.

**RMC**  See IBM Rational Method Composer.

**Role**  A definition of the behavior and responsibilities of an individual or set of individuals working together as a team.

**RUP**  See Rational Unified Process.

**Scenario** (from UML)  A specific sequence of actions that illustrates behaviors. A scenario may be used to illustrate an interaction or the execution of one or more use-case instances.

**Scrum**  An agile software project management process introduced by Ken Schwaber and Jeff Sutherland. Scrum is known for self-organized teams, thirty-day iterations called Sprints, daily team meetings called Scrum, and a to-do list called *Product Backlog*.

**Service** (In service-oriented architecture)  A published capability that can be discovered and used dynamically.

**Sprint Backlog**  The subset of a *product backlog* targeted for implementation within a sprint, which is Scrum's term for *iteration*.

**Task**  Tasks define how to move the project forward by creating or updating one or more *work products*. The work is performed by one or more people in specific *roles* and involves creating or updating one or more work products.

**Transition**    The fourth and last phase of the *Unified Process lifecycle*, which results in a final product release.

**Unified Process**    A family of processes and process frameworks, including *OpenUP* and *RUP,* sharing a common set of characteristics; adherence to the *Unified Process lifecycle,* iterative, architecture-centric, and use-case-driven development.

**Unified Process lifecycle**    A management lifecycle common for processes in the Unified Process family. It divides a project into four *phases: Inception, Elaboration, Construction,* and *Transition.* Each phase is further divided into one or several *iterations.*

**Use case** (from Kroll 2003)    A sequence of actions a system performs that yields an observable result of value to a particular *actor.* A use-case class contains all main, alternate, and exception flows of events related to producing the "observable result of value."

**User Story**    A user-specified requirement used to plan and track a project. A user story comes from XP and should be able to be implemented within a single *iteration* by a pair of programmers.

**XP**    See eXtreme Programming.

**Waterfall Development**    An approach to software development in which the requirements, architecture, design, implementation, integration, and testing are sequentially defined.

**Work Item**    A to-do item used to plan and assign work. Some examples are requirements to implement, defects to fix, tasks to perform, and work products to produce.

**Work Item List**    A list of *work items* used in *OpenUP/Basic,* corresponding to *Scrum*'s concept of *product backlog.*

**Work Product**    Something that is produced, or a desired outcome. The most common type of work product is an artifact, which is a physical piece of information that is used or produced by a software development process, such as a document, model, or model element.

# BIBLIOGRAPHY

Allen 2002. Eric E Allen. "Diagnosing Java Code: Assertions and Temporal Logic in Java." Found online in IBM's *developerWorks* Web site at http://www-106.ibm.com/developerworks/java/library/j-diag0723.html.

Ambler 2002. Scott W. Ambler and Ron Jeffries. *Agile Modeling: Effective Practices for Extreme Programming and the Unified Process.* Hoboken, NJ: John Wiley & Sons, 2002.

Ambler 2003. Scott W. Ambler. *Agile Database Techniques: Effective Strategies for the Agile Software Developer.* Hoboken, NJ: John Wiley & Sons, 2003.

Ambler 2004. Scott W. Ambler. *The Object Primer: Agile Model-Driven Development with UML 2.0.* Cambridge, UK: Cambridge University Press, 2004.

Ambler 2005. Scott W. Ambler, John Nalbone, and Michael J. Vizdos. *The Enterprise Unified Process: Extending the Rational Unified Process.* Upper Saddle River, NJ: Prentice Hall, 2005.

Ambler 2006. Scott W. Ambler and Pramodkumar J. Sadalage. *Refactoring Databases: Evolutionary Database Design.* Boston: Addison-Wesley, 2006.

Arlow 2002. Jim Arlow and Ila Neustadt. *UML and the Unified Process: Practical Object-Oriented Analysis and Design.* Boston: Addison-Wesley, 2002.

Arnold 1993. Robert S. Arnold. *Software Reengineering (IEEE Computer Society Press Tutorial).* Institute of Electrical & Electronics Engineers, 1993.

Astels 2003. David Astels. *Test-Driven Development: A Practical Guide.* Upper Saddle River, NJ: Prentice Hall, 2003.

Augustine 2005. Sanjiv Augustine. *Managing Agile Projects.* Boston: Addison-Wesley, 2005.

Bass 2003. Len Bass, Paul Clements, and Rick Kazman. *Software Architecture in Practice, Second Edition.* Boston: Addison-Wesley, 2003.

Beck 2000. Kent Beck. *Extreme Programming Explained: Embrace Change.* Boston: Addison-Wesley, 2000.

Beck 2001. Kent Beck and Martin Fowler. *Planning Extreme Programming.* Boston: Addison-Wesley, 2001.

Beck 2003. Kent Beck. *Test-Driven Development: By Example.* Boston: Addison-Wesley, 2003.

Beck 2004. Kent Beck with Cynthia Andres. *Extreme Programming Explained: Embrace Change, Second Edition.* Boston: Addison-Wesley, 2004.

Beizer 1995. Boris Beizer. *Black Box Testing.* Hoboken, NJ: John Wiley & Sons, 1995.

Bellagio 2004. David Bellagio and Ana Giordano. *UCM Stream Strategies and Best Practices.* Grapevine, TX: Rational Software Development User Conference, July 2004.

Bellagio 2005. David Bellagio and Tom Milligan. *Software Configuration Management Strategies and IBM Rational ClearCase: A Practical Introduction, Second Edition.* IBM Press, 2005.

Bennett 1997. Douglas W. Bennett. *Designing Hard Software: The Essential Tasks.* Chicago, IL: Independent Publishers Group, 1997.

Berczuk 2002. S. Berczuk and B. Appleton. *Software Configuration Management Patterns: Effective Teamwork, Practical Integration.* Addison-Wesley, 2002.

Bergström 2004. Stefan Bergström and Lotta Råberg. *Adopting the Rational Unified Process: Success with the RUP.* Boston: Addison-Wesley, 2004.

Bittner 2002. Kurt Bittner and Ian Spence. *Use Case Modeling.* Boston: Addison-Wesley, 2002.

Boehm 1988. Barry W. Boehm. "A Spiral Model of Software Development and Enhancement." *IEEE Computer* 21 (5), May 1988, pp. 61–72.

Boehm 1991. Barry W. Boehm, "Software Risk Management: Principles and Practices." *IEEE Software*, January 1991, pp. 32–41.

Boehm 2000. Barry W. Boehm et al. *Software Cost Estimation with COCOMO II*. Upper Saddle River, NJ: Prentice Hall, 2000.

Boehm 2002. Barry W. Boehm. "Get Ready for Agile Methods, with Care." *IEEE Computer*, Volume 35, January 2002.

Boehm 2003. Barry Boehm and Richard Turner. *Balancing Agility and Discipline*. Boston: Addison-Wesley, 2003.

Booch 1996. Grady Booch. *Object Solutions: Managing the Object-Oriented Project*. Reading, MA: Addison-Wesley, 1996.

Brooks 1995. Frederick P. Brooks, Jr. *The Mythical Man-Month, Anniversary Edition*. Reading, MA: Addison-Wesley, 1995.

Bryson 2001. Brian Bryson. "Quality by Design: Enabling Cost-Effective Comprehensive Component Testing." *The Rational Edge,* January 2001.

Buschmann 1996. F. Buschmann et al. *Pattern-Oriented Software Architecture: A System of Patterns*. Hoboken, NJ: John Wiley & Sons, 1996.

Cantor 2001. Murray Cantor. *Software Leadership: A Guide to Successful Software Development*. Boston: Addison-Wesley, 2001.

Carnegie 1990. Dale Carnegie. *How to Win Friends and Influence People, Revised Edition*. New York: Pocket Books, 1990.

Carr 1993. Marvin Carr et al. *Taxonomy Based Risk Identification*. Technical report #93-TR-006. Pittsburgh, PA: Software Engineering Institute, June 1993.

Chaos 2003. *Chaos Chronicle v3.0*. The Standish Group International, Inc., 2003.

Charette 1989. Robert Charette. *Software Engineering Risk Analysis and Management*. New York: McGraw-Hill, 1989.

Cheesman 2000. John Cheesman and John Daniels, *UML Components: A Simple Process for Specifying Component-Based Software*. Boston: Addison-Wesley, 2000.

Chonoles 2003. Michael Chonoles. *UML 2 for Dummies*. Hoboken, NJ: John Wiley & Sons, 2003.

Clements 2002. Paul Clements and Linda Northrop. *Software Product Lines: Practices and Patterns*. Boston: Addison-Wesley, 2002.

Cockburn 2000. Alistair Cockburn and Laurie Williams. "The Costs and Benefits of Pair Programming." Found online at http://collaboration.csc.ncsu.edu/laurie/Papers/XPSardinia.PDF.

Cockburn 2001. Alistair Cockburn. *Writing Effective Use Cases*. Boston: Addison-Wesley, 2001.

Cockburn 2002. Alistair Cockburn. *Agile Software Development*. Boston: Addison-Wesley, 2002.

Cockburn 2005. Alistair Cockburn. *Crystal Clear: A Human-Powered Methodology for Small Teams*. Boston: Addison-Wesley, 2005.

Cooper 1999. Alan Cooper. *The Inmates Are Running the Asylum*. Indianapolis, IN: Sams, 1999.

de Bono 1970. Edward de Bono. *Lateral Thinking: Creativity Step by Step*. New York: Harper & Row, 1970.

de Bono 1993. Edward de Bono. *Serious Creativity: Using the Power of Lateral Thinking to Create New Ideas*. New York: HarperBusiness, 1993.

DeMarco 2003. Tom DeMarco and Timothy Lister. *Waltzing with Bears: Managing Risk on Software Projects*. New York: Dorset House, 2003.

Denne 2004. Mark Denne and Jane Cleland-Huang. *Software by Numbers*. Upper Saddle River, NJ: Prentice Hall, 2004.

Devlin 1995. M. T. Devlin and W. E. Royce. *Improving Software Economics in the Aerospace and Defense Industry*. Technical paper TP-46. Santa Clara, CA: Rational Software Corp., 1995.

Dustin 1999. Elfriede Dustin, Jeff Rashka, and John Paul. *Automated Software Testing: Introduction, Management, and Performance.* Reading, MA: Addison-Wesley, 1999.

Eeles 2003. Peter Eeles, Kelli Houston, and Wojtek Kozaczynski. *Building J2EE™ Applications with the Rational Unified Process.* Boston: Addison-Wesley, 2003.

Eeles 2004. Peter Eeles. "Capturing Architectural Requirements." *The Rational Edge*, April 2004. Found online at http://www.ibm.com/developerworks/rational/library/4706.html.

Evans 2004. Eric Evans. *Domain-Driven Design: Tackling Complexity in the Heart of Software.* Boston: Addison-Wesley, 2004.

Esselink 2000. Bert Esselink. *A Practical Guide to Localization.* Amsterdam: John Benjamins, 2000.

Fagan 1976. Michael Fagan. "Design and Code Inspections to Reduce Errors in Program Development." *IBM Systems Journal*, Volume 15, No. 3, pp. 182–211. Found online at www.mfagan.com/ibmfagan.pdf.

Feathers 2005. Michael C. Feathers. *Working Effectively with Legacy Code.* Upper Saddle River, NJ: Prentice Hall, 2005.

Ferm 2003. Fredrik Ferm. "The What, Why, and How of a Subsystem." *The Rational Edge,* 2003. Found online at http://www.ibm.com/developerworks.

Fewster 1999. Mark Fewster and Dorothy Graham. *Software Test Automation: Effective Use of Test Execution Tools.* Reading, MA: Addison-Wesley, 1999.

Fowler 1999. Martin Fowler et al. *Refactoring: Improving the Design of Existing Code.* Reading, MA: Addison-Wesley, 1999.

Fowler 2000. Martin Fowler. *Is Design Dead?* Keynote XP 2000 conference. Found online at http://www.martinfowler.com/.

Fowler 2003. Martin Fowler. *Patterns of Enterprise Application Architecture.* Boston: Addison-Wesley, 2003.

Gamma 1995. Erich Gamma et al. *Design Patterns: Elements of Reusable Object-Oriented Software*. Reading, MA: Addison-Wesley, 1995.

Gilb 1988. Tom Gilb. *Principles of Software Engineering Management*. Reading, MA: Addison-Wesley, 1988.

Glass 2003. Robert R. Glass. *Facts and Fallacies of Software Engineering*. Boston: Addison-Wesley, 2003.

Gottesdiener 2003. Ellen Gottesdiener. "Team Retrospectives for Better Iterative Assessment." *The Rational Edge*, April 2003.

Goldratt 2004. Eliyahu M. Goldratt and Jeff Cox. *The Goal, Third Edition*. Great Barrington, MA: North River Press, 2004.

Grady 1997. Robert Grady. *Successful Software Process Improvement*. Englewood Cliffs, NJ: Prentice Hall, 1997.

Greenfield 2004. Jack Greenfield et al. *Software Factories: Assembling Applications with Patterns, Models, Frameworks, and Tools*. Hoboken, NJ: John Wiley & Sons, 2004.

Harvey 1996. Jerry Harvey. *The Abilene Paradox and Other Meditations on Management*. San Francisco: Jossey-Bass, 1996.

Herzum 1999. Peter Herzum and Oliver Sims. *Business Component Factory: A Comprehensive Overview of Component-Based Development for the Enterprise*. Hoboken, NJ: John Wiley & Sons, 1999.

Highsmith 2004. James A. Highsmith. *Agile Project Management: Creating Innovative Products*. Boston: Addison-Wesley, 2004.

Hohpe 2004. Gregor Hohpe and Bobby Woolf. *Enterprise Integration Patterns*. Boston: Addison-Wesley, 2004.

IEEE 1998. IEEE Standard 1490-1998. *IEEE Guide Adoption of PMI Standard: A Guide to the Project Management Body of Knowledge*. New York: Software Engineering Standards Committee of the IEEE Computer Society, 1998.

Ishigaki 2003. Doug Ishigaki and Cheryl Jones. "Practical Measurement in the Rational Unified Process." *The Rational Edge*, January 2003.

Jacobson 1992. Ivar Jacobson et al. *Object-Oriented Software Engineering: A Use Case Driven Approach.* Reading, MA: Addison-Wesley, 1992.

Jacobson 1995. Ivar Jacobson, Maria Ericsson, and Agneta Jacobson. *The Object Advantage: Business Process Reengineering with Object Technology.* Reading, MA: Addison-Wesley, 1995.

Jacobson 1997. Ivar Jacobson, Martin Griss, and Patrik Jonsson. *Software Reuse: Architecture, Process, and Organization for Business Success.* Reading, MA: Addison-Wesley, 1997.

Jacobson 1999. Ivar Jacobson et al. *The Unified Software Development Process.* Reading, MA: Addison-Wesley, 1999.

Jones 1994. Capers Jones. *Assessment and Control of Software Risks.* Englewood Cliffs, NJ: Yourdon Press, 1994.

Kaner 2001. Cem Kaner, James Bach, and Bret Pettichord. *Lessons Learned in Software Testing.* Hoboken, NJ: John Wiley & Sons, 2001.

Karolak 1996. Dale Karolak. *Software Engineering Risk Management.* Washington, DC: IEEE Computer Society Press, 1996.

Katzenbach 2003. Jon R. Katzenbach and Douglas K. Smith. *The Wisdom of Teams: Creating the High-Performance Organization.* New York: HarperBusiness, 2003.

Kerievsky 2005. Joshua Kerievsky. *Refactoring to Patterns.* Boston: Addison-Wesley, 2005.

Kerth 2001. N. Kerth. *Project Retrospectives: A Handbook for Team Reviews.* New York: Dorset House, 2001.

Kircher 2004. Michael Kircher and Prashant Jain. *Pattern-Oriented Software Architecture: Patterns for Resource Management.* Hoboken, NJ: John Wiley & Sons, 2004.

Kit 1999. Edward Kit. "Integrated, Effective Test Design and Automation." *Software Development Magazine* (online version), February 1999.

Knuth 1992. Donald E. Knuth. *Literate Programming.* Center for the Study of Language and Information, 1992.

Knuth 1993. Donald E. Knuth and Silvio Levy, *The CWEB System of Structured Documentation, Version 3.6*. Reading, MA: Addison-Wesley, 1993.

Krafzig 2005. Dirk Krafzig, Karl Banke, and Dirk Slama. *Enterprise SOA: Service-Oriented Architecture Best Practices*. Upper Saddle River, NJ: Prentice Hall, 2005.

Kroll 2001. Per Kroll. "The RUP: An Industry-Wide Platform for Best Practices." *The Rational Edge*, 2001.

Kroll 2003. Per Kroll and Philippe Kruchten. *The Rational Unified Process Made Easy: A Practitioner's Guide to the RUP*. Boston: Addison-Wesley, 2003.

Kroll 2004. Per Kroll. "Iterative Development Requires a Different Mindset." *The Rational Edge*, March 2004.

Kroll 2005. Per Kroll and Walker Royce. "Key Principles for Business-Driven Development." *The Rational Edge*, October 2005.

Kruchten 1995. Philippe Kruchten. "The 4+1 view model of architecture." *IEEE Software* 6 (12), 1995, pp. 45–50.

Kruchten 1999. Philippe Kruchten. "The Software Architect and the Software Architecture Team." In *Software Architecture*, P. Donohue, ed. Boston: Kluwer Academic Publishers, 1999, pp. 565–583.

Kruchten 2001. Philippe Kruchten. "Using the RUP to Evolve a Legacy System." *The Rational Edge*, May 2001. http://www.therationaledge.com/content/may_01/t_legacy_pk.html.

Kruchten 2003. Philippe Kruchten. *The Rational Unified Process—An Introduction, Third Edition*. Boston: Addison-Wesley, 2003.

Larman 2004. Craig Larman. *Agile and Iterative Development: A Manager's Guide*. Boston: Addison-Wesley, 2004.

Larman 2005. Craig Larman. *Applying UML and Patterns, Third Edition: An Introduction to Object-Oriented Analysis and Design and Iterative Development*. Upper Saddle River, NJ: Prentice Hall, 2005.

Leffingwell 2000. Dean Leffingwell and Don Widrig. *Managing Software Requirements: A Unified Approach*. Boston: Addison-Wesley, 2000.

Lehman 2000. M. M. Lehman and J. F. Ramil. "Software Evolution in the Age of Component-Based Software Engineering." *Software, IEE Proceedings*, Volume 147, No. 6, December 2000, pp. 249–255.

Lencioni 2000. Patrick Lencioni. *The Four Obsessions of an Extraordinary Executive*. San Francisco: Jossey-Bass, 2000.

Lencioni 2002. Patrick Lencioni. *The Five Dysfunctions of a Team*. San Francisco: Jossey-Bass, 2002.

Leonard 2003. Jason Leonard. "Simplifying Product Line Development Using UCM Streams." *The Rational Edge*, http://www.ibm.com/developerworks/rational/library/1748.html.

McConnell 2004. Steve McConnell. *Code Complete: A Practical Handbook of Software Construction, Second Edition*. Microsoft Press, 2004.

McFeeley 1996. Robert McFeeley. *IDEAL: A User's Guide for Software Process Improvement*. Pittsburgh, PA: Software Engineering Institute, CMU/SEI-96-HB-001, 1996.

Mili 2002. Hafedh Mili, *Reuse-Based Software Engineering: Techniques, Organizations, and Controls*. Hoboken, NJ: John Wiley & Sons 2002.

Moore 2004. Bill Moore et al. *Eclipse Development Using the Graphical Editing Framework and the Eclipse Modeling Framework*, IBM 2004. Found online at http://ibm.com/redbook.

Padburg 2003. Frank Padburg and Matthias M. Muller. "Analyzing the Cost and Benefit of Pair Programming." Proceedings of the Ninth International Software Metrics Symposium (METRICS'03), 2003.

Pettichord 2001. Bret Pettichord. "Seven Steps to Test Automation Success." June 2001. Found online at http://www.io.com/~wazmo/papers/seven_steps.html.

Ross 2003. Ronald G. Ross. *Principles of the Business Rule Approach*. Boston: Addison-Wesley, 2003.

Rothman 2004. Johanna Rothman. *Hiring the Best Knowledge Workers, Techies & Nerds: The Secrets & Science of Hiring Technical People*. New York: Dorset House, 2004.

Royce 1998. Walker Royce. *Software Project Management: A Unified Framework*. Reading, MA: Addison-Wesley, 1998.

Rumbaugh 2004. James Rumbaugh, Ivar Jacobson, and Grady Booch. *The Unified Modeling Language Reference Manual, Second Edition*. Boston: Addison-Wesley, 2004.

Santayana 1905. George Santayana. *The Life Of Reason, Volume 1*. New York: Scribner's, 1905.

Schmidt 2000. Douglas Schmidt, Michael Stal, et al. *Pattern-Oriented Software Architecture, Volume 2: Patterns for Concurrent and Networked Objects*. Hoboken, NJ: John Wiley, 2000.

Schneider 2001. Geri Schneider and Jason P. Winters. *Applying Use Cases: A Practical Approach, Second Edition*. Boston: Addison-Wesley, 2001.

Schwaber 2002. Ken Schwaber and M. Beedle. *Agile Software Development with SCRUM*. Upper Saddle River, NJ: Prentice Hall, 2002.

Schwaber 2004. Ken Schwaber. *Agile Project Management with Scrum*. Redmond, WA: Microsoft Press, 2004.

Senge 1990. Peter M. Senge. *The Fifth Discipline*. New York: Doubleday, 1990.

Stapleton 2003. Jennifer Stapleton and DSDM Consortium. *DSDM: Business Focused Development, Second Edition*. Boston: Addison-Wesley, 2003.

Stojanovic 2005. Zoran Stojanovic and Ajantha Dahanayake, eds. *Service-Oriented Software System Engineering: Challenges and Practices*. Hershey, PA: Idea Group Publishing, 2005.

Ulrich 2002. William M. Ulrich. *Legacy Systems Transformation Strategies*. Upper Saddle River, NJ: Prentice Hall, 2002.

White 2005. Stephen A. White. *Introduction to BPMN*. White Plains, NY: IBM Corporation, 2005.

Whittaker 2003. James Whittaker. *How to Break Software: A Practical Guide to Testing*. Boston: Addison-Wesley, 2003.

Wideman 2003. R. Max Wideman. "Progressive Acquisition and the RUP Part I–V." *The Rational Edge,* December 2002–April 2003.

Wiegers 2002. Karl Wiegers. *Peer Reviews in Software: A Practical Guide.* Boston: Addison-Wesley, 2002.

Williams 1998. Laurie Williams et al. "Strengthening the Case for Pair Programming." Communications of the ACM, Volume 41, pp. 105–108, 1998, and online at http://collaboration.csc.ncsu.edu/laurie/Papers/ieeeSoftware.PDF.

Yourdon 2004. Edward Yourdon. *Death March, Second Edition.* Upper Saddle River, NJ: Prentice Hall, 2004.

Zurkowski 2002. John Zurkowski. "Magic with Merlin: Working with Assertions." Found online in IBM's *developerWorks* Web site at http://www-106.ibm.com/developerworks/java/library/j-mer0219.html.

# INDEX

# Get
# *The*
# *Rational*
# *Edge*

# Rational Minds and Addison-Wesley
# What a Combination!

 0-321-32127-8

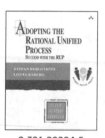 0-321-20294-5

 0-321-26888-1

 0-321-32130-8

 0-805-35340-2

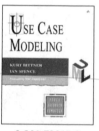 0-201-70913-9

 0-201-57168-4

 0-201-73038-3

 0-201-79166-8

 0-201-42289-1

 0-201-54435-0

 0-201-92476-5

 0-201-57169-2

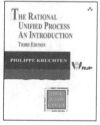 0-321-19770-4

 0-321-12247-X

 0-201-72163-5

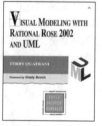 0-201-72932-6

 0-201-30958-0

 0-321-16609-4

 0-321-24562-8

 For more information on these books, please go to **www.awprofessional.com**

# Register
## Your Book
### at www.awprofessional.com/register

You may be eligible to receive:

- Advance notice of forthcoming editions of the book
- Related book recommendations
- Chapter excerpts and supplements of forthcoming titles
- Information about special contests and promotions throughout the year
- Notices and reminders about author appearances, tradeshows, and online chats with special guests

## Contact us

If you are interested in writing a book or reviewing manuscripts prior to publication, please write to us at:

Editorial Department
Addison-Wesley Professional
75 Arlington Street, Suite 300
Boston, MA  02116  USA
Email: AWPro@aw.com

Addison-Wesley

Visit us on the Web: http://www.awprofessional.com

# THIS BOOK IS SAFARI ENABLED

## INCLUDES FREE 45-DAY ACCESS TO THE ONLINE EDITION

The Safari® Enabled icon on the cover of your favorite technology book means the book is available through Safari Bookshelf. When you buy this book, you get free access to the online edition for 45 days.

Safari Bookshelf is an electronic reference library that lets you easily search thousands of technical books, find code samples, download chapters, and access technical information whenever and wherever you need it.

**TO GAIN 45-DAY SAFARI ENABLED ACCESS TO THIS BOOK:**

- Go to **http://www.awprofessional.com/safarienabled**
- Complete the brief registration form
- Enter the coupon code found in the front of this book on the "Copyright" page

If you have difficulty registering on Safari Bookshelf or accessing the online edition, please e-mail customer-service@safaribooksonline.com.

Addison
Wesley